Jet Black Futures

CW01669615

Keith Piper

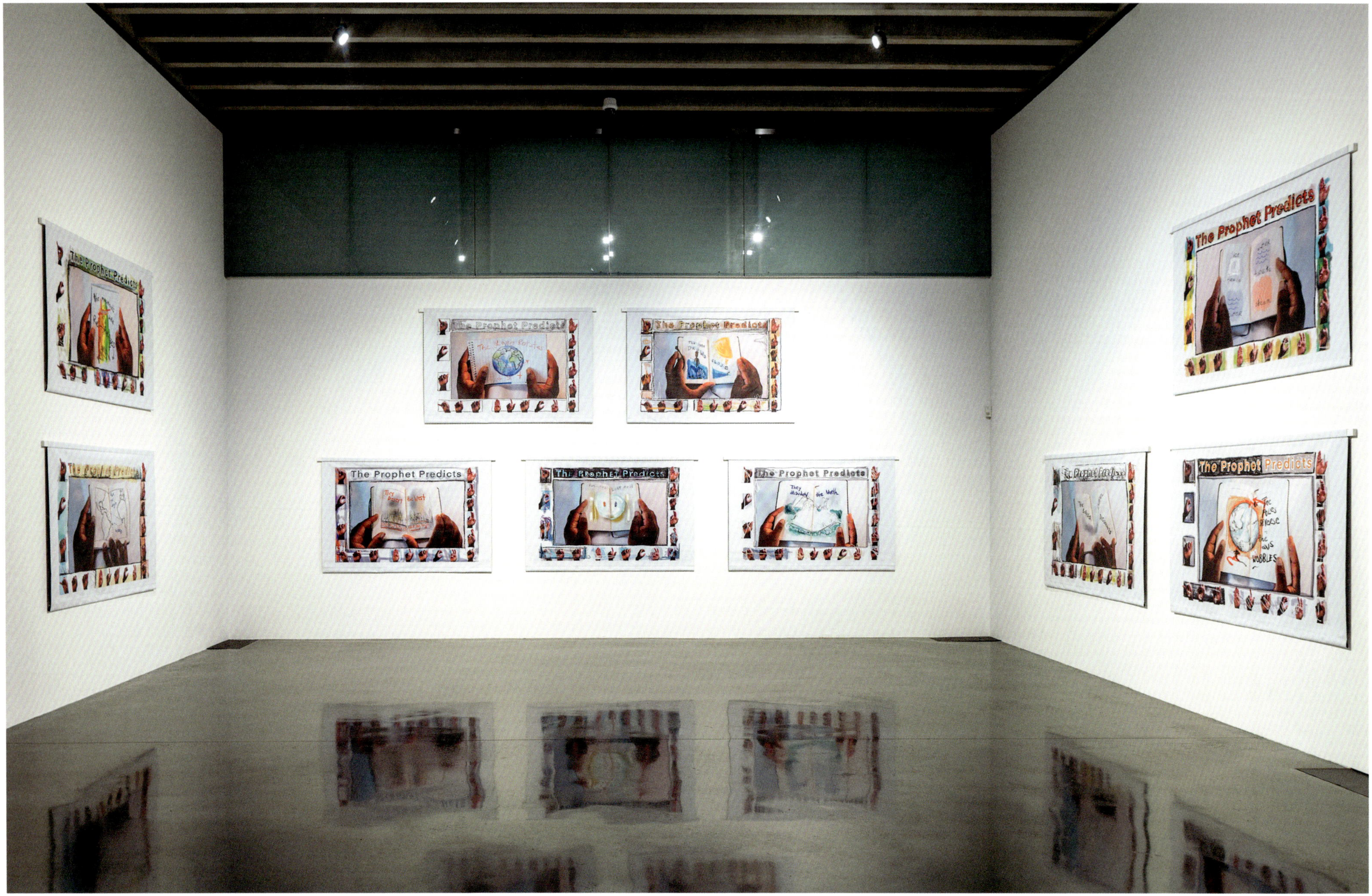
The Prophet Predicts
The Prophet Predicts
The Prophet Predicts
The Prophet Predicts
The Prophet Predicts
The Prophet Predicts

Introduction

DEBORAH ROBINSON Head of Exhibitions, The New Art Gallery Walsall

On behalf of The New Art Gallery Walsall and our partners, Wolverhampton Art Gallery and Middlesex University London, I am delighted to introduce this publication. Remarkably, it is the first monograph on the artist Keith Piper since *Re-locating the Remains*, published by InIVA in 1997. Considering Piper's position in the art world, both past and present, this project feels much overdue.

The publication focuses on two complementary exhibitions of Piper's work; *Jet Black Futures* at The New Art Gallery Walsall (14 January – 24 April 2022) and *Body Politics: Works from 1982-2007* at Wolverhampton Art Gallery (10 October – 1 December 2019). Previously the two exhibitions were programmed a year apart but like many creative projects planned over the last couple of years, the pandemic has severely impacted the development and production of new work and has forced the rescheduling of projects. Added to this, seismic recent events such as Covid-19, Brexit, the murder of George Floyd and the renewed vigour towards tackling climate change and social and racial inequalities, have all continued to fuel Piper's practice and activism.

Jet Black Futures is an ongoing project, which, in Piper's words, "encompasses a number of existing and proposed works, texts and interventions, exploring issues of race, speculative futurism and technology in an age of anxiety." The title of the exhibition is deliberately ambiguous. "Blackness" could relate to social, cultural, political and racial categories but also alludes to modernity and technology as well as the absence of light. As time has gone by and significant world events have impacted on all of us, the direction of the work has gently shifted. Piper reflects on his first ever solo exhibition *Past Imperfect, Future Tense* at The Black-Art Gallery in London 1984. The exhibition was indicative of Piper's interest in the way histories are written and interpreted and the ways in which we imagine the future which speaks about contemporary concerns.

The exhibition *Jet Black Futures* focuses on brand new work which, for Piper, is characteristically research-based and confronts current hopes, fears and anxieties for the future. *In Search of Four Horses* is an ambitious and epic four-screen video installation based around an exploration of the myth, metaphor and symbolism of the biblical story of The Four Horsemen of the Apocalypse. These riders are usually associated with warnings of impending catastrophe. Animation is combined with the filming of a series of interviews with a diverse range of participants considering their predictions for the future.

At the heart of a multi-layered narrative is Kassandra. According to Greek mythology, Apollo developed a sexual interest in Cassandra and enticed her with the gift of prophecy. When she spurned his advances, he added a cruel twist. Though she would clearly be able to predict the future, she would always be disbelieved and faced with scepticism and mistrust. In 1949, Gaston Bachelard coined the phrase, the Cassandra Syndrome, in which valid warnings are dismissed by others. There is a resounding connection to current debates around climate change, environmental degradation, the mass extinction of species and social and economic equalities. In Piper's work, Kassandra is a calm and confident Black woman, rigorously conducting interviews.

Piper has drawn on this rich metaphorical imagery in previous works, notably *The Four Horsemen of the Apocalypse* (1984). Here, the Horsemen were articulated as a Tory Voter, A Police Officer, a US General and Ronald Reagan with his finger on the button. This new work is less explicit, tapping into the particular social, political and economic context. It is also a work that is borne out of the coronavirus pandemic. Kassandra conducts her interviews via Zoom. Each participant is framed within these now familiar boxes, their backgrounds revealing details of their home environment which in most cases, has also become their office environment. Exquisite still lifes reflect this hybrid work/home combination. The outdoor landscape has become abstracted and constructed from memory and imagination. Piper himself completed this work during the festive holidays when he was sick with Covid and was self-isolating.

A new series of banners also entitled *Jet Black Futures* (2021-22) expands and develops the themes explored through this installation. Characteristically, Piper alludes to traditions of storytelling, whether biblical, mythological or otherwise, to weave together elusive yet compelling narratives. Stylistically, he employs a mixture of painting, drawing, photography and digital tools to create images clearly influenced by the visual language of cartoons, graphic novels, graffiti and memes, and in particular, the works of the late Jean-Michel Basquiat. The use of banners also connotes activism, collective energy and anti-establishment practices.

In this series of works, Piper imagines a group of apostles, each of whom make a prophecy about the future. The transatlantic triangle is inverted, the poles reverse and Earth's axis wobbles, borders dissolve, monuments are re-purposed and the majority rules. Each prophecy is presented on the pages of a book which is held by the artist. Many include the artist's hands spelling out in sign language, "I see a Jet Black Future".

An additional body of existing work included in the exhibition is the series of nine prints entitled *Pulp Fictions*, originally showed as part of the exhibition *Unearthing the Banker's Bones* (2016-17). The prints appear like covers of well-thumbed paperback science fiction books. These are imagined novels which draw on characters and themes that relate to the broader exhibition. Science fiction plays on our fears of infiltration, invasion or disruption and remains a significant influence on Piper's work. He is particularly interested in the assumed fear of a rampaging "other" which often manifests itself in many science fiction and horror genres as well as political rhetoric.

Body Politics at Wolverhampton Art Gallery brought together seminal works by the artist, largely from the 1980s and 90s. Through a powerful and influential body of work, Piper explores issues around race, class, identity, history, colonialism and empire. These rich and varied works also demonstrate Piper's gradual transition from painting, print and collage through to new media. Works such as *The Four Horsemen of the Apocalypse* and *The Black Assassin Saints* (1982) took the form of large paintings on un-stretched canvas, allowing for ease of movement.

Piper regarded such works as guerrilla interventions. Also represented is the highly complex work *The Seven Rages of Man* (1984 and revisited in 2018). Piper reinterprets "The Seven Ages of Man" to address the experiences of Black communities, starting from an imagined recollection of life in pre-colonial Africa through to slavery and its legacies, the Windrush generation and the disillusionment that followed, culminating in a symbolic return to a liberated and united continent of Africa. These works are discussed at length in Anjalie Dalal-Clayton's compelling essay.

In the late 1980s, the rise of home computing enabled the collaging of video, images and sound, allowing Piper to develop his famous and pioneering "cut and paste" aesthetic which has continued to evolve, taking advantage of increasingly sophisticated technologies. Works such as *Go West Young Man* (1996) and *Trade Winds* (1992) highlighted Britain's role in the Transatlantic Slave Trade and the price paid by enslaved Africans for the development of global capitalism. *The Trophies of Empire* (1985) addressed colonial histories and narratives. *The Nation's Finest* (1990) explores preconceptions and prejudices relating to the racialised body and notions of national belonging. The most recent of works in this exhibition, *The Perfect City* (2007) reflects on institutional and organisational powers regulating urban space and society.

Both exhibitions have included the installation *Surveillance: Tagging the Other* (1992). This work was created in response to issues arising in the run-up to the instigation of the European Union in 1992. The four monitors, installed in a row, show the artist's head being a target of surveillance and control. His body is scrutinised in terms of ethnicity, gender, citizenship and appearance.

The soundtrack features fragments of news reports relating to the rise of racist attacks, anti-Semitism and right-wing tendencies across Europe. Although it was made in 1992, the work remains hauntingly pertinent, following the death of George Floyd and the urgent demands for racial equality that have followed. The work also connects with wider issues around surveillance and control with the cultural dominance of the internet and social media and the exploitation of personal data to manipulate and monitor. It also connects with wider issues around surveillance and control in the wake of the coronavirus pandemic. In the longer term, the work bears witness to turbulent times in British history and the struggles for racial equality but remarkably, given such recent significant global events over the past couple of years, potential readings of the work have become more fluid and extensive. The New Art Gallery was able to acquire this work for its Collections through support from the Contemporary Art Society's Rapid Response Fund in 2020.

The two exhibitions together celebrate Piper's hugely powerful and influential practice, from his earlier works to his current practice. Of course, Piper has a long and significant connection to the West Midlands. He grew up in Birmingham with his parents who were part of the Windrush generation and studied in Coventry, Nottingham and the Royal College of Art, London. He was a founder member of what came to be known as the Blk Art Group which was formed in Wolverhampton in the early 1980s with a range of artists including Eddie Chambers, Claudette Johnson, Donald Rodney and Marlene Smith. Against a context of political unrest and widespread racial discrimination, these artists fought for their place in the art world and paved the way for the career development of many other artists as well as forcing the sector to confront the harsh reality of institutional racism. These enterprising young students were inspired by America's Black Arts Movement

(BAM), part of the larger Black Power movement and closer to home, by renowned cultural theorist Stuart Hall.

Piper participated in the hugely important exhibition *Black Art an' Done* at Wolverhampton Art Gallery in 1981 which also featured Eddie Chambers, Andrew Hazel, Dominic Dawes and Ian Palmer. It was followed on 28 October 1982 by the First National Black Art Convention at the Faculty of Art at what was then Wolverhampton Polytechnic. This was something of a rallying cry to all Black artists "to discuss the form, functioning, and future of Black Art". A further exhibition, *The Pan-Afrikan Connection* was shown at both London's Africa Centre and Ikon Gallery in Birmingham who have continued to support Piper's work, presenting the important exhibition *A Ship called Jesus* in 1991. I worked at Ikon Gallery at the time and this powerful and challenging exhibition still remains one of the most impactful shows I have seen.

Both Keith Piper and Anjalie Dalal-Clayton will go on to elaborate on the works represented across both exhibitions and the themes and issues explored. Dalal-Clayton has focused largely on four works; the two versions of *The Seven Rages of Man* (1984 and 2018) along with *The Four Horsemen of the Apocalypse* (1984) and *In Search of Four Horses* (2021-2) to look at the evolution of Piper's practice in terms of content, materiality and artistic strategy whilst exploring the ways in which he revisits and reshapes work in relation to the contemporary context.

There are many people to thank with regard to the realisation of this project. Thank you to all our partners who have worked collaboratively with us on this publication. From Wolverhampton Art Gallery, we must thank Marguerite Nugent, Roma Piotrowska and Carol Thompson as well as Neus Miro, the original curator of *Body Politics*. From Middlesex University London, we especially thank Dr Kene Igweonu, Professor Paul Cobley and the Middlesex ACI Faculty Research Funding Group for their support, not just of the publication but for supporting the development and production of works through additional resources such as expertise, equipment and enabling students to develop their skills and experience in such an exciting project. We are also incredibly grateful to the Paul Mellon Centre for Studies in British Art for their generous support of the publication.

We also thank our partners Departure Lounge and Revoluton Arts in Luton who have supported the project and facilitated the involvement of young people. We plan to show the installation in some form in Luton. Special thanks go to Matthew Shaul and Samantha Maitland at Departure Lounge and Johanne Hudson-Lett and Jenny Williams at Revoluton Arts.

Thank you to all those who participated as interviewees in the installation *In Search of Four Horses*. They are; Felicity Allen, Louise Beer, Berrisford Boothe, Lisa Bradley, Rachel Garfield, Shreela Ghosh, Manick Govinda, Magdalene Kourti, Fran Ledonio Flaherty, Sonia Lopes, Joanne Moore, Glynis Neslen and Roderick Ryan. Thank you also to our very own Kassandra, actor Karol Dolores Malcolm.

We are grateful to both Anjalie Dalal-Clayton and Keith Piper for their insightful, illuminating and thoughtful contributions to this publication as well as designer Victoria Bithell for her creativity, responsiveness and patience in the design and production. We are grateful to Dr Alice Correia for her support, particularly with copy editing.

Thank you as ever to Stephen Snoddy and all the team at The New Art Gallery Walsall and to the team at

Wolverhampton Art Gallery for the realisation of both exhibitions. Special thanks should go to the Technical teams at each organisation, led respectively by Kevin Storrar and Naomi Greaves. I would also like to thank my team, Hannah Anderson and Zoë Lippett for their ongoing support. By extension, we thank Arts Council England, Walsall Council and Wolverhampton Council for their continued support. Thanks also go to Ilona Zielinska (Elona Photographer) for her photographic documentation of both exhibitions and to Mark Hinton (Blend Films) for associated videography.

I would also like to extend our gratitude to the Contemporary Art Society who, through the Rapid Response Fund, have enabled the acquisition of *Surveillance: Tagging the Other* for The New Art Gallery's Permanent Collection. We look forward to revisiting this work for the benefit of future generations.

Lastly but certainly not least, I would like to thank the incredible and hugely significant artist Keith Piper for his creativity, his warmth and humour. He continues to shine a light on contemporary issues and remains committed to the fight to combat social and racial inequalities through his practice, through rich and powerful works that are underpinned by rigorous research, compelling storytelling and powerful immersive experiences.

***The Black Assassin Saints* (detail)**
1982

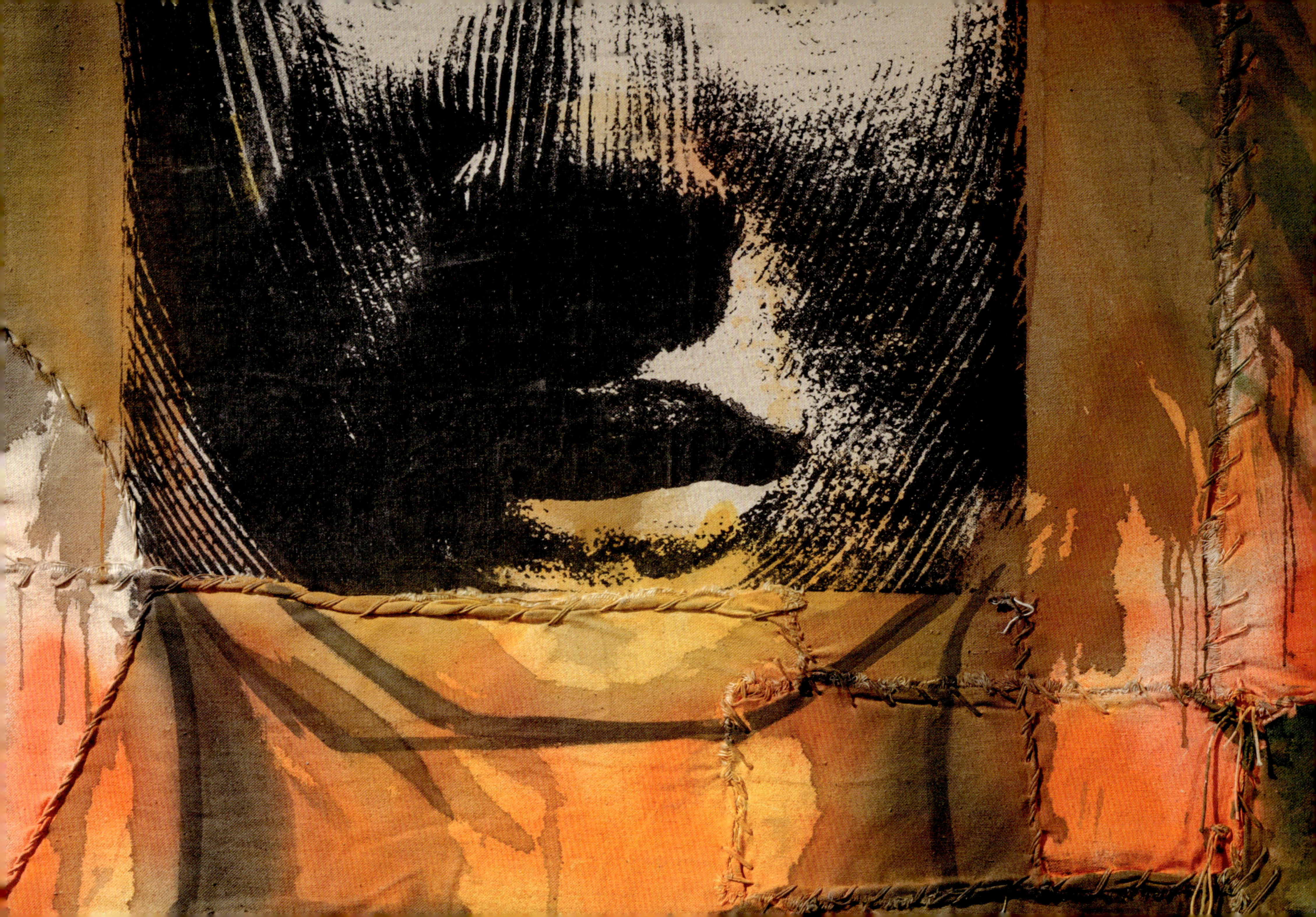

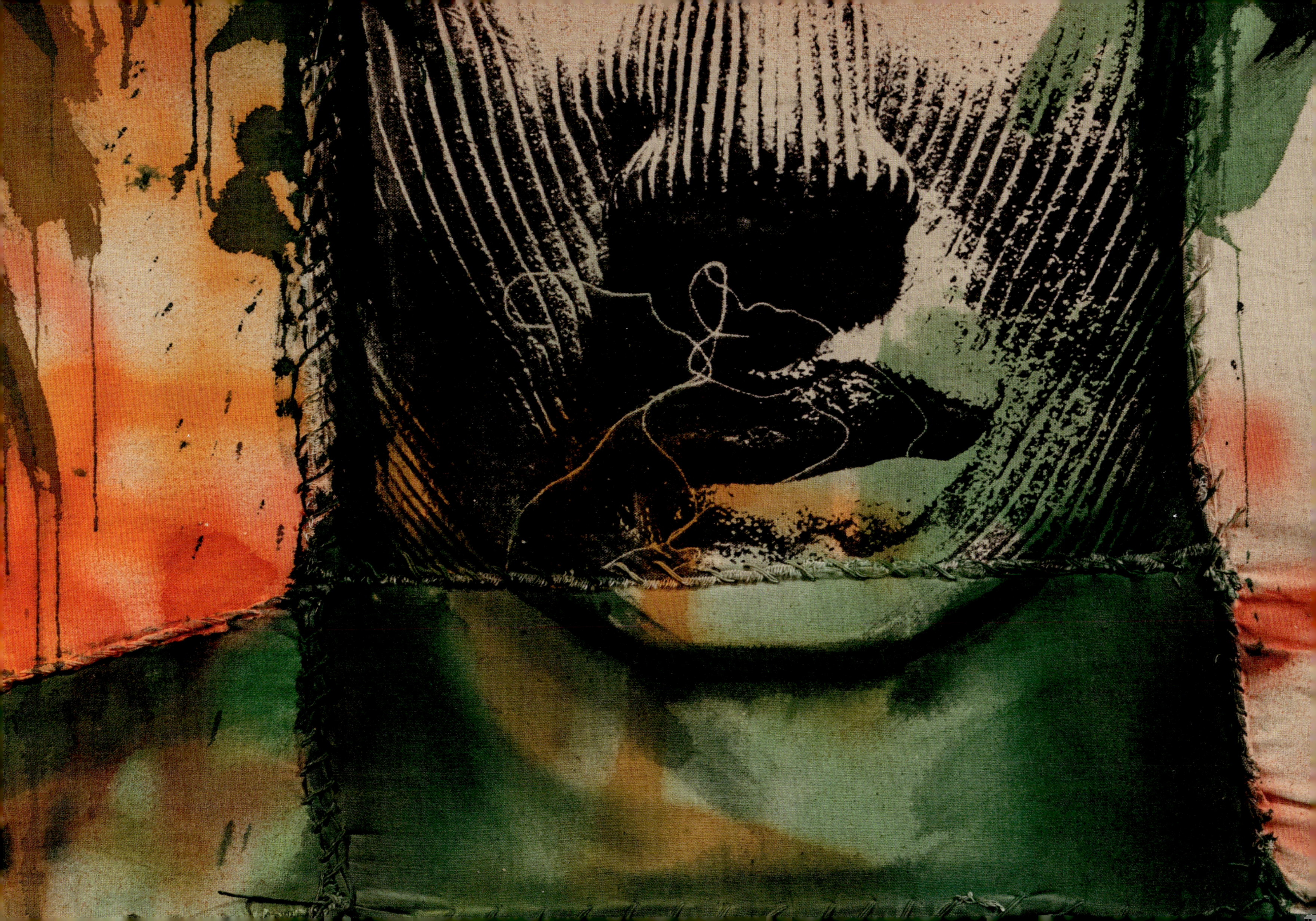

Obscured Black Histories/ Jet Black Futures

KEITH PIPER, 2022

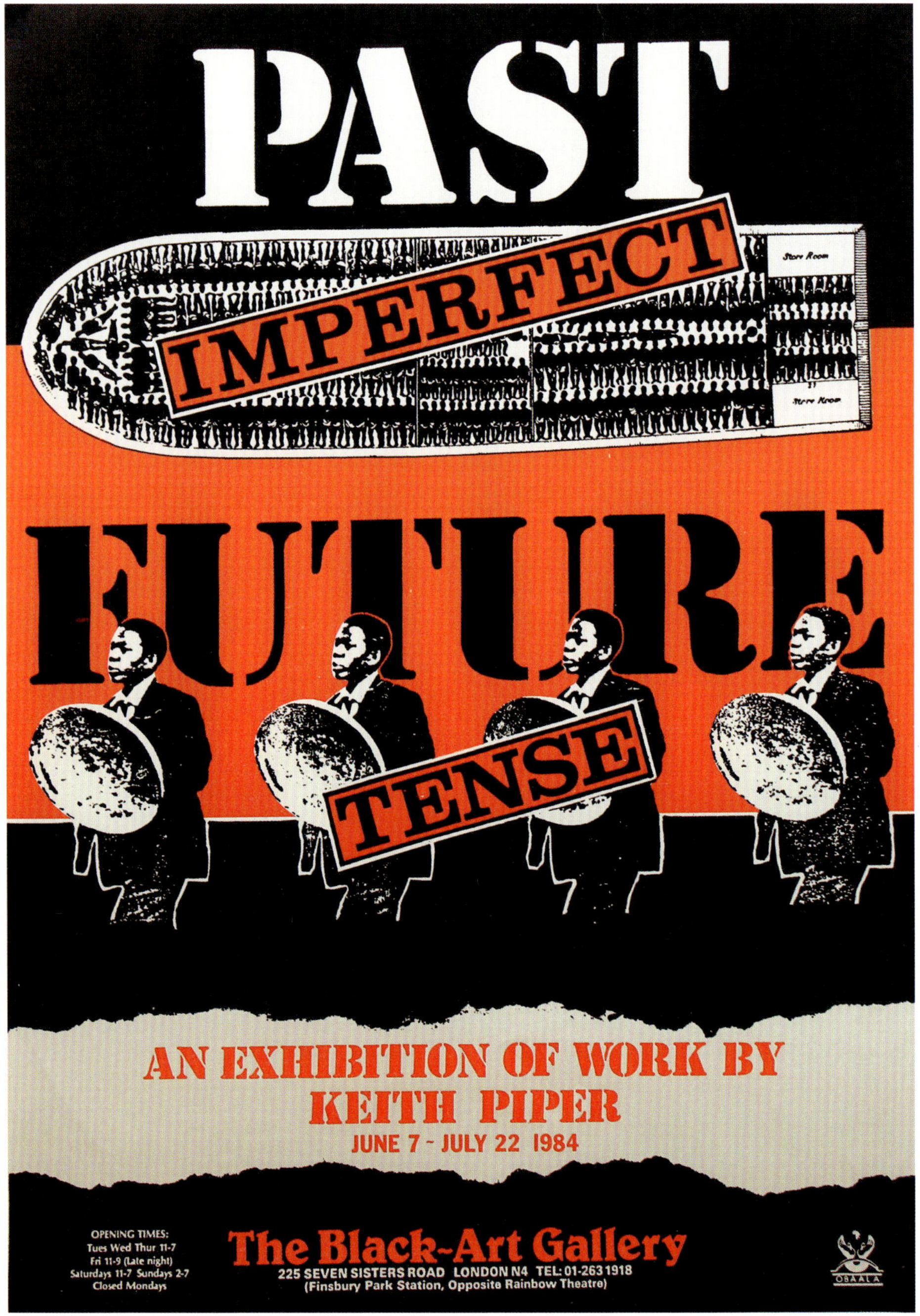

Poster for *Past Imperfect Future Tense*, The Black-Art Gallery
1984

My practice over the past four decades has been continuously punctuated by two separate but interlocking concerns. The first is how we excavate, assemble and articulate history. The second is how we imagine the future.

The paralleling of these two concerns was made explicit in the title and framing of my first ever solo exhibition, staged in June 1984 at the iconic, but sadly short-lived 'Black-Art Gallery' in London's Finsbury Park.

The exhibition was entitled *Past Imperfect, Future Tense*, a play, not only on grammatical conventions, but also on how our emerging political consciousness of the day was being impacted by our reading of history on one hand, and our concerns, expectations, and predictions around the unfolding political struggles of the time, on the other.

This was articulated around the use of two totemic images on the exhibition poster. The 'Past Imperfect' was denoted by the re-use of the notorious diagram of 454 Black bodies crammed into the hold of the Slave Ship "Brookes" dated from 1787 and deployed in Abolitionist campaigning of the time.[1]

For 'Future Tense', an image was derived from Peter Magubane's iconic photo-documentation of the Anti-Apartheid unrest in 1976[2], of a youth with a dustbin-lid striding purposely towards confrontation. Although from the previous decade, Magubane's work was being widely requoted into the early 1980s by graphic and visual artists to express the outrage that we felt at the stark and unmediated racist violence of the South African Apartheid regime and its Western apologists, and our solidarity with those engaged on the 'front line' of that struggle. Magubane's photo image embodied a spirit of defiant resistance in a way that resonated not only as historical document, but as a marker of predictive future struggles to be played out, regionally and globally, and it was this combination of historical excavation and futurological speculation that informed much of the content of the show.

During this exhibition, I was drawn into a critical conversation with a middle-aged man from the local West Indian community, who had ventured into the space and took exception to some of the political content of the exhibition. After a lively exchange, he boiled his objections down to a simple critique. In his view the exhibition spoke about 'The Past (Imperfect)' and speculated about 'The Future (Tense) but ignored what he described as the 'Present'. As a 23-year-old, I lacked the verbal or conceptual dexterity to adequately counter his position, but our conversation has remained with me. At this moment I am reminded of the familiar line from George Orwell's 1949 novel *Nineteen Eighty-Four*, "Who controls the past controls the future: Who controls the present controls the past"[3]. The dystopian implications of this assertion can perhaps in this context be shifted from the totalitarian setting of 'Oceania-Airstrip One' with its emphasis on 'who controls', to something that becomes more useful to an understanding of how history is re-read, and futures are projected.

The 'Present' becomes a shifting and 'subject specific' location from which historical narratives can be shifted, re-ordered and rearticulated dependant on the orientation of the 'history-teller'. The concrete remains, fossils and fragments that litter the archive are continuously repositioned for emphasis. Individual pieces are selected and subjected to microscopic scrutiny, or left to sit semi-obscured amidst the jumble and noise that surrounds them. In the case of the project *Jet Black Futures*, the 'present' from which we cast our gaze back through the archive,

[1]https://www.bl.uk/collection-items/diagram-of-the-brookes-slave-ship
[2] Peter Magubane, *Fighting bullets with stones in Alexandra Township June 17 1976'* (1976) Goodman Gallery

and forward into predictive speculation, is saturated by key epochal concerns that colour the project and accent its aesthetics, approaches and themes.

The period after 25th of May 2020 has been marked by the aftermath of the murder of George Floyd made searingly graphic and immediate by Darnella Frazier's unflinching camera phone documentation of the atrocious act. Frazier's decision to upload the video to Facebook at 1.46am on the 26th May[4] effectively demonstrated how the new networks of 'Social Media' could effectively short-circuit the dominant narrative building of the established and empowered channels of 'Main-stream media', as the video went globally 'viral'.

Frazier's act would also revive and reamplify another call made initially via Facebook, which would resonate into the present in the wake of Floyd's death. It was on July 13th 2013, that Oakland based community activist Alicia Garza posted a message, once again via Facebook, containing the line "I continue to be surprised at how little Black lives matter"[5] in response to the acquittal of neighbourhood vigilante George Zimmerman, who had been on trial for the killing of Black teenager Trayvon Martin. Rearticulated into the hashtag, #BlackLivesMatter with the help of Garza's collaborative partners, Patrisse Cullors and Opal Tometi, the sentiment became a local, national, and later global rallying call highlighting incidents and legacies of state endorsed violence against Black bodies.

It has been the role of on-line messaging in these moments, that has, I would argue come to characterise how we view our present. Alongside and supplementing the constant and cyclical official messaging from mainstream news channels, we sit in an era which is increasingly information drenched, much of it conflicting and requiring careful sifting.

The moment of #BlackLivesMatter spilt over into conversations around how historical figures are venerated, especially through their public memorials, when the statue of the slave trader Edward Colston was toppled in June 2020[6], echoing a wave of statue toppling's in the USA and beyond. It further resonated through conversations around the role of Museums as repositories for colonial loot through calls to #ReturnTheIcons. Echoes of these conversations wash through the work in this exhibition, especially through the messages presented by the 'Twelve Apostles' featured in the series of digital drawings entitled *Jet Black Futures* (2022).

Alongside these concerns that colour our present, two others loom large, overlapping with and impacting the production of the work in this exhibition. The first was a news cycle and popular consciousness dominated by our growing awareness of the scale of the climate emergency. The fragile ecosystem that has provided a sustaining envelope for human societal development since the subsiding of the last major 'Ice Age', is currently reeling in response to our activities. The production of this exhibition took place against the cacophony of voices assembled around the 'UN Climate Change Conference UK 2021', more commonly known as COP26, held in Glasgow between 31st October and the 12th November[7]. This highlighted a moment at which the scale of these issues was coming into the sharpest of focus, even though the absence of agreed solutions would further heighten our shared anxieties around the future.

The final epoch shaping set of events that would impact the development of this project would be first identified in the city of Wuhan, China in late 2019[8]. Coronavirus Disease 2019 (COVID-19) would impact the ways in which we think about the tension between public and private space, notions of bodily autonomy versus interdependence through shared social systems, and at its most profound, our own mortality and that of our nearest and dearest. Our plans for social engagement and physical interaction were suddenly put on hold as sequential 'social distancing' and 'Lock Downs' became our lived reality between March 2020 and most of 2021.

The developmental arch of the work *In Search of Four Horses* was transformed by the new realities of 'Lock Down' unfolding through the spring and summer of 2021. A project initially conceived as a series of filmed interactions in various geographic locations across North London and Luton, morphed into a series of remote conversations negotiated over the virtual networks of 'Facebook' and conducted through the virtual spaces of 'Zoom'. The central role of the researcher and journalist Kassandra, modelled after the mythical priestess of Apollo who is gifted the ability of seeing the future, but robbed of the ability to be believed, shifts in the work from moving through and around a series of physical locations and social spaces, to echoing 'home-working' by conducting her research from the claustrophobia and clutter of a domestic desktop. The subjects of her interviews shift from a group of physically proximate young people in the City of Luton, to an internationally disparate and socially diverse group of commentators who come to the work through a series of recorded on-line interviews, carrying a complex and wide-ranging array of predictions of the future reflective of their diverse political positions.

The final shift in the work is an aesthetic one. Originally conceived as a work extending the denser visual collaging of earlier video works such as *UnEarthing the Bankers Bones* (2016) *Mic Drop* (2017) and *A Ship Called Jesus Redux* (2021), *In Search of Four Horses* deploys a wider visual canvas of four conjoined video screens but becomes more minimal in pacing and tone. The underlying metaphor, referring to the biblical allegory of the 'Four Horsemen of the Apocalypse' is hinted at through the occasional flickering into view of sparsely rendered hand drawn animations, but the bulk of the work is played out against a single 'imagined' landscape, emptied of detail, echoing the threatening and unvisited landscapes beyond our hermetically sealed domestic spaces. These aesthetic shifts in the work evolved in part to draw focus to the rich contributions bought to the work by the interviewees and their multiple perspectives but are also an unexpected outcome of testing positive for Covid myself during a key production phase of the work. Although by no means a severe case, the impact of the virus seemed to push me towards a more minimalist aesthetic in the structure and pacing of the work. This I would argue, leaves the project marked with the memory of its moment of production, reflecting the concerns and anxieties of that time across a very specific set of social, symbolic, logistical and aesthetic registers.

I would like to give my heartfelt thanks to my 'Facebook friends' who volunteered to generously share their predictions of the future during a series of Zoom conversations held between October and December 2021 against the backdrop of pandemic and lockdown. These were, Rachel Garfield, Manick Govinda, Louise Beer, Magdalene Kourti, Glynis Neslen, Joanne Moore, Shreela Ghosh, Roderick Ryan, Lisa Bradley, Fran Ledonio Flaherty, Felicity Allen, Sonia Lopes and Berrisford Boothe. I would also like to thank Karol Dolores Malcolm for generously stepping into the role of Kassandra.

[3] George Orwell. *Nineteen Eighty-Four*. Published by Secker and Warburg 1949
[4] Alexander, Elizabeth (June 15, 2020). "The Trayvon Generation: For Solo, Simon, Robel, Maurice, Cameron, and Sekou". *NewYorker*.
[5] Laurie Collier Hillstrom (2018). *Black Lives Matter: From a Moment to a Movement*. ABC-CLIO. p. 22. ISBN 9781440865718.
[6] https://theconversation.com/edward-colston-statue-toppled-how-bristol-came-to-see-the-slave-trader-as-a-hero-and-philanthropist-140271
[7] https://ukcop26.org/
[8] Page J, Hinshaw D, McKay B (26 February 2021). "In Hunt for Covid-19 Origin, Patient Zero Points to Second Wuhan Market – The man with the first confirmed infection of the new coronavirus told the WHO team that his parents had shopped there". *The Wall Street Journal*.

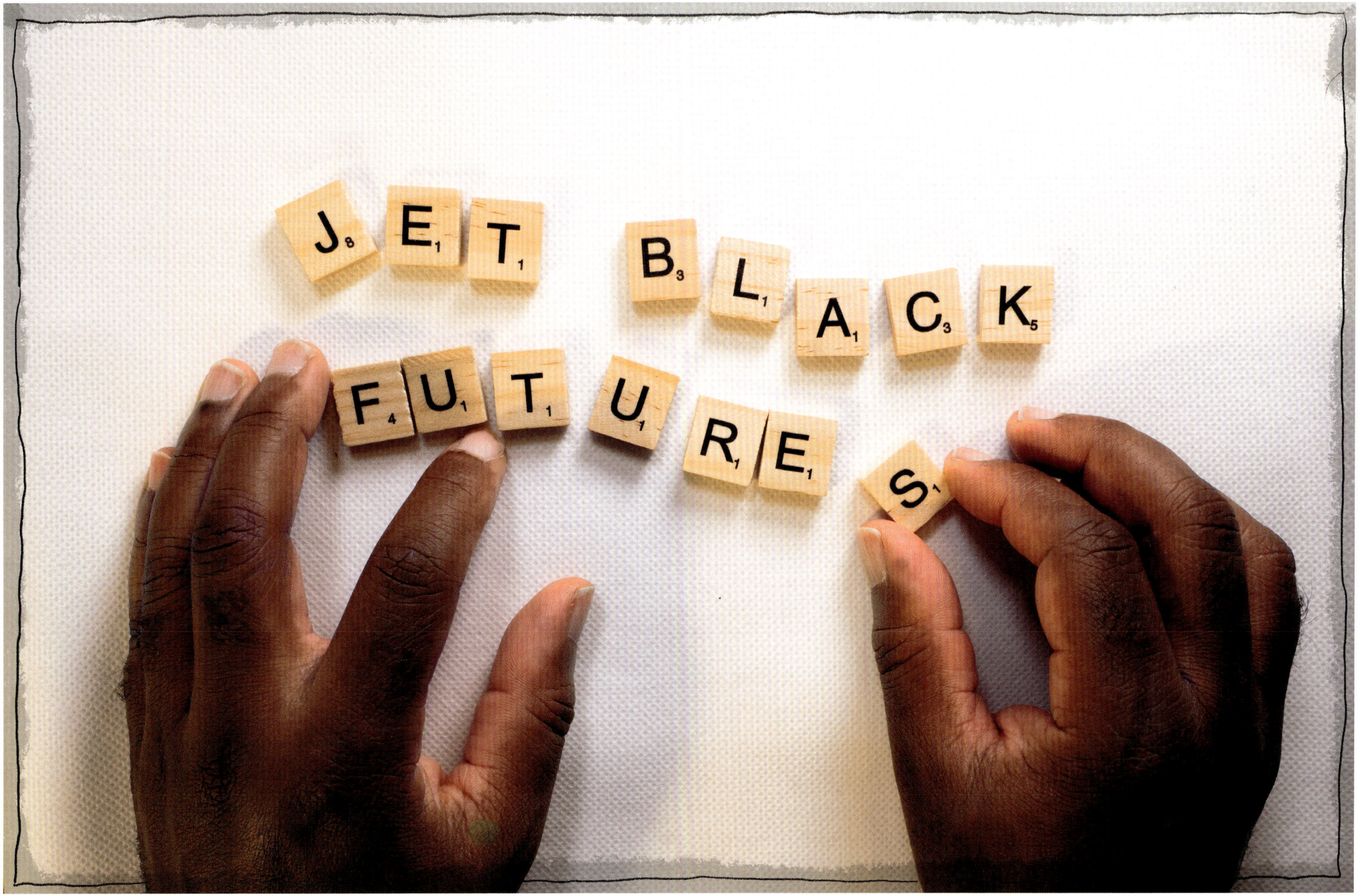
JET BLACK
FUTURES

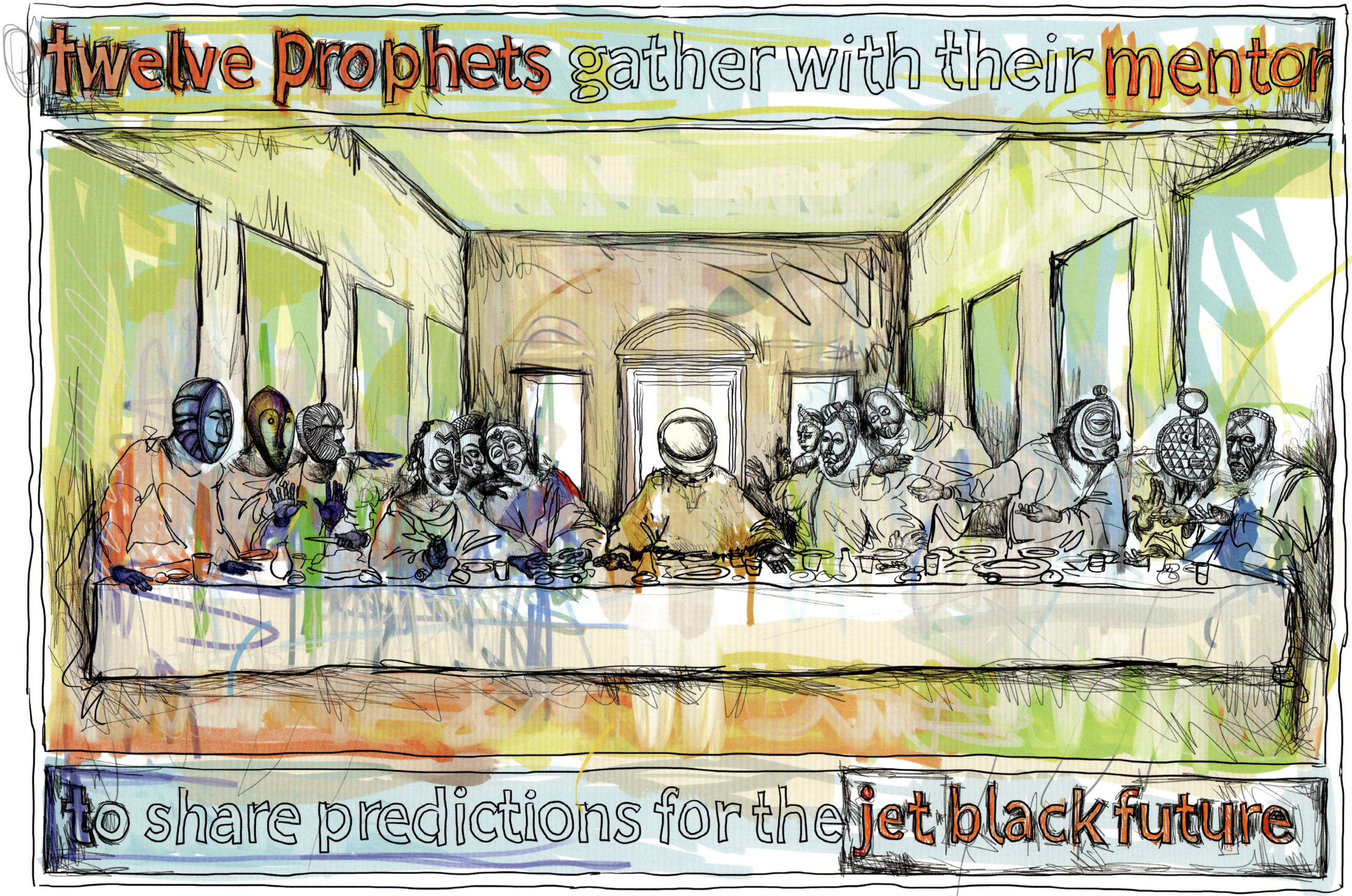
twelve prophets gather with their mentor
to share predictions for the jet black future

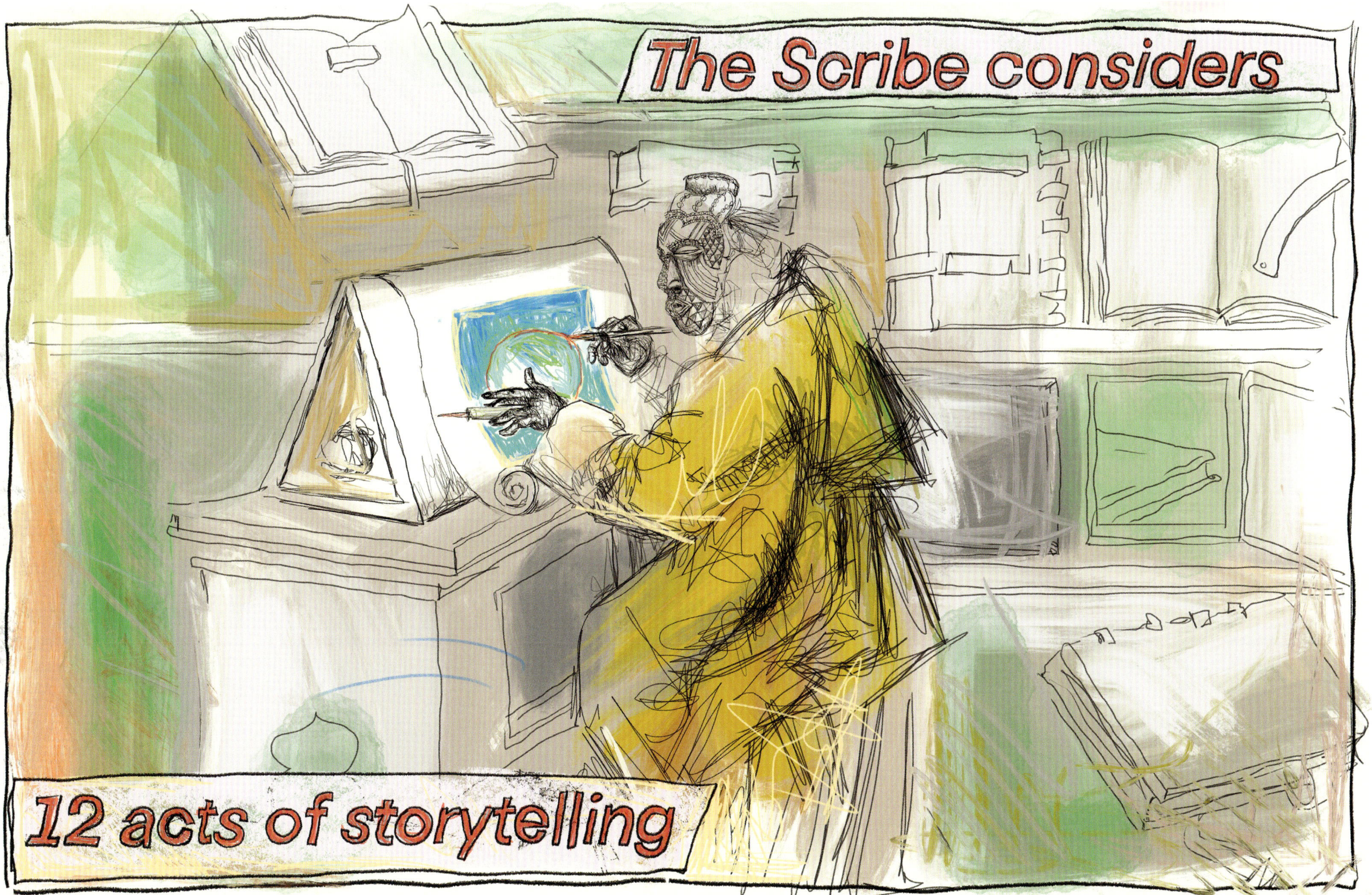
The Scribe considers
12 acts of storytelling

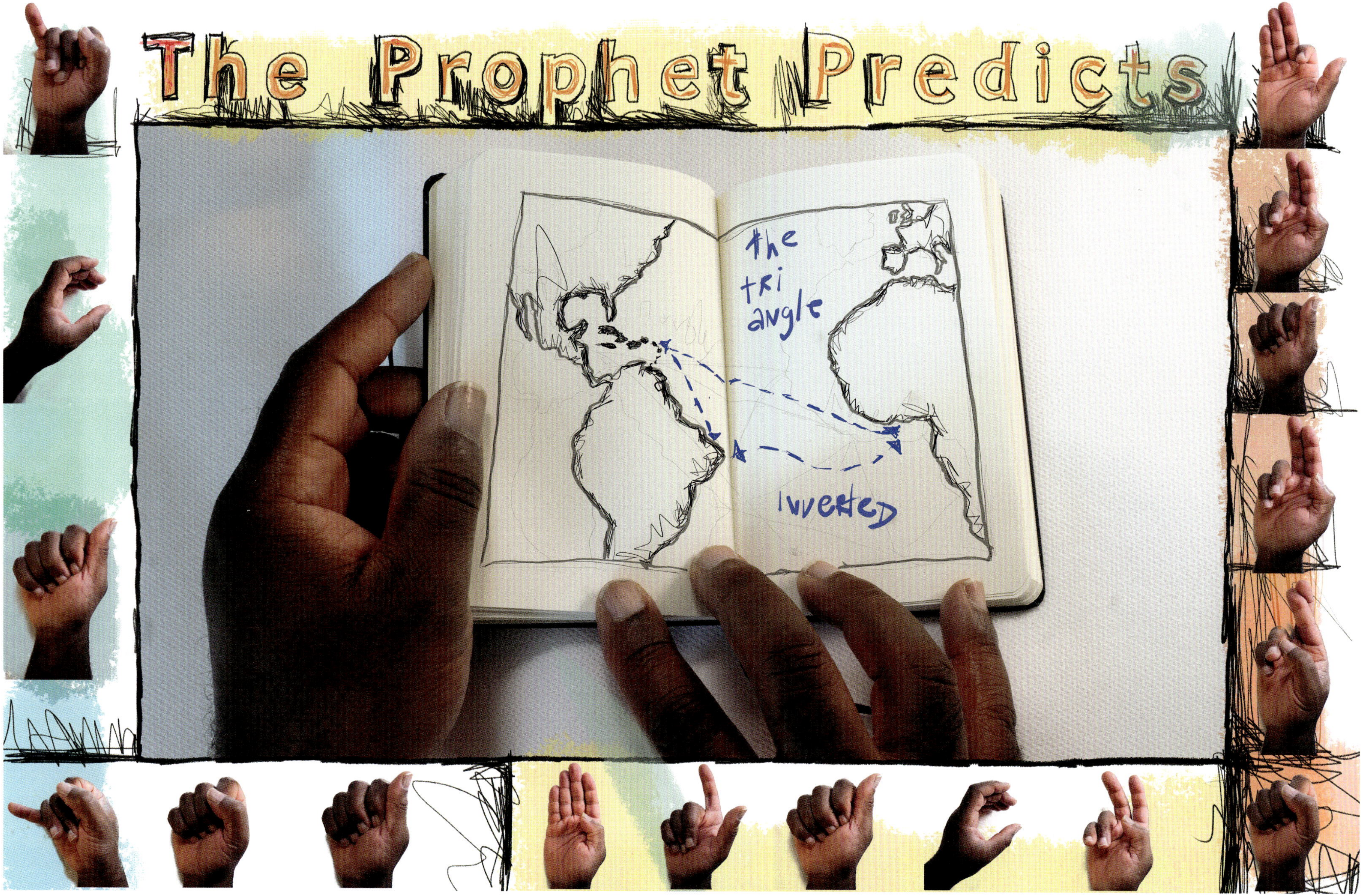
The Prophet Predicts
the tri angle
inverted

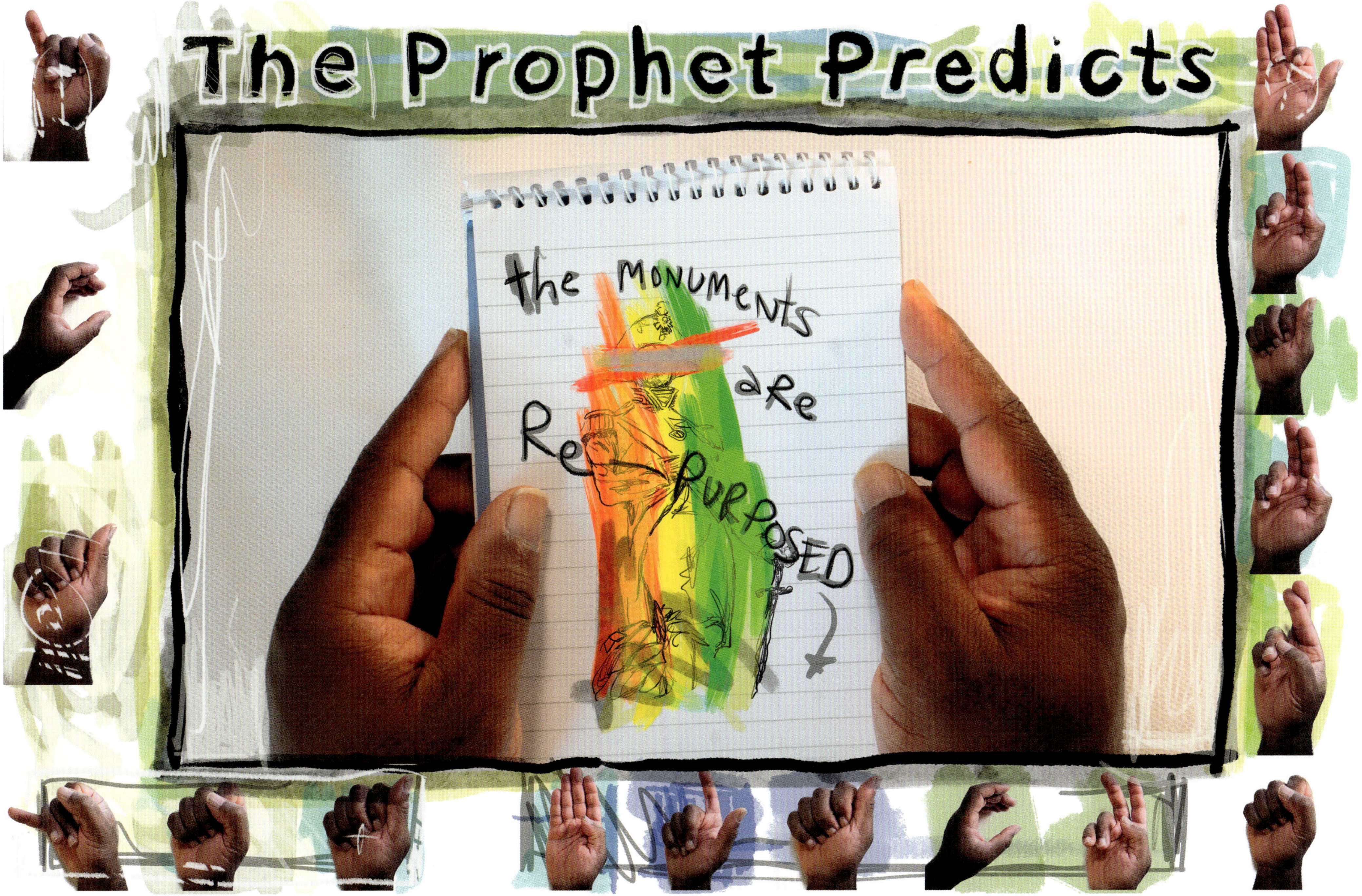
The Prophet Predicts
the MONUMENTS
are
RePURPOSED

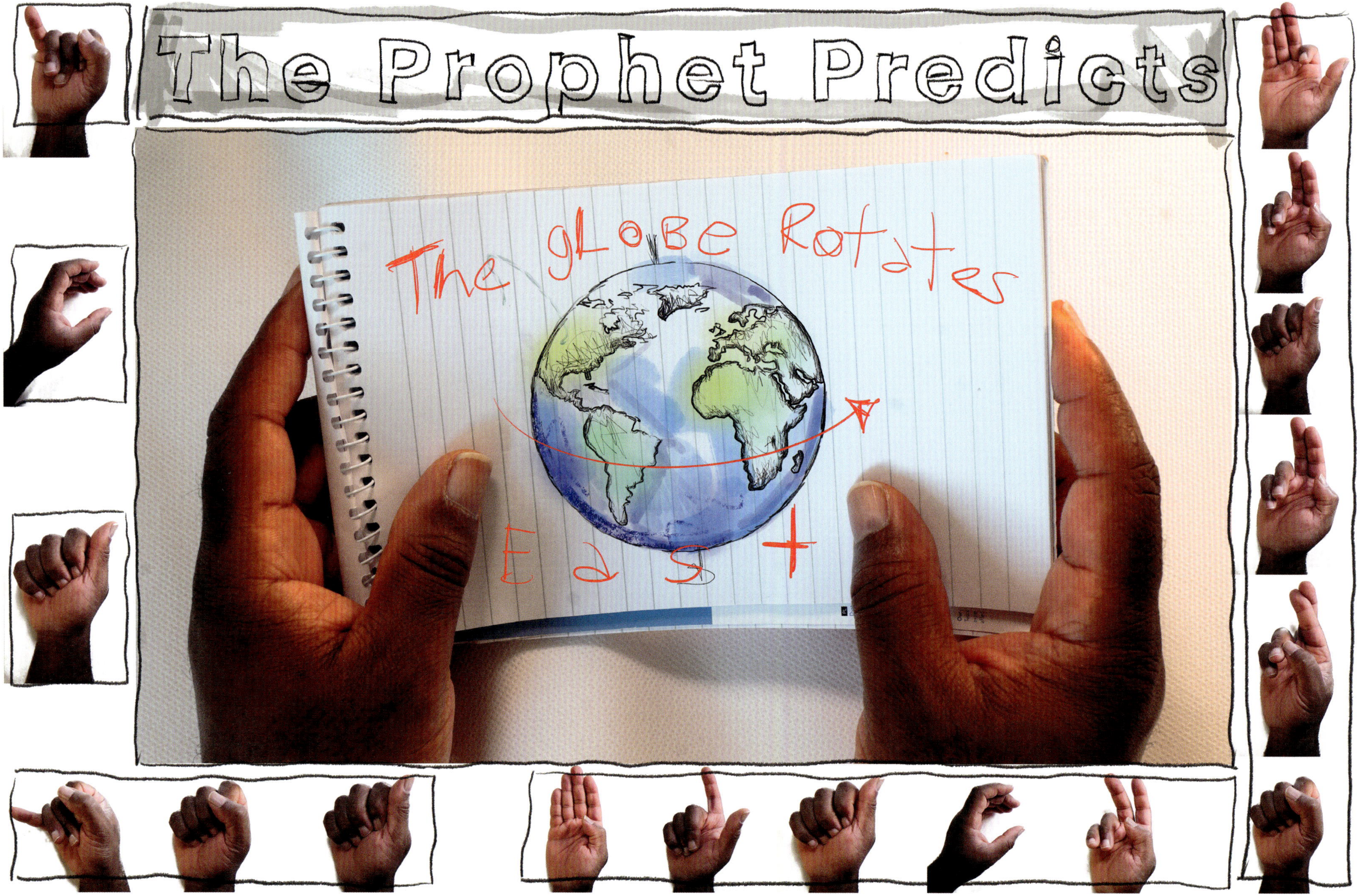
The Prophet Predicts
The globe Rotates
East

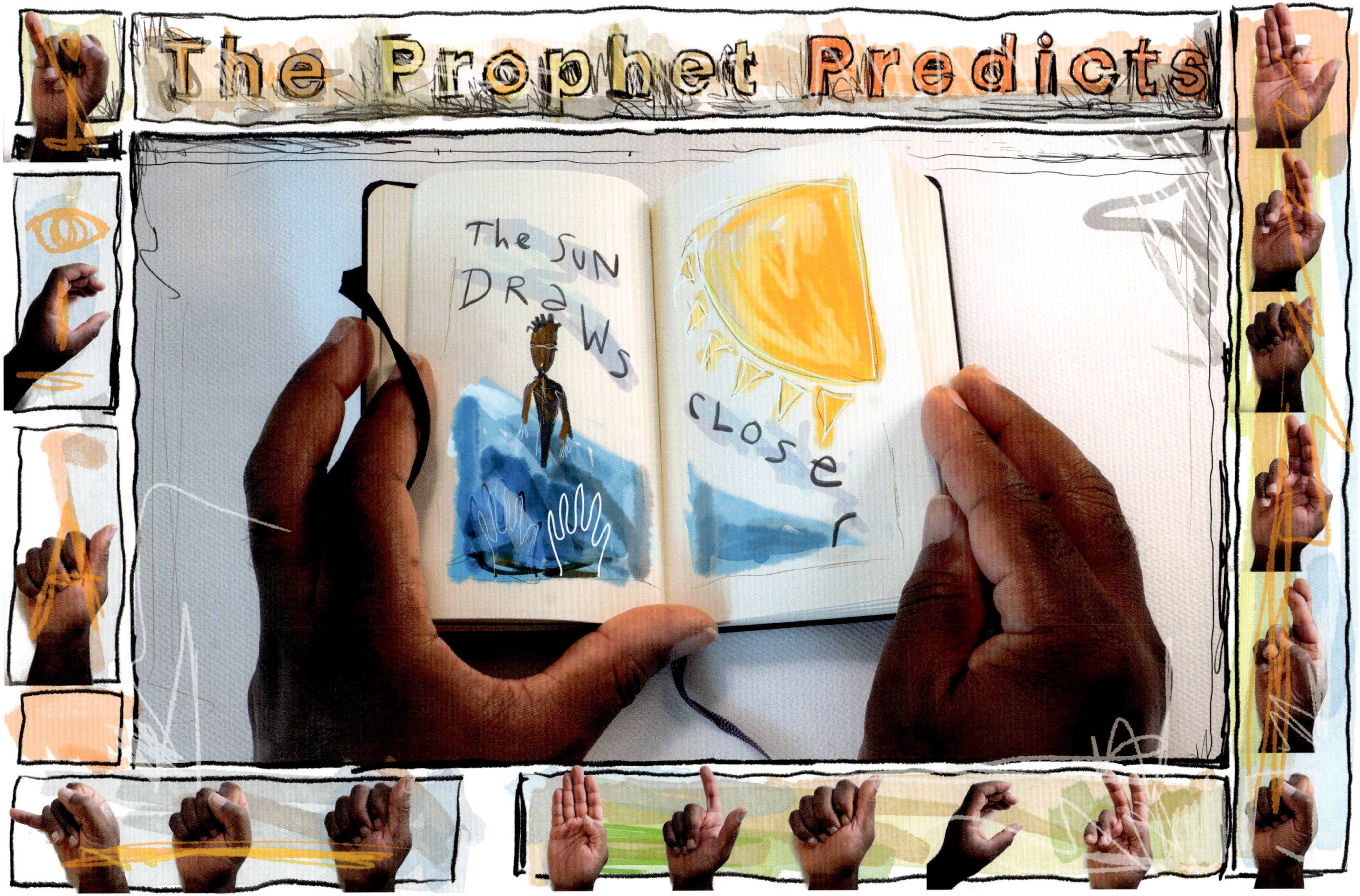
The Prophet Predicts
The Sun Draws closer

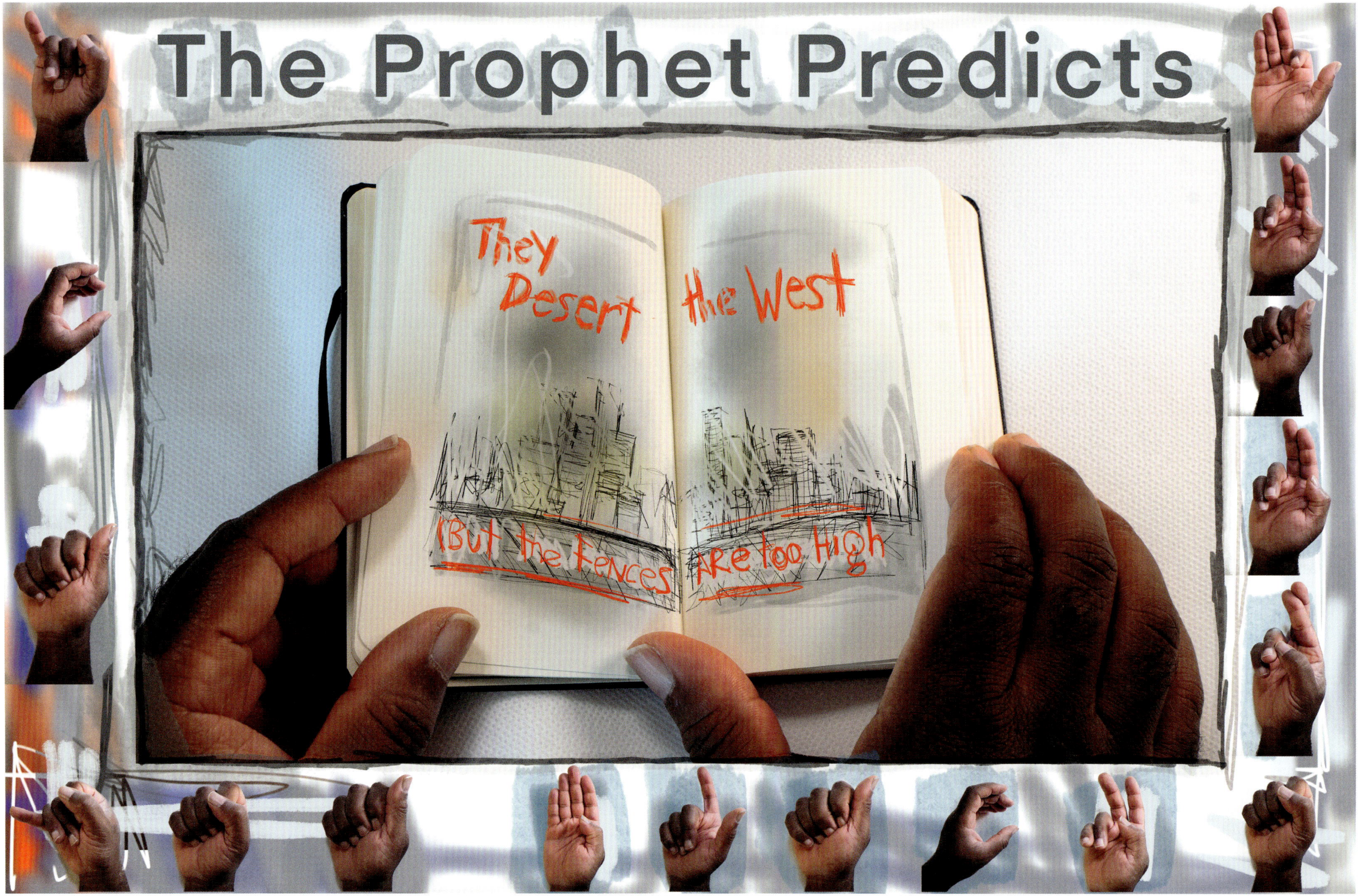
The Prophet Predicts
They Desert the West
(But the Fences Are too High

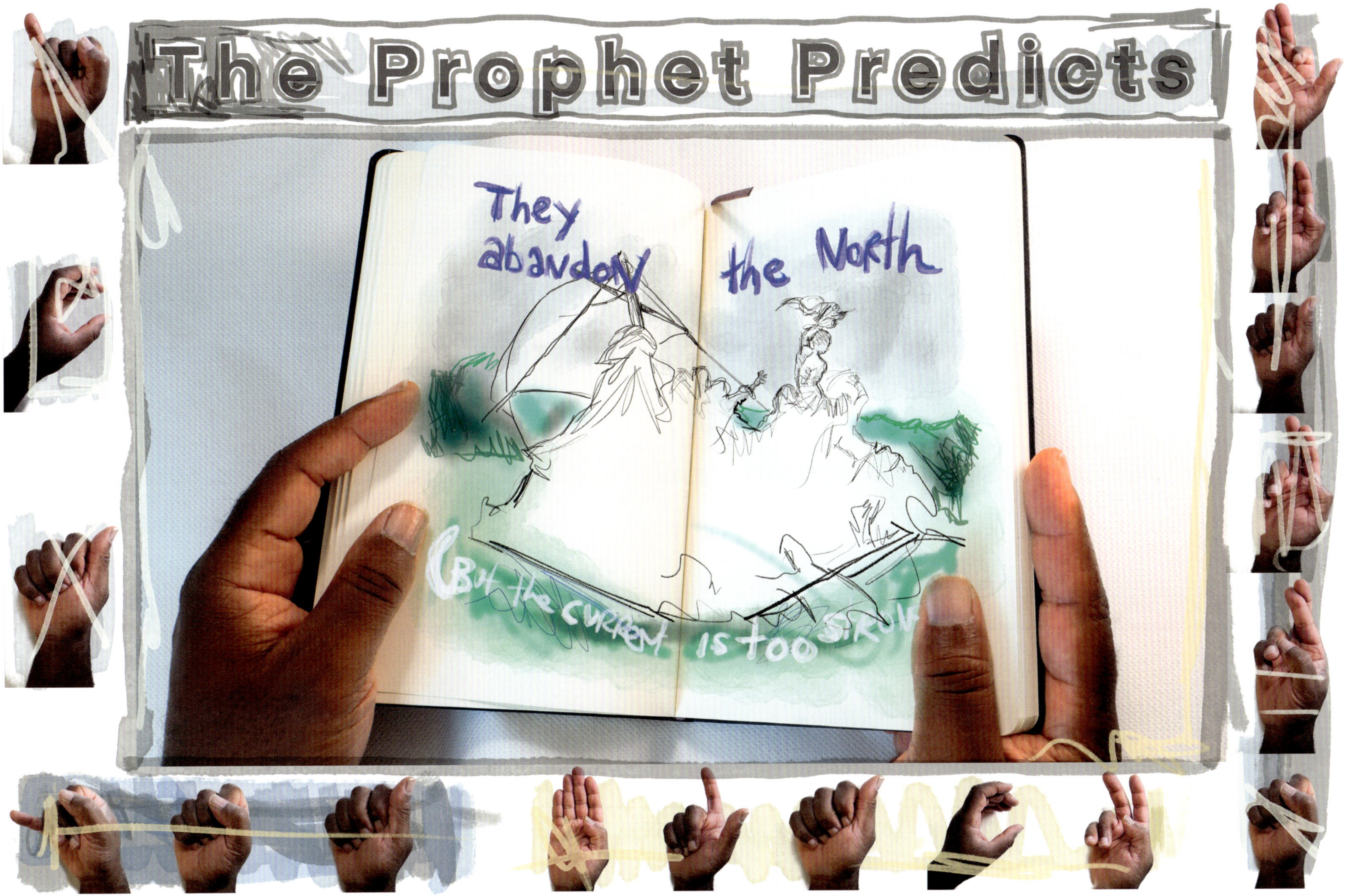
The Prophet Predicts
They abandon the North
But the current is too

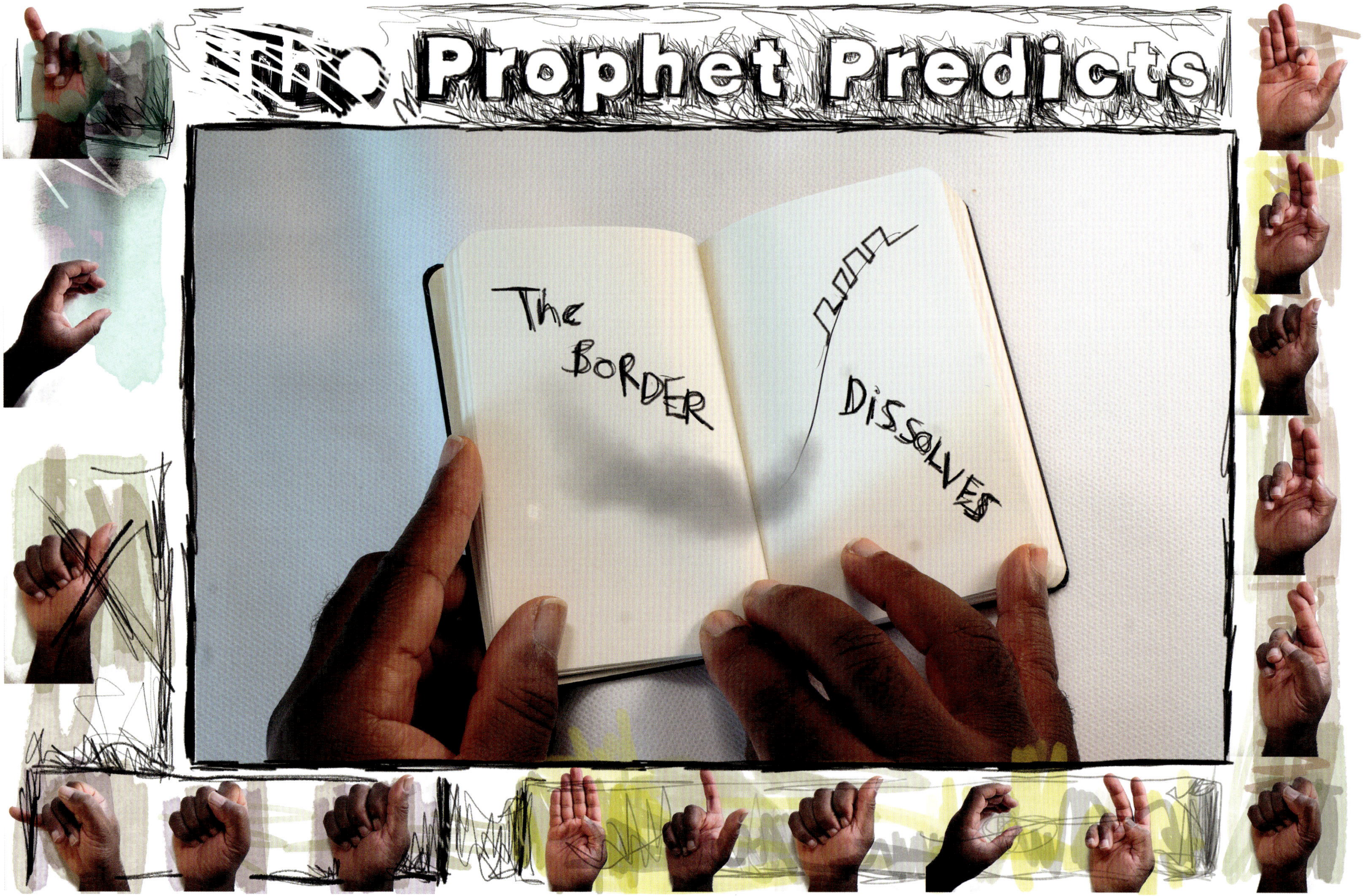
Prophet Predicts
The
BORDER
DISSOLVES

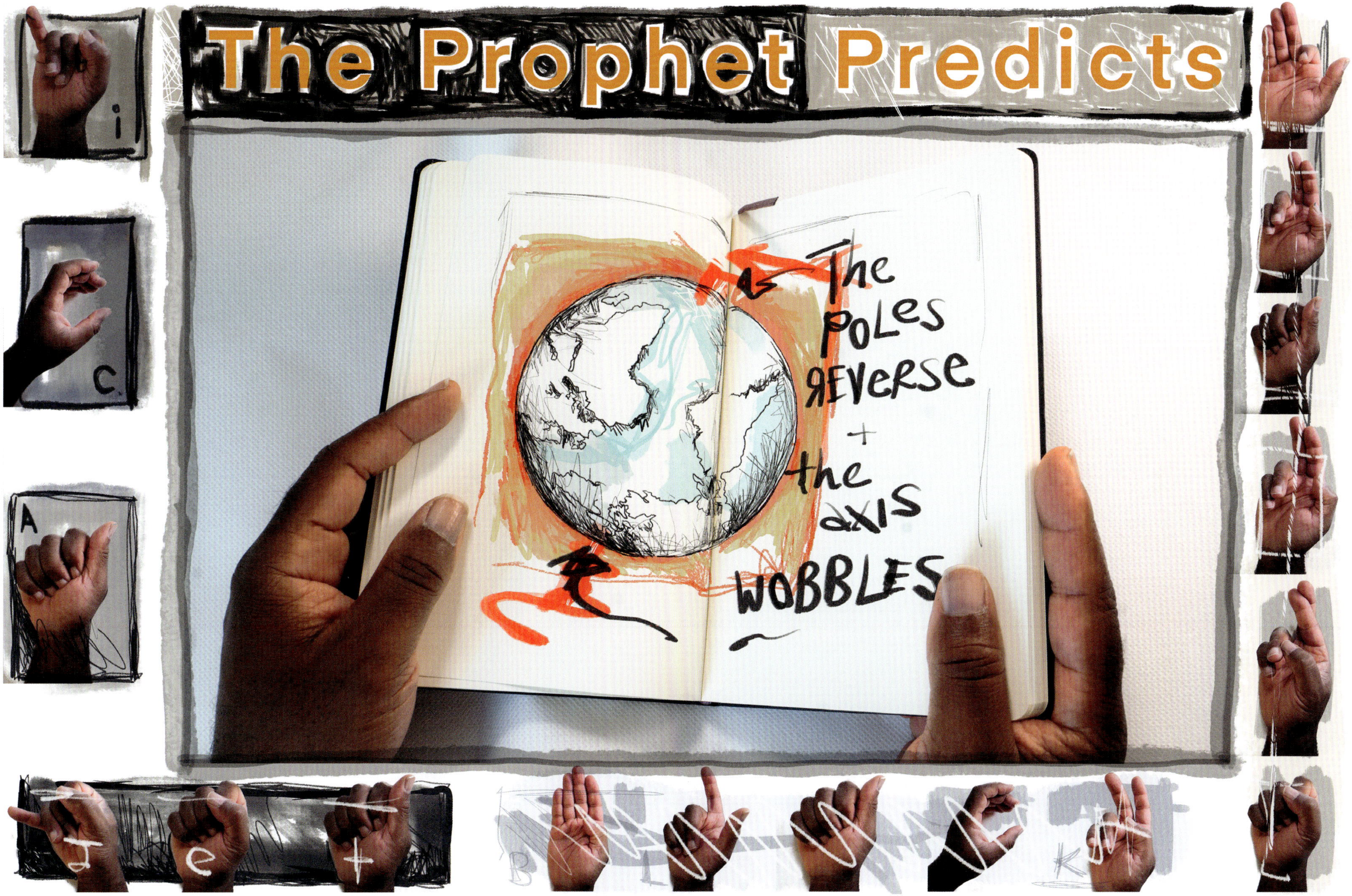
The Prophet Predicts
The poles reverse
+
the axis
wobbles

The Prophet Predicts

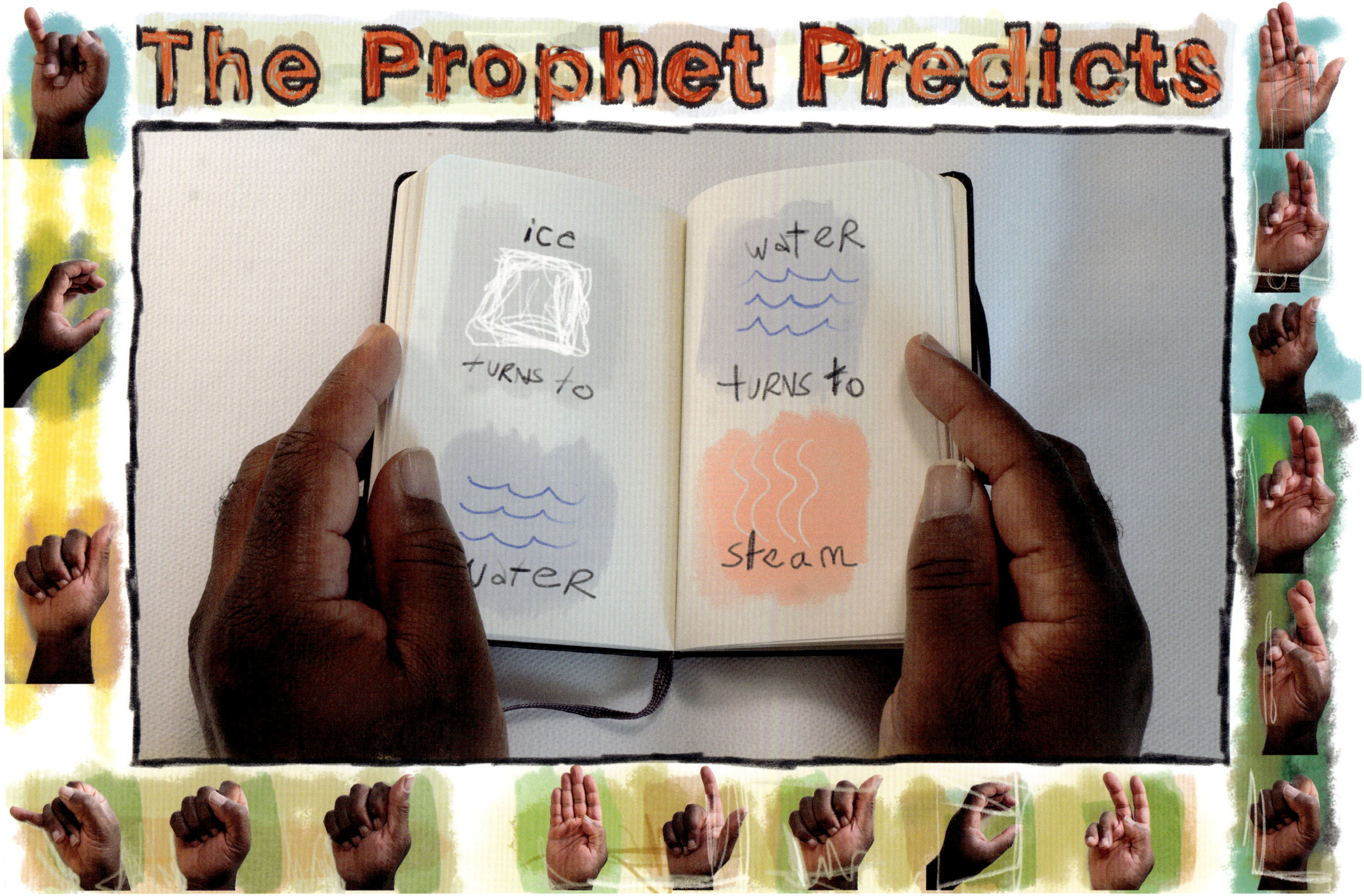

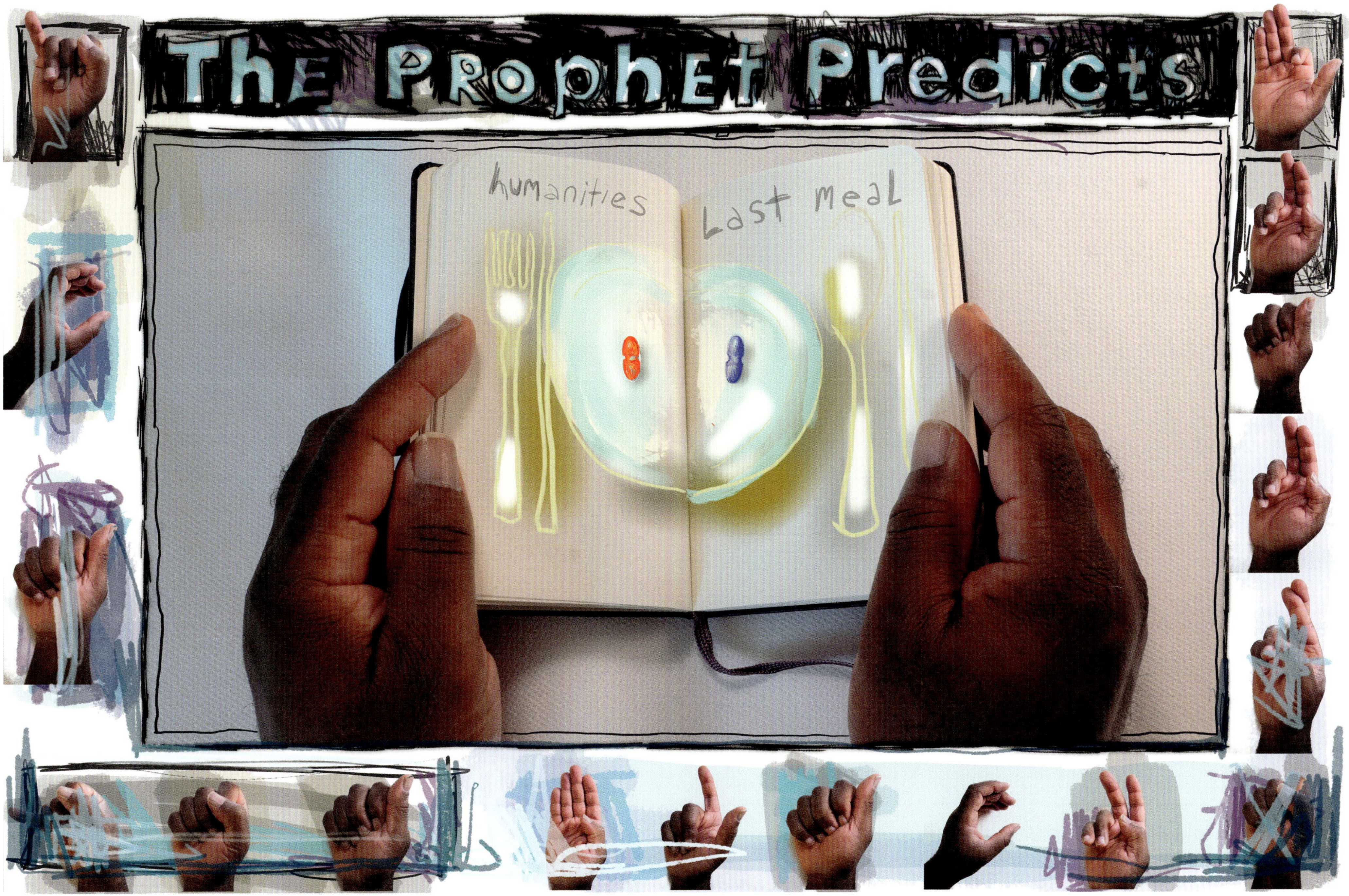
The Prophet Predicts
humanities
Last meal

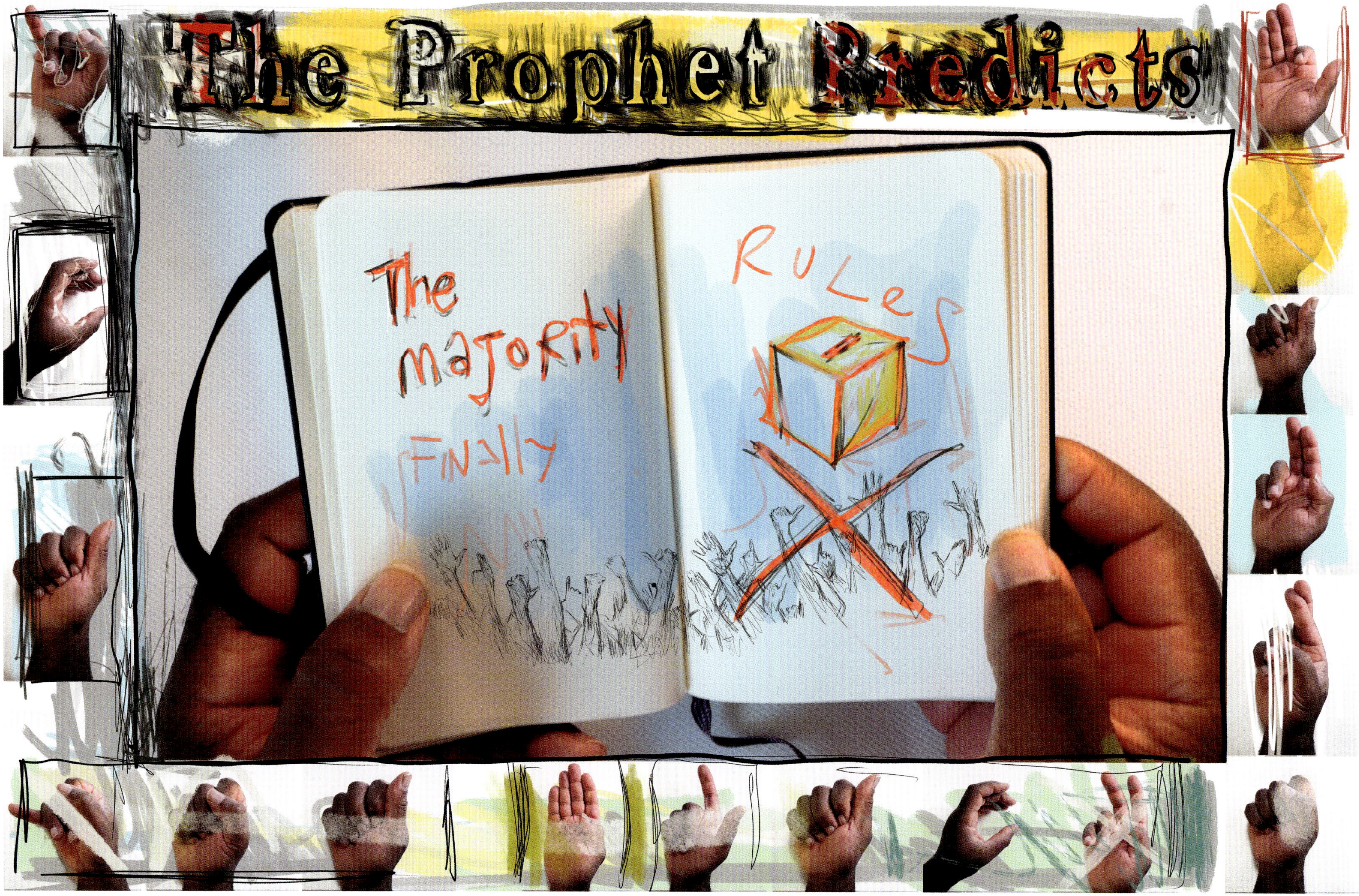
The Prophet Predicts
The majority
Finally
RULES

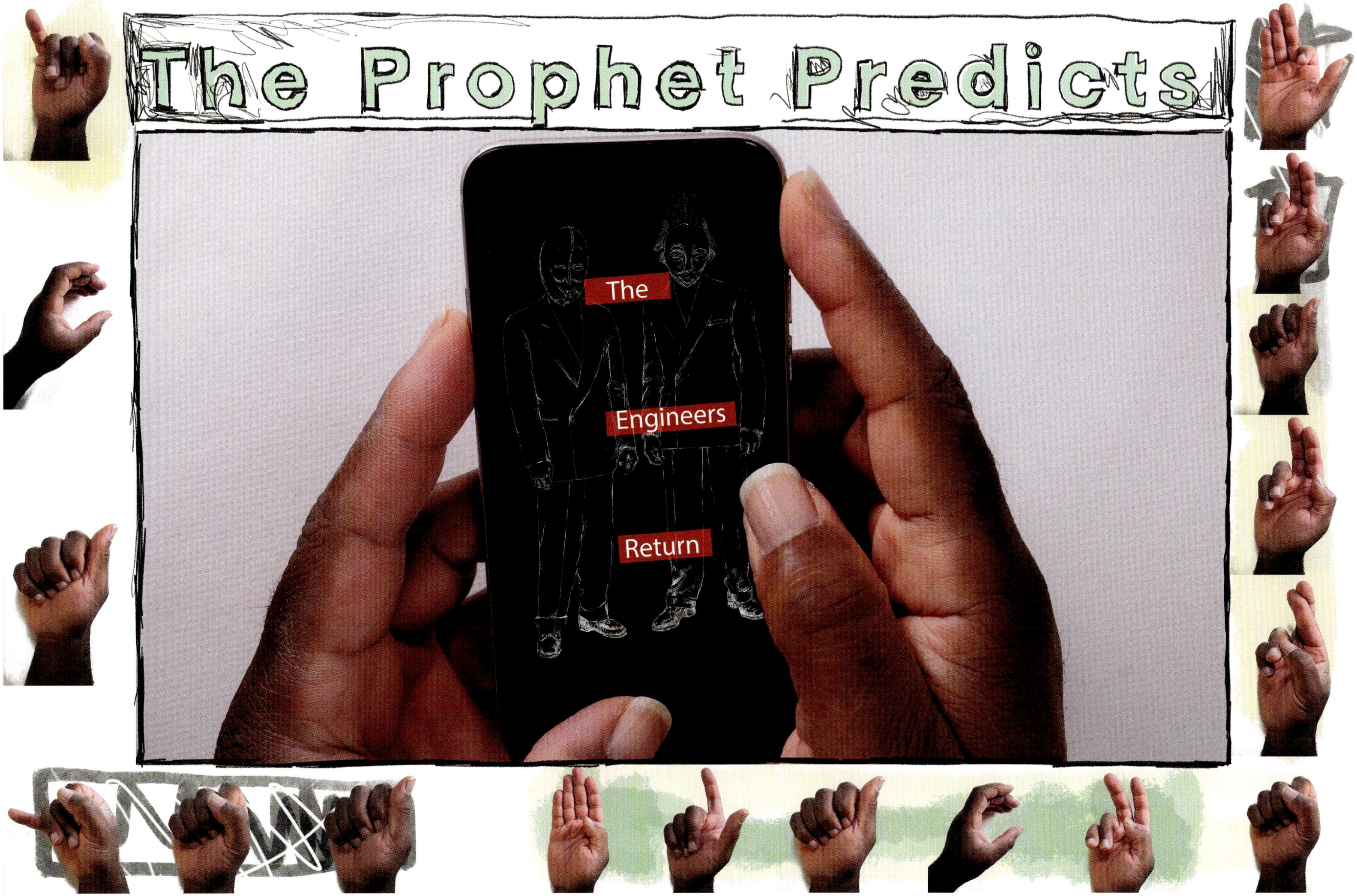
The Prophet Predicts
The
Engineers
Return

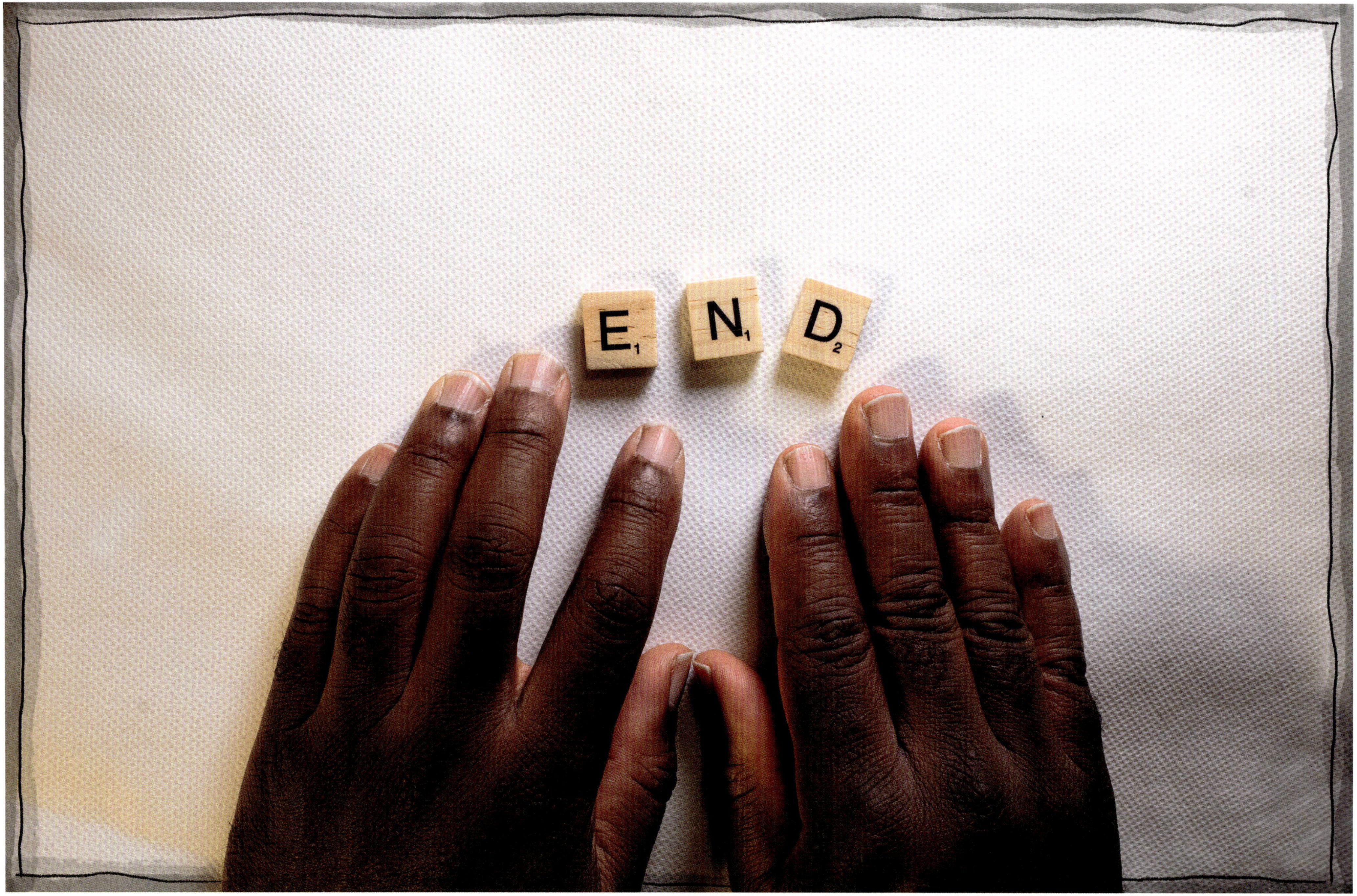
END

Time looping: cyclical pasts and speculative futures in the work of Keith Piper

ANJALIE DALAL-CLAYTON, 2022

'Contemporary society gives man a sense, on a scale hitherto unknown, of connections, of cause and effect, of the conditions from which an event arises, of other events occurring simultaneously. His world is one of constantly increasing multiplicity of relations between himself, immense mechanical constructions and social organizations of world-wide scope'[1]

(C.L.R. JAMES)

[1] C.L.R. James, 'Popular art and the cultural tradition' (translation of a talk delivered at a discussion on mass culture held under the auspices of The Congress of Cultural Freedom, on 9 March 1954, at the offices of the French magazine, *Preuves*, Paris), *Third Text*, 4 (10): 3-10, 3.

The experience of engaging with Keith Piper's (b.1960) artworks is consistently multi-sensory. Their visual complexity and richly layered content, anchored in an array of references from the historical to the literary, and the religious to the socio-political, cause our eyes to dart rapidly across the visual field and our minds to leap across time and space, prompting connections in unexpected ways. An additional layer of complexity results from Piper's tendency to circle back within his own practice, whereby he revisits artworks, artistic strategies, visual tropes, themes and concepts. New works almost invariably involve self-quotation, reiteration or reverberation, so that it becomes difficult to consider his newer work without looking back, and similarly, to contemplate earlier works without looking forward to witness them subtly rematerializing several decades later. When looking at Piper's work, it is almost impossible, therefore, to examine just one artwork at a time, or indeed one period of art-making. So, here, I focus on two sets of artworks, each produced four decades apart: the mixed media installation *The Seven Rages of Man* made in 1984 and the later version of the same title made in 2018; and two iterations of the painting *The Four Horsemen of the Apocalypse*, both created in 1984, as well as Piper's newest work, *In Search of Four Horses*, of 2021-22. Seen together, these artworks are wonderfully indicative of the way Piper loops time and narratives, and revisits and reconsiders the past and future in his artistic practice.

Although Piper's work can be interpreted from numerous angles and perspectives thanks to its multiple layers and reference points, my critical and art-historical analysis is consciously grounded in the acts of active listening and close looking. That is, my understanding is guided by several interviews with Piper and repeated visual inspection of artworks, both with and without the presence of the artist. My objective in taking this two-pronged approach is to develop an interpretation that is both initiated by the art object, and directed by its maker. My aim then, is to offer a reading of Piper's work that is representative and respectful of his intentions. It is a curious thing, however, to write about an artist's work, when the artist writes about their own work as part of their practice. For many years, Piper has written and posted reflective essays about his practice on his website, providing unmediated insights into his artistic process and interpretations of his artworks.[2] This leaves me wondering what I, as an art historian, as a respondent, can offer in terms of original but compatible appraisal. My answer is to suggest how Piper's work might be positioned within both the histories of art, and contemporary artistic practice - something Piper is too unassuming to do in his own writing.

Thus, in the following pages I first present a close and highly descriptive reading of *The Seven Rages of Man*, 1984, and Piper's 2018 updated work of the same title, drawing attention to similarities and differences between the two iterations and considering how we might locate these artworks in relation to the techniques, genres and movements of art's histories, including gestural mark making, photomontage, narrative art, commemorative art, and Afrofuturism. Then, I examine the two versions of *The Four Horsemen of the Apocalypse* that Piper created in 1984, and *In Search of Four Horses*, 2021-22, to suggest how these artworks might be understood in relation to comic strip art, political satire, Pop Art, history painting, apocalyptic art, and socially-engaged practices. Analysing some of the many art historical genealogies to which Piper belongs helps disclose how his oeuvre loops in and around itself, showing how he uses his past work to drive his artistic practice forward.

Δ

[2] See *Keith Piper's website*, available at http://www.keithpiper.info/ (accessed 4 March 2022).

Keith Piper's artistic career began in 1979 whilst undertaking a Foundation Diploma in Art at Lanchester Polytechnic in Coventry. Initially, his practice was conceptual, involving the production of temporary sculptures using found objects and ironic text-only pieces. However, once he became engaged in the Blk Art Group in the first years of the 1980s, his practice took a turn towards the figurative and highly referential.[3] The Blk Art Group was primarily concerned with engaging in Black political struggle, empowering Black artists, and encouraging white artists to incorporate more social relevance into their practices. Crucially, they were critical of high-modernist and conceptual artistic practices that were self-referential, and instead sought to profile artists and produce art forms that addressed the needs of the Black community and which would raise Black consciousness.[4] Heavily committed to the concerns and objectives of the group, Piper began developing his practice in directions that made it easier to display, and in which it could communicate the most direct of messages. This typically involved the combining of image and text, plaster casts, painting, and collaged photocopies in powerful, referential works that visualised Black political struggle. In 1984, Piper brought these artistic strategies and concerns together as part of his burgeoning interest in history, narrative and British imperialism in the installation *The Seven Rages of Man*.

The Seven Rages of Man was a 10m (approx.) wall-based mixed-media frieze comprising eight plastic-covered panels that combined text and pasted photocopied images on sugar paper. Mounted onto seven of these panels were sculptural portrait busts of the artist, made in plaster. The title referenced a monologue in William Shakespeare's play *As You Like It* (c.1599), which describes how a person's lifespan can be understood as comprising seven unique stages. For Piper this concept was useful for conceiving and articulating Black history as a series of seven epochs, as experienced through the various incarnations of one person. The first of the eight panels functioned as an introduction to this idea, presenting the hand-painted words, 'The Seven Rages of Man. I have lived and died and lived again. I have struggled through centuries'. The seven remaining panels, together with plaster casts of the artist's head and shoulders, combined text and image to elucidate the different epochal moments through which the protagonist was, and would be reincarnated. Viewed from left to right, the figure is positioned in the periods of pre-colonial Africa; the Middle Passage; the era of the American slave plantation; post-War migration to Britain from its colonies in the Caribbean; Black British cultural nationalism in the early 1980s; Black revolutionary struggle; and finally, an imagined future in a united, socialist Africa.[5] Reflecting on the installation in a 2016 essay, Piper summarised that, 'the work attempted to reference a sequence of historical "(r)ages" through which the African diasporic subject had passed, and speculate/ advocate around futurological moments to come'.[6]

In 1984 Piper achieved two related objectives in *The Seven Rages of Man*. The first was to express historical, global struggles in terms of a personal struggle.[7] This approach is rooted in Feminist conceptual practices of the 1970s, arguably best characterised by the artist Mary Kelly (b.1941), whose works sought to critically engage Conceptual Art with the wider world in pursuit of activist agendas, including the oft-cited slogan that 'the personal is political'.[8] For Piper, hand-written text played a pivotal role in realising this aim. In earlier text-only conceptual works, text appeared as part of an exploration into the arbitrariness between words and their meanings, or as in *Many People Have Died in Political Struggle* (1980), as signs of impersonal formalities. In *The Seven Rages of Man*, however, text is utilised to locate

The Seven Rages of Man
1984

[3] For more information and discussion of this stage in Piper's artistic career see: Keith Piper, 'Artist's statement', *Black Art An' Done* (Wolverhampton: Wolverhampton Art Gallery, 1981), available at https://issuu.com/blkres/docs/wolverhampton (accessed 28 February 2022); Eddie Chambers, *Black Artists in British Art: A History since the 1950s* (London: IB Tauris, 2014) 105-113; Kobena Mercer, 'Witness at the Crossroads: An Artist's Journey in Postcolonial Space', *Keith Piper: Relocating the Remains* (London: Institute of International Visual Arts, 1997); and Anjalie Dalal-Clayton, 'Legacy Media › Digital Revolution › Analogue Revival: Technological Journeys in the Work of Keith Piper' in *After the Black Arts Movement in Britain: Framing the Critical Decade*, eds. Dorothy Price and Elizabeth Robles (London: Routledge, 2022) [page numbers not available at time of publication].
[4] See Eddie Chambers, 'Black Artists for Uhuru', *Moz-Art: The Arts Magazine of the West Midlands*, March-July 1983, available at https://issuu.com/blkres/docs/blkartgroup1983 (accessed 4 March 2022) and Piper, 'Artist's statement', 1981.
[5] No critical responses to the original iteration of *The Seven Rages of Man* (1984) exist, and therefore, my knowledge and experience of the installation, as a whole, is based on a small number of digitised slides of its installation at the Bluecoat in 1985; images from Piper's 1997 CD Rom, *Relocating the Remains*; and the artist's descriptions of it during interview. For a more in-depth discussion of the content of the original 1984 artwork see Keith Piper, 'Strategic Remembering and Tactical Forgetfulness in Depicting the Plantation: A Personal Account, in *Visualising Slavery: Art Across the African Diaspora*, eds. Celeste Marie Bernier and Hannah Durkin (Liverpool: Liverpool University Press, 2016), 62-78.
[6] Piper, 'Strategic Remembering,' 66.
[7] *Keith Piper*, unpublished interview by Anjalie Dalal-Clayton, 28 October 2015.
[8] For example, Mary Kelly's *Post-Partum Document* (1973-79) featured, amongst many elements, several annotations that detailed her relationship with her infant son over six years in order to explore the issues and contradictions involved in being both an artist and a mother. See 'Post-Patrum Document (1973-79)', Mary Kelly's website at https://www.marykellyartist.com/post-partum-document-1973-79 (accessed 5 March 2022).

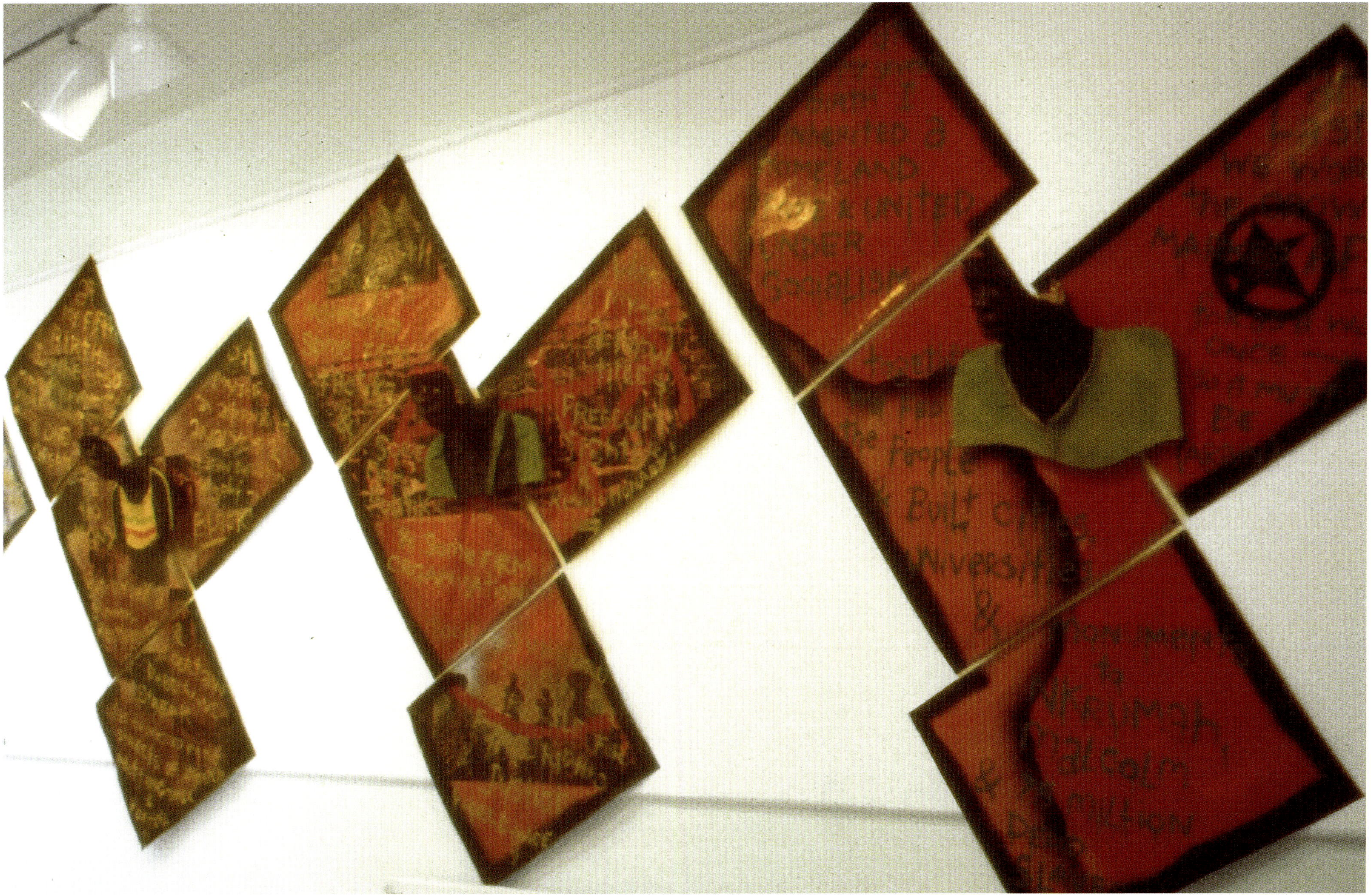
UNDER
FREEDOM
the People
Universities
Malcolm

the image and narrative in a particular moment in time and in an imagined individual's personal experience. By using text in this way, Piper presented and underscored a personal narrative in each part of the installation that simultaneously conveyed a much longer, global history across the entire piece.[9] What Piper described as the 'notion of the symbolic experiencing of historical epochs as personally "lived" moments', would reappear in his multi-part photographic tableaux *Go West Young Man* (1987).[10]

The second objective that Piper achieved in *The Seven Rages of Man* was to challenge the perception that history occurs in discrete stages and that the past is distinguishable from the present.[11] He did this by placing a narrative at the heart of the installation that evoked the idea of historical progression, whilst also challenging it. Narrative art can take different forms, from the simultaneous, the monoscenic, the synoptic, and the continuous, to the panoramic, the progressive and the sequential.[12] *The Seven Rages of Man* is sequential in that it deploys enframement – where each scene or moment is presented in its own frame – to indicate temporal progression, as seen in graphic novels and comics.[13] However, unlike most sequential narratives, *The Seven Rages of Man* disrupts the notion of linear progression by repeating a map motif of West Africa in the second and last panels. Although these sections, or stages, in the protagonist's narrative differ in colour, and contain different temporally located textual statements, both are geographically situated by the black outline of the African continent. These references to the coastal regions of West Africa are suggestive of the Pan-Africanist and Black cultural nationalist vision of a return to the African continent - the 'homeland' of Black, African diasporic people - and thereby, a circularity in the paths of human migration over time.[14]

Piper's investment in the philosophies and objectives of Black cultural nationalism during the early 1980s is also evident by the fact that *The Seven Rages of Man* was first shown in his solo show, *Past Imperfect Future Tense*, staged at The Black-Art Gallery, London, from 7 June to 22 July 1984. Run by Shakka Dedi and Eve-I Kadeena, The Black-Art Gallery was founded according to a Pan-African political ethos, with the specific aim of supporting artists from the African diaspora.[15] Panels 5, 6 and 7 of *The Seven Rages of Man*, which reference self-definition, revolutionary Black struggle and a return of Black diasporic people to a united, socialist Africa, would have been in concert with the gallery's principles.[16] Subsequently, *The Seven Rages of Man* was included in the large survey show *Into the Open: New Paintings, Prints and Sculptures by Contemporary Black Artists* (Mappin Art Gallery, Sheffield, 4 August to 9 September 1984), followed by *Black Skin/Bluecoat* (Bluecoat, Liverpool, 4 April to 4 May 1985), *Depicting History: For Today* (Leeds Art Gallery, Rochdale Art Gallery and Mappin Art Gallery, between March and November 1988). The installation then remained on informal loan from the artist in the Mappin Art Gallery's store for nineteen years, until new-in-post curator, Louisa Briggs, discovered the plaster casts by chance in a box labelled 'Keith Sekou Piper' in 2007.[17] The plaster casts had deteriorated and the eight accompanying panels were nowhere to be found. However, with Piper's permission, Sheffield Museums restored the plaster casts in 2012, after which they remained in storage.

Four years later, in 2016, Briggs asked Piper if he would consider remaking the eight lost panels so that *The Seven Rages of Man* could be included in *Hope is Strong* - an exhibition that would open at Museums Sheffield in 2018.[18] Rather than producing a facsimile of the original, Piper took this as an opportunity to revisit and respond to it in a new installation that could incorporate the restored plaster casts. That the original plaster casts had

[9] For example, in the third panel relating to the Middle Passage, the text reads, 'At my second birth I inherited a chain for my quick black limbs, a whip for my broad black back & a mission to bloat European coffee with the fruits of my unpaid black labour. I was christened with a red hot brand & a new Christian name → slave'. In the final eighth panel the text reads 'At my seventh birth I inherited a homeland free and united under socialism. Together we fed the people & built cities, universities & monuments to Nkrumah, Malcolm & 75 million dead slaves. At last we wore the crown marked Afrikan, for as it was once → so it must be (again)'.
[10] Piper, 'Strategic Remembering', 73. For more on *Go West Young Man* (1987), see Fiona Anderson, 'Keith Piper, Go West Young Man, 1984', *Tate*, available at https://www.tate.org.uk/art/artworks/piper-go-west-young-man-t12575 (accessed 4 March 2022).
[11] Keith Piper, unpublished interview by Anjalie Dalal-Clayton, 28 October 2015.
[12] For an overview of narrative art, see Dominique Collon, G. A. Gaballa, Guy Hedreen, Marianna S. Simpson, D. A. Swallow, David M. Jones, Paula D. Leveto and Randy R. Becker, 'Narrative art', *Grove Art Online*, available at https://www.oxfordartonline.com/groveart/view/10.1093/gao/9781884446054.001.0001/oao-9781884446054-e-7000061028 (accessed 4 March 2022).
[13] Connections may also be drawn with the Stations of the Cross, a series of fourteen images depicting the Passion of Christ, from Jesus' betrayal in the garden of Gethsemane, his condemnation to death, his journey carrying the cross, and his crucifixion. The Stations are commonly found in Christian churches, marking stages in a processional route that worshippers follow in their contemplation of Christ's suffering and his journey towards his resurrection and salvation. In Piper's work, an equivalent journey from suffering to freedom may be found, while the placement of its sculptural elements encourages a similar meditative physical progression. Thanks to Alice Correia for alerting me to this potential reading.
[14] The idea of Black diasporic people from around the globe 'returning' to Africa first developed in the eighteenth and nineteenth centuries as part of the abolitionist movement in the United States. This idea became instilled in the 'Back to Africa' movement. Although the movement did not result in large numbers of formerly enslaved African-Americans moving to Africa, the idea remained popular into the twentieth century through the work of Black political activists including Marcus Garvey (1887-1940), who envisioned himself as leader of Africa as a unified, one-party state. For more on this history, see Stuart A. Kallen, *Marcus Garvey and the Back to Africa Movement* (New York: Greenhaven Publishing, 2006).

***The Seven Rages of Man* (detail)**
2018

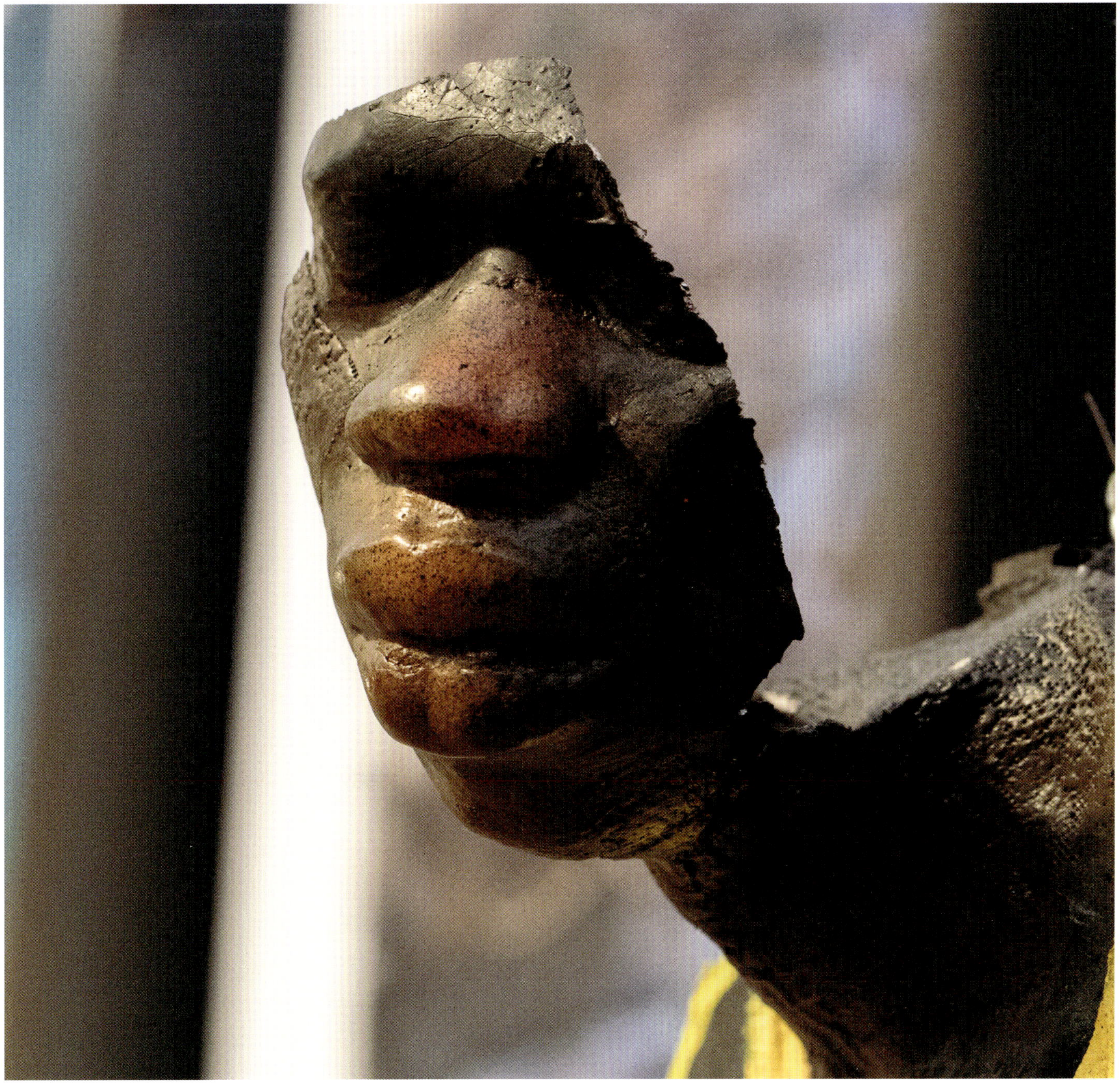

[15] For more information, see 'The Black-Art Gallery', Diaspora-artists.net, available at http://new.diaspora-artists.net/display_item.php?table=venues&id=14 (accessed 4 March 2022).
[16] The text on panel 5 read, 'At my birth I inherited more misinformation, more misprogramming & one great white lie too many. Got myself a growing restlessness & a certain rebellious streak (as expressed on the streets of Brixton, Notting Hill & Toxteth). Got myself an alternative analysis & a new definition of myself – Black.' The text on panel 6 read, 'At my sixth birth I inherited some firm tactics & some firm politics & some firm organisation. Took a vanguard role in the struggle for equal rights & justice worldwide. Won myself a new title – Freedom Fighter & Revolutionary'. The text on panel 7 read, 'At my seventh birth I inherited a homeland, free & united under socialism. Together we fed the people & built cities, universities & monuments to Nkrumah, Malcolm & 75 million dead slaves. At last we wore the crown marked 'Afrikan', for as it was once, so it must be (again)'.
[17] It is likely that the components of the installation remained in storage in, and recorded as on loan to, Sheffield Museums because Piper did not have the space to store it himself at the time; Donald Rodney's *The House that Jack Built* (1987), remained on loan to Sheffield for several years for this reason. However, Piper was not aware of Rodney's arrangement and assumed that his installation had been lost in transit.
[18] *Hope is Strong*, Millennium Gallery, Sheffield, 17 February to 10 June 2018.

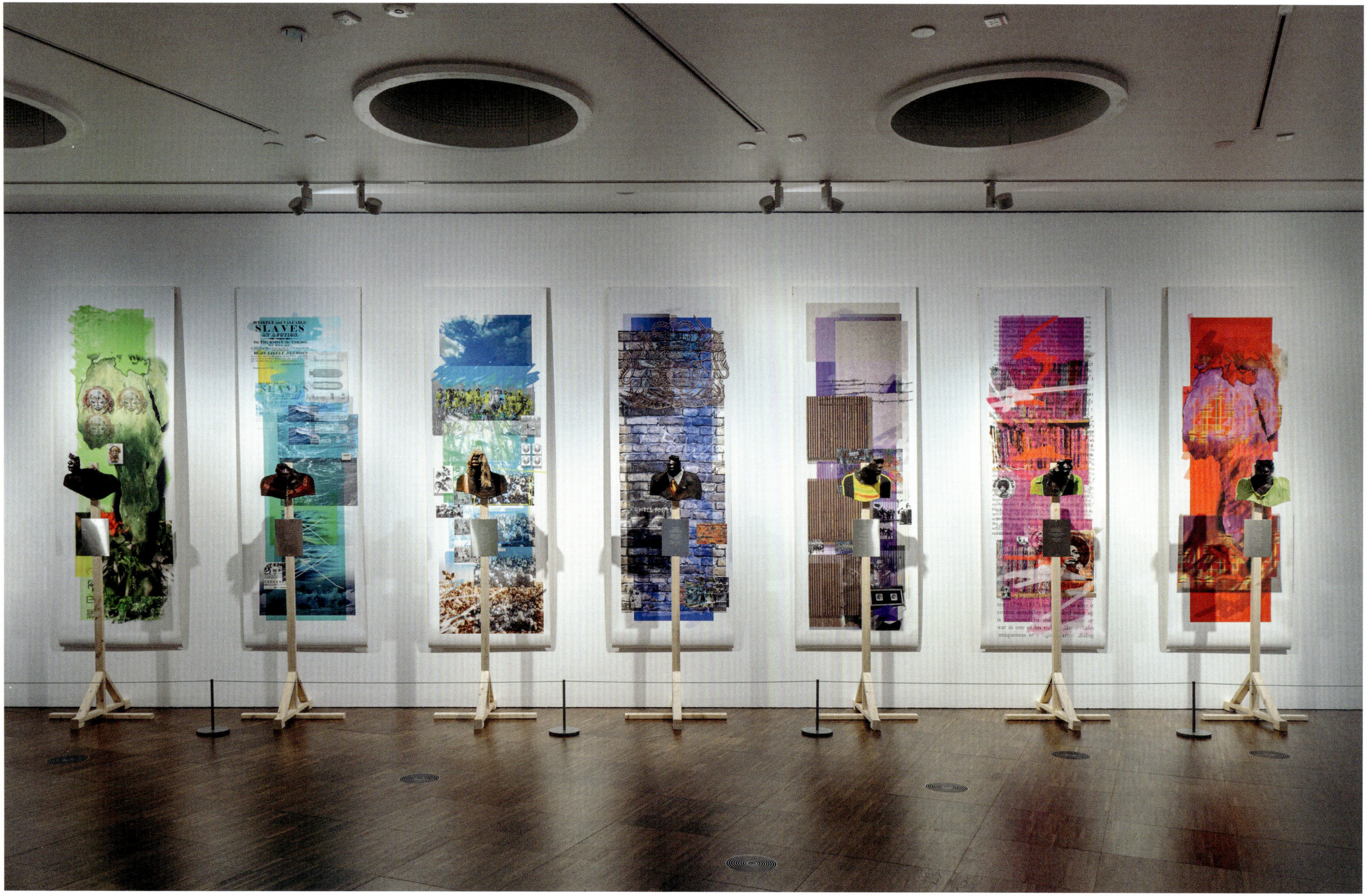
SLAVES

The Seven Rages of Man
2018

been found in a box labelled 'Keith Sekou Piper' was an immediate reminder to him of his engagement in the politics of Black cultural nationalism in the early 1980s, and prompted a reflection on how his politics had since shifted. Although he would later stop using it, during the 1980s Piper adopted the West-African, Fulani-origin name 'Sekou' as his middle name as a sign of his allegiance to Black cultural nationalist politics.[19] As Piper explained in 2020, when he was approached to remake the missing panels, he was not interested in reproducing the original panels exactly because his political worldview had altered.[20] He therefore set about creating new panels that would critically respond to the politics of the first installation.

The 2018 iteration of *The Seven Rages of Man* is easily comparable to the 1984 version in that it is an installation with sequenced components, including the seven original plaster casts of the artist's head and shoulders. However, the colour scheme, aesthetic, and theme of each panel also remains similar to the corresponding original, including the reuse of several visual signifiers such as: the diagram of the Brookes slave ship[21]; photographs of enslaved workers on American plantations; and the outline of the African continent in the first and final segments. However, there are several significant differences between the two iterations.

The most obvious distinction lies in the fact that each plaster cast bust is mounted on a free-standing wooden post, and each post is accompanied by an engraved metal plaque bearing the text of the corresponding 1984 panel. The physical separation of the busts from the panels establishes a distance between the three-dimensional, reincarnated individuals and the two-dimensional wall panels behind. Although this altered physical arrangement may have had more to do with the fragility of the busts than Piper's desire to allude to his critical distance from the politics of the original installation, in this separation of old and new, it may also be possible to regard a conceptual distance between Piper's politics and aesthetic concerns, then and now. The highly reflective plaques have a commemorative quality - reminiscent of the brass memorial plaques found on park benches, or even perhaps the blue plaques found on the former residences of notable historic individuals or at historic sites – thus representing a new dimension to Piper's engagement with history and notions of the historical. In conversation, Piper commented that it is difficult to read the text on the plaques due to their reflective surfaces, particularly in a gallery setting where there are often multiple light sources.[22] Consequently, the viewer is forced to adjust their position several times in order to be able to read each text in full, thus disrupting the still, contemplative and commemorative quality of the plaques. For Piper, these plaques function as 'a memory'[23] of the original iteration, not only commemorating the historical moment and imagined individual in each segment, but also the first version of the artwork itself - lost but not forgotten. Comparing the hand-painted text on the 1984 panels with the more delicate, yet impersonal and constrained engraved text on the 2018 metal plaques, Piper commented that the former was 'like a shout' whereas 'these new things are like a ghostly whisper of the original text',[24] evoking the commemorative as well as something more official and impersonal, and thereby his own critical distance from the raw and fervent politics of the first iteration.[25]

The second notable difference is that the new panels no longer comprise paint and photocopied images, but are instead digital prints on canvas, presenting high-resolution 'photoshopped' photomontages or composite images. A photomontage is a combination of several photographs brought together in a single frame for artistic effect and

[19] The philosophies and tenets of Black Nationalism, and Black cultural nationalism within it, are too complex and varied to rehearse here. However, the adoption of African or Arabic names was one way that those engaged in its politics, and those of the Black Power movement more generally, chose to exercise self-definition, self-determination and achieve psychological liberation from the identity of the their ancestor's slave masters.
[20] Keith Piper, unpublished interview by Anjalie Dalal-Clayton, 29 May 2020.
[21] 'The Brooks Ship' is a 1788 drawing depicting the horrific way that enslaved African people were transported to the Americas on the British slave ship, which launched from Liverpool in 1781. For more information on this image, see 'Diagram of the "Brooks" slave ship', British Library, available at https://www.bl.uk/collection-items/diagram-of-the-brookes-slave-ship (accessed 4 March 2022).
[22] Keith Piper, unpublished interview by Anjalie Dalal-Clayton, 29 May 2020.
[23] Keith Piper, unpublished interview by Anjalie Dalal-Clayton, 29 May 2020.
[24] Keith Piper, unpublished interview by Anjalie Dalal-Clayton, 29 May 2020.
[25] Since 2020, this particular element might also take on new significances in relation to the Rhodes Must Fall movement and the toppling of commemorative statues of historical figures involved in the Transatlantic Slave Trade, such as the removal of a statue of Edward Colston in Bristol, 2020.

has origins in nineteenth century collage. However, the technique notably became a tool for the German Dadaists in their protests against World War I, thus entering the sphere of modern art as a mode for artistic social and political protest and also enabled artists to make important strides in their respective fields.[26] During the 1960s for example, the African-American artist Romare Bearden (1911-1988) combined cut paper, photographs and paintings in photomontages such as *The Dove* (1964), in order to depict Black life in America in unusual and thought-provoking juxtaposed images. Bearden's use of the photomontage technique was significant in that, as Kobena Mercer has astutely observed, it 'resolved the apparent dichotomy between abstraction and figuration in African-American debates on art's relation to politics'.[27]

Just as the photograph had been ground-breaking in the nineteenth century for its ability to represent alternative, or arguably more accurate versions of reality, the photomontage had revolutionary potential at the end of the twentieth century, particularly for artists who used it to create visions of the future. Digital image editing software and programmes such as Adobe Photoshop and Paint Shop Pro made the process of assembling photographic components faster and much easier, enabling artists to realise their artistic visions by combining highly divergent visual elements within a single image. Today, numerous artists, including Stacey Robinson (b.1972), Damon Davis (b.1985) and Manzel Bowman (b.1990), are using digital composite images or photomontages to imagine alternative histories and to speculate about the future with visually-convincing and sometimes magical realist images.[28] Although Piper uses the same technologies as these artists to consider different moments in history and to envision a future Africa in the 2018 iteration of *The Seven Rages of Man*,

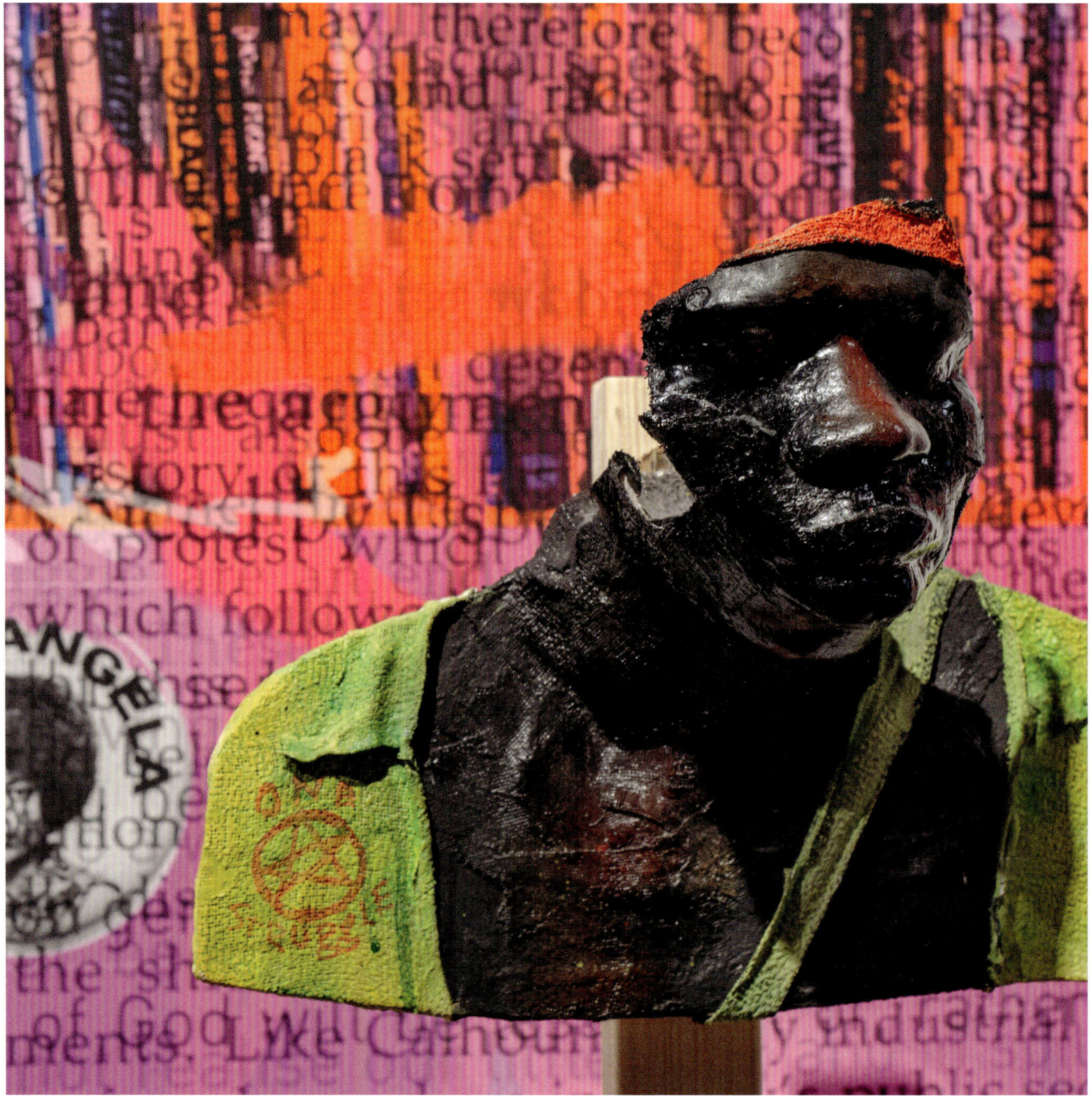

***The Seven Rages of Man* (detail)**
2018

interestingly, he remains broadly faithful to the raw, cut and paste aesthetic of his earlier version, with a discernible layering of images and an echo of the artist's hand at work.

Despite the absence of paint and hand-painted text in the 2018 version of *The Seven Rages of Man*, 'the mark of the hand, an unconstrained hand',[29] as Piper has put it, remains present through his inclusion of lines and scribbles within the collages on the new panels, which he created using a digital stylus and iPad. Piper describes these elements as 'playing around with the aesthetics of the scribble', and as 'a haptic, hand-marking thing'.[30] Mark-making – a form of expression as old as human existence – has a gestural quality. For many Impressionist artists at the start of the twentieth century, the mark, line or dash was used to suggest movement, and often, it implied the presence of emotion in the creative process - a materialisation of the artist's mind. Later in the century, for artists such as Yayoi Kusama (b.1929) and Bernard Cohen (b.1933), mark-making was controlled, systematic and methodical. For others, such as Jean-Michel Basquiat (1960-1988) and Jackson Pollock (1912-1956), it was improvisational, intuitive and impulsive. Piper applied marks by hand directly onto the canvas in his 1984 iteration of *The Seven Rages of Man*, and similar marks reappear in the 2018 version thanks to his digital stylus, which enabled him to retain some of the haptic, gestural quality of the original despite his remove from the physical object via the digital process.

Reflecting on the differences between the two iterations of *The Seven Rages of Man*, Piper has commented,

> '[The first version] was absolutely grounded in the political moment...when I did that show in 1984 [*Past Imperfect Future Tense*] that was the point at which I was most engaged with a very particular politics. So in looking back at the work now, I'm very much about how it sat within that moment... [I want] to re-examine those politics...to look at those politics from a distance... The politics of a young Black British people of specifically Caribbean descent in the early 80s, who were re-orienting themselves towards a notion of African-ness – an Africa of our romantic imagination'.[31]

Piper's re-examination of those politics, and particularly his recognition of the way they produced and engaged with a romantic construction of Africa represents another important difference between the two iterations of *The Seven Rages of Man*. This manifests in his use of Adrinka symbols and Kente cloth in panels 1 and 7 of the 2018 version as signifiers of 'Africa' as an ideal.[32] Adinkra and Kente both originate from Ghana – the first African nation to gain independence from British colonial rule – and these new additions in the panels serve a dual purpose.[33] Together with images of Fidel Castro standing alongside Ghana's first President and a leading figure in African socialism, Kwame Nkrumah; the Marxist scholar and political activist Angela Davis; and the spines of several editions of *Race & Class*, a leading British sociology journal in panel 6, they underscore the importance of socialism within the broader framework of Black nationalism and Black revolutionary struggle. However, the inclusion of Adinkra symbols and Kente cloth may also reflect Piper's ambivalence towards his past politics. Adinkra and Kente are among some of the West African cultural traditions that became popular emblems of Afrocentrism, Pan-Africanism and Black cultural nationalism in late-twentieth century Europe and North America, so much so that their commodification and misapplication outside Ghana, and West Africa, became signifiers of a romantic idealism. Arguably these forms of cultural

[26] See Dawn Ades, *Photomontage* (London: Thames and Hudson, 2021).
[27] Kobena Mercer, 'Witness at the Crossroads: An Artist's Journey in Postcolonial Space', *Keith Piper: Relocating the Remains* (London: Institute of International Visual Arts, 1997), 28. For further discussion of Romare Bearden's use of photomontage, see Kobena Mercer, 'Romare Bearden 1964 Collage as Kunstwollen', *Cosmopolitan Modernities*, ed. Kobena Mercer (London: INIVA, 2005), 124-145.
[28] Robinson, Davis and Bowman's practices are located within the canon of Afrofuturism, discussed below.
[29] Keith Piper, unpublished interview by Anjalie Dalal-Clayton, 29 May 2020.
[30] Keith Piper, unpublished interview by Anjalie Dalal-Clayton, 29 May 2020.
[31] Keith Piper, unpublished interview by Anjalie Dalal-Clayton, 29 May 2020.
[32] According to Kobena Mercer's assessment of Piper's earlier work, in which symbolic references to Africa frequently appear, 'Piper is alluding not to Africa as it is but to an idea of "Africa" as it exists in the diaspora imagination as the signifier of a lost origin reconstructed in collective memory as a presiding symbol for the production of a new identity' (Kobena Mercer, 'Witness at the Crossroads: An Artist's Journey in Postcolonial Space', *Keith Piper: Relocating the Remains*. (London: Institute of International Visual Arts, 1997), 28).
[33] Adinkra symbols represent concepts, aphorisms or proverbs and are typically found on pottery and cloth, and more recently on t-shirts and jewellery aimed at the tourist market. Kente cloth is a distinctive hand-woven textile often used for the purposes of commemoration.

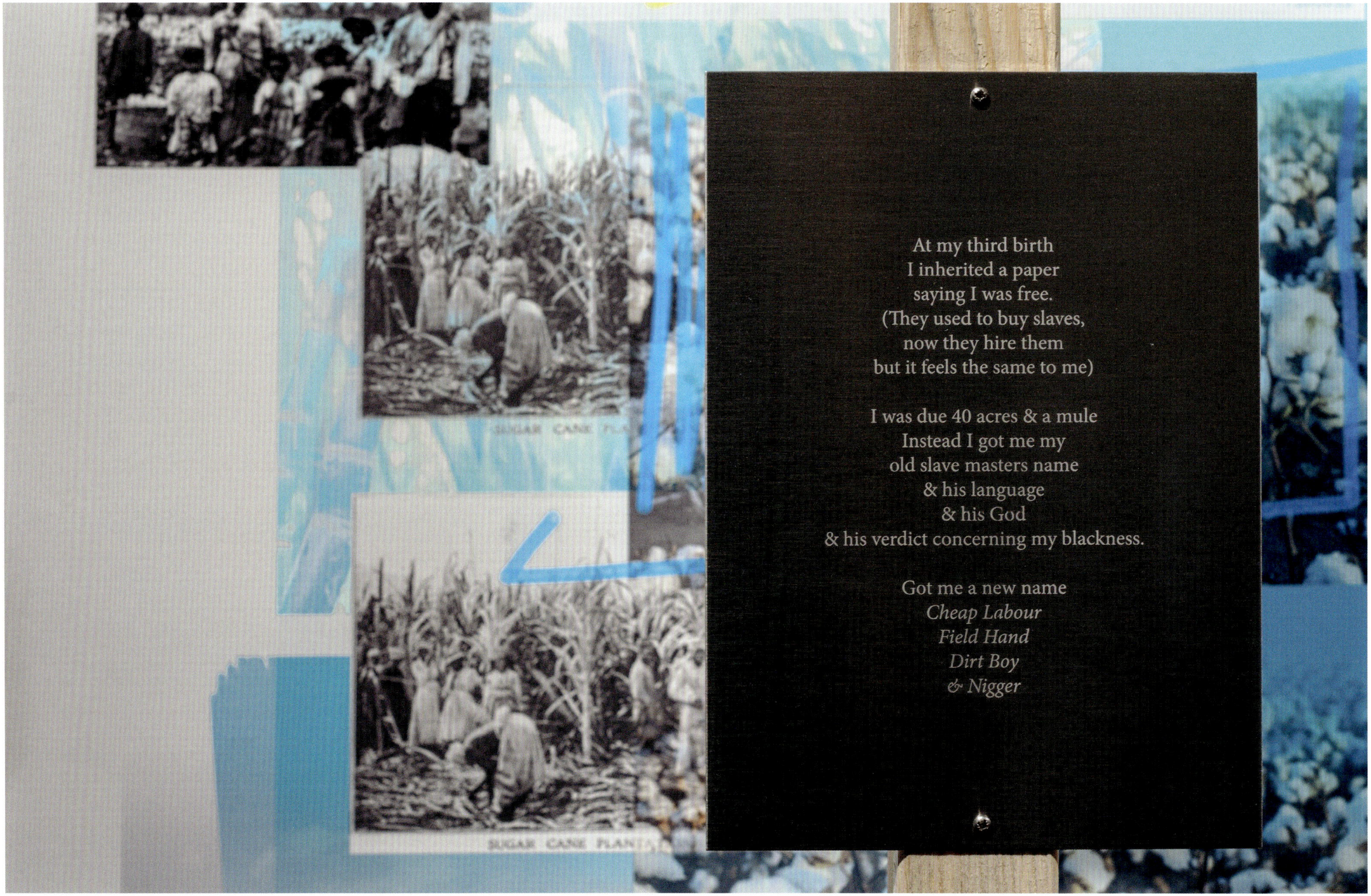
At my third birth
I inherited a paper
saying I was free.
(They used to buy slaves,
now they hire them
but it feels the same to me)

I was due 40 acres & a mule
Instead I got me my
old slave masters name
& his language
& his God
& his verdict concerning my blackness.

Got me a new name
Cheap Labour
Field Hand
Dirt Boy
& Nigger

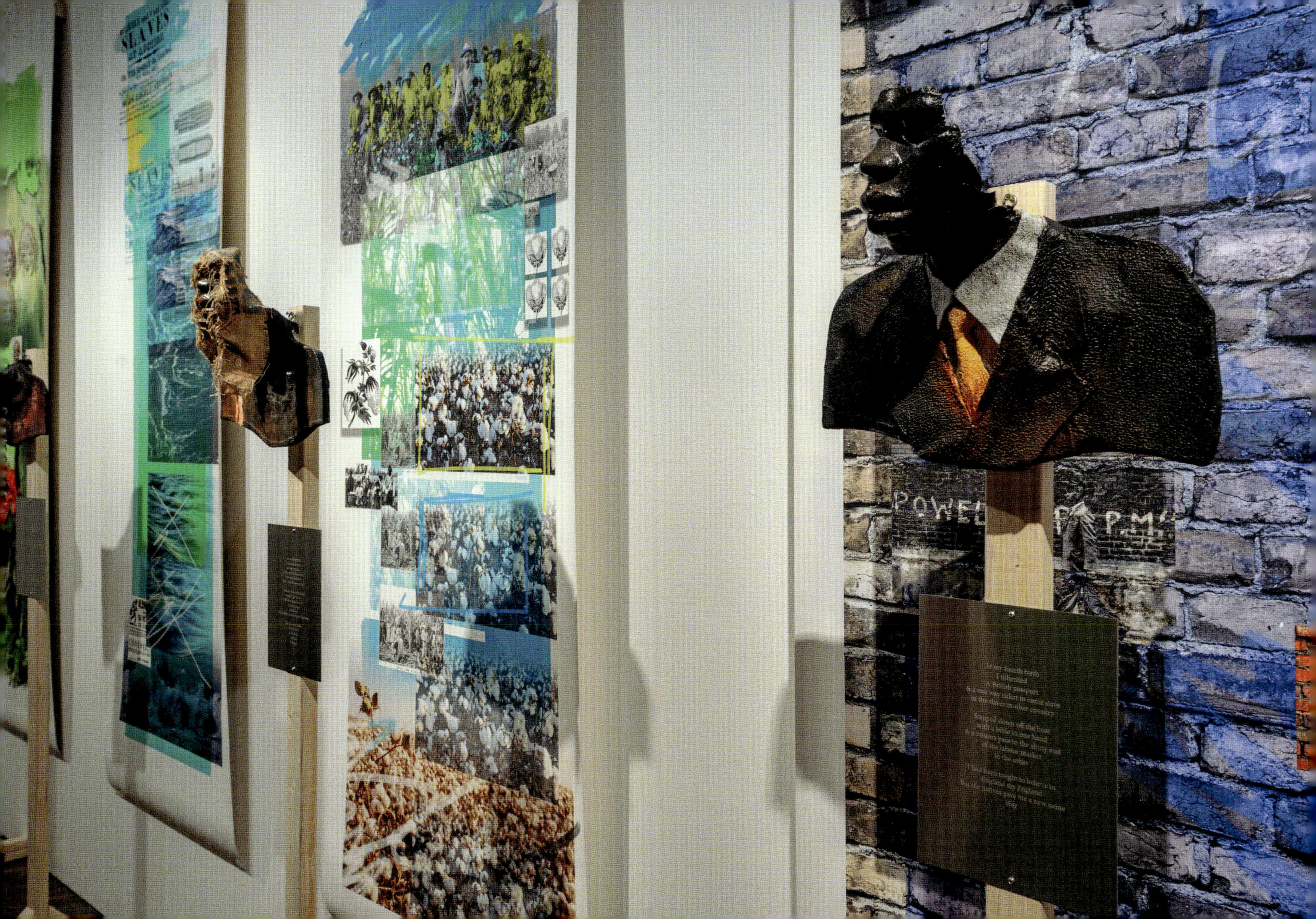
SLAVES
POWELL
P.M.
At my fourth birth
I inherited
A British passport
& a one way ticket to come slave
in the slaves mother country
Stepped down off the boat
with a bible in one hand
& a visitors pass to the shitty end
of the labour market
in the other
I had been taught to believe in
England my England
but the natives gave me a new name
Wog

expression, within a Euro-American context, became symbolic of a displaced diasporic imagining of Africa that was not rooted in the lived realities on the African continent.[34] In 2020 Piper was reluctant to discuss exactly how his politics have shifted since the early 1980s, stating, 'That's a whole other conversation!', but he acknowledged a move away from some of the certainties of Pan-Africanism.[35] A shift in Piper's thinking may also be identified in his removal of any mention of socialism in panel 7. In the 1984 version, the hand-painted text read, 'At my seventh birth I inherited a homeland, free & united under socialism', whereas in the second version the words 'under socialism' are omitted from the inscribed metal plaque.

This is not to say that Piper has abandoned idealised imaginings of Africa within his practice altogether. In panel 7, collaged images of computer circuitry form map-like pathways within the cartographic outline of the African continent and may be read as a reference to neocolonial developments in Africa, whereby rare minerals and metals are being mined by predominantly Chinese corporations for use in the production of electronics.[36] But, this visual motif is better understood as an Afrofuturist vision of Black liberation.[37] As both a philosophy of history and science and a cultural aesthetic, Afrofuturism explores the future of African and African diasporic cultures and peoples in relation to advancements in science and technology. It has a significant visual history in which artists and filmmakers have pictured Black people not only within, but at the forefront of technological progress and future thinking. Panel 7 of the second iteration of *The Seven Rages of Man* does not present the fantastical or magical realist vision of Africa that characterises the practices of numerous Afrofuturist artists, including Stacey Robinson, Damon Davis and Manzel Bowman, mentioned above. Africa's role in advancing technologies, which is acknowledged by Piper's inclusion of computer circuit imagery, is a reality rather than a fantasy. Nonetheless, his combination of these images and reference points, and his envisioning of Africa's 'technologically driven [rather than socialist] future',[38] unquestionably positions him within an Afrofuturist canon.

Despite the differences between the two versions of *The Seven Rages of Man*, there is a continuum between them. Both present Black struggle as global and personal by depicting seven epochs as experienced through the incarnations of a single individual and expressed through a first person narrative. Further, by presenting a narrative that finishes - geographically – where it starts, both contest the notion that history is linear. Finally, despite being produced in different media, both are expansive, multi-layered and visually complex installations. It is significant that Piper retained some of the discordant cut and paste aesthetic of the original version in his 2018 iteration through his use of digital mark-making, while also harnessing the possibilities of digital technology. The transparent layering of images that was enabled through digital photomontage techniques has created a lattice-like appearance that is more ambiguous and less assertive than the bold solidity of the original panels. This, combined with the inclusion of the commemorative plaques, has resulted in a work that speaks in a quieter voice, acting as a site of contemplative remembrance of what the installation once was, and of the politics that Piper was once engaged in. At the same time, the work also points to a speculative future – this time, one that is based less in an idealised African past, but which is driven by technological developments that are already underway. As such, the non-linearity of the original installation develops into a more obvious circularity in the updated version thanks to its gentle but critical revisionism.

Δ

***The Seven Rages of Man* (detail)**
1984

***The Seven Rages of Man* (detail)**
1984

[34] For example, the wearing of Kente cloth that was printed and mass-produced, rather than 'authentically' woven by hand, or the tattooing of Adinkra symbols onto the body without knowing their meaning.
[35] Keith Piper, unpublished interview by Anjalie Dalal-Clayton, 29 May 2020.
[36] For more on the mining of rare earth metals and minerals in Africa, see, Mark Esposito, Terence Tse and Merit Al-Sayed, 'Recolonizing Africa: A modern Chinese story?', CNBC, 2014, available at https://www.cnbc.com/2014/12/30/recolonizing-africa-a-modern-chinese-story.html (accessed 2 February2022), and Vladimir Basov, 'The Chinese Scramble to Mine Africa', *Mining.Com*, 2015, available at https://www.mining.com/feature-chinas-scramble-for-africa/ (accessed 2 February 2022).
[37] For more, see: Kodwo Eshun, 'Further considerations on Afrofuturism', *CR: The New Centennial Review*, 3 (2),287-302; Edward George, 'Last Angel of History', *Third Text*, 35 (2), 205-226; and Paul Gilroy, 'Third Stone from the Sun', *Against Race: Imagining Political Culture Beyond the Colour Line* (Cambridge: Harvard University Press, 2001).
[38] Keith Piper, unpublished interview by Anjalie Dalal-Clayton, 29 May 2020.

In 1984, the same year that Piper produced *The Seven Rages of Man*, he began making another multi-panelled wall-based piece titled *The Four Horsemen of the Apocalypse*. While the former was a narrative sequence depicting several different historical moments occurring over several centuries, the latter provided a snapshot of four contemporaneous and foreboding socio-political moments of the early 1980s. Taking the form of a quadriptych, it combined a diverse range of conceptual and visual references and presented four terrifying figures with both human and equine features. Piper's idea for the figures derived from two sources: the symbolic warnings of death from the New Testament's book of Revelation; and the work of artist Malcolm Poynter (b. 1946).

Poynter is an international sculptor who has been active since the 1960s with a wide-ranging practice that has also incorporated the design of record covers, restaurants, theatres and even jewellery. Several of his sculptures are produced through life casting and integrate unusual materials and objects, such as rubbish, pebbles and toy guns and soldiers, resulting in figures that are as repulsive as they are intriguing.[39]

In the early 1980s, Poynter supplemented his income by working on the UK's art school lecture circuit, and it was at one of his lectures at Trent Polytechnic in Nottingham that Piper became inspired by his work – in particular, his sculptures of human figures with horses' heads, including *Second Horseman of the Apocalypse* (1981). These surreal, life-size, male forms, cast from Poynter's own body are presented in standing or kneeling positions, sometimes alongside other human figures so as to raise questions about power, intimacy and relationality. For Piper, these sculptures spoke to 'our relations with so many issues of that time, from the USSR to missiles, nuclear war'.[40]

However, it was not Poynter's sculptural approach that particularly drew Piper's attention. Piper frequently acknowledges the influence of his Christian upbringing on his practice,[41] and Christian themes and references are evident in several of his works, including *A Ship Called Jesus* (1991), *The Ghosts of Christendom* (1992), and *The Twelve Disciples* (1996). Thus, when introduced to Poynter's horse-headed sculptures, it was the biblical reference in their titles that intrigued Piper and prompted him to explore how the ancient allegory of the four horsemen of the apocalypse might become both a visual and conceptual device for contemporary social commentary within his own practice.

In the book of Revelation, God is described as holding a scroll secured by seven seals. When opened, each of the first four seals summons a being riding on a horse. Together, the four horsemen are sent by God to patrol the earth as harbingers of the Last Judgement. The first is a crowned figure of conquest upon a white horse, who carries a bow and whose role is to invoke pestilence - fatal, epidemic disease. The second carries a sword, rides a red horse, and is an instigator of war. The third rides a black horse, carries a set of scales, and initiates famine. Finally, the fourth rides a pale or grey horse, and simply triggers death. Within Christian visual culture, images of the four horsemen of the apocalypse, such as Albrecht Dürer's (1471-1528) series of prints made in 1498, were potent visual representations of this biblical narrative. Although the religious symbolism of each horseman would undoubtedly have been resonant for Piper given his upbringing, very little of it appeared in his painting. Rather, the biblical allegory provided a loose framework through which he could depict four ominous and relatively contemporaneous socio-political events and circumstances. Piper produced an initial version of *The Four Horsemen of the Apocalypse* early in 1984 while living in Nottingham with fellow artist Donald Rodney

[39] Life casting is a moulding technique using resin that results in hyper-realist representation, especially of the human form.
[40] Melissa Chemam and Keith Piper, 'Keith Piper: on the history of the Black Art Group', Art UK, 2021, available at https://artuk.org/discover/stories/keith-piper-on-the-history-of-the-black-art-group (accessed 19 February 2022).
[41] See Keith Piper, 'A Short History Pt.1', *Keith Piper's website*, available at, http://www.keithpiper.info/statement.htm (accessed 4 March 2022); Chemam and Piper, 'Keith Piper: On the History of the Black Art Group', 2021; and Keith Piper and Robert Beckford in conversation, Ikon Gallery, Birmingham, published 20 August 2021, available at https://www.youtube.com/watch?v=gqwW2LPMt7Q (accessed 19/02/2022).

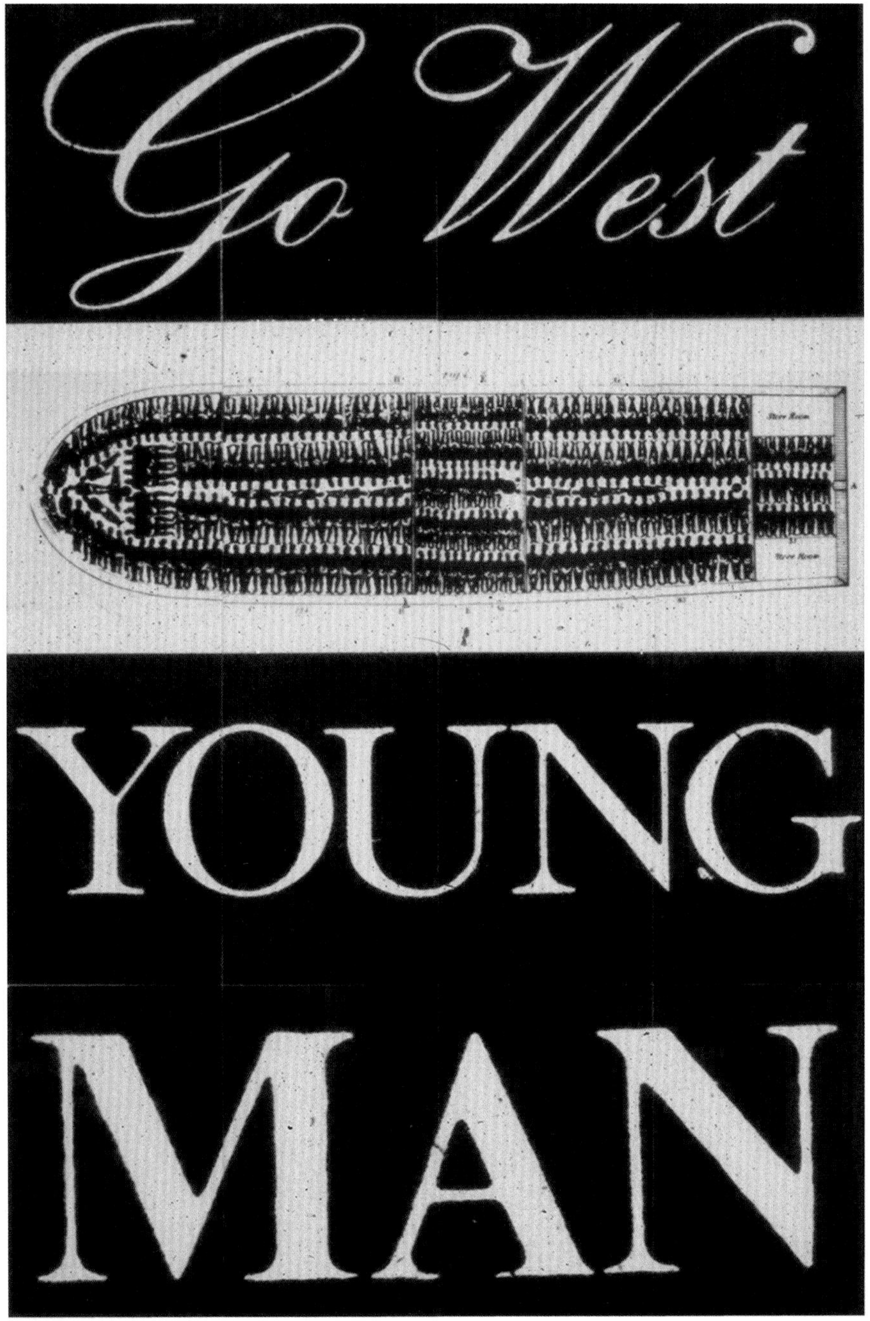

Go West Young Man
1987

The Four Horsemen of the Apocalypse
1984 (earlier version)

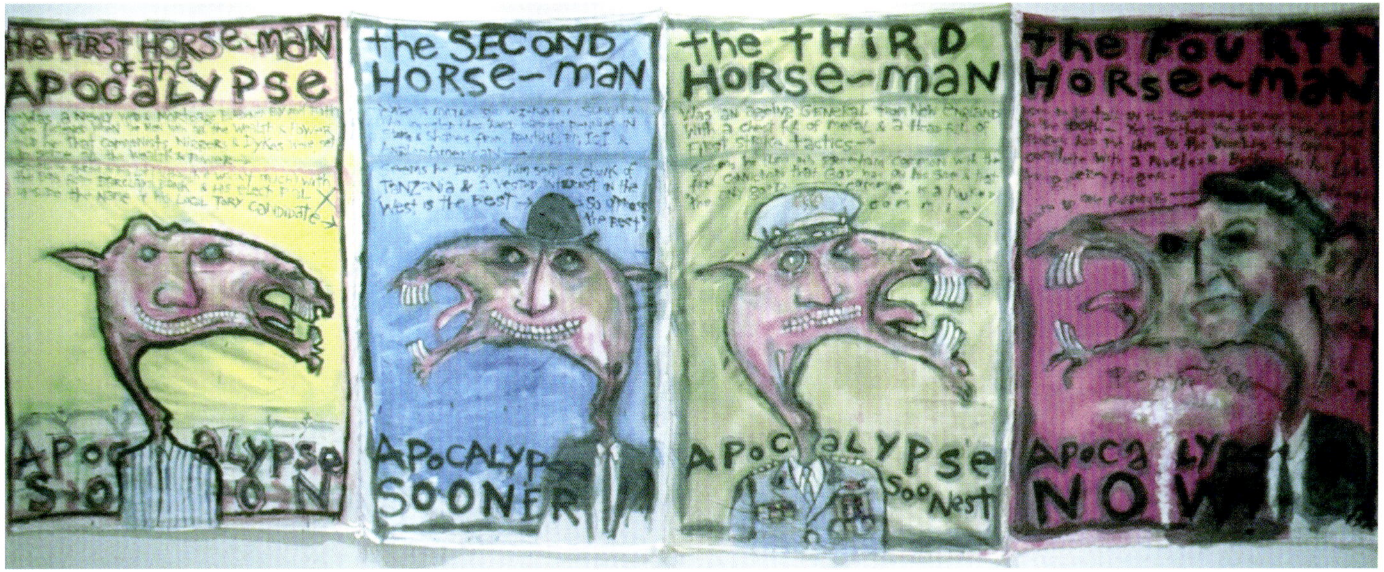

(1961-1998). He would then create a second iteration later that same year. In 2021 Piper returned to the subject in a four-channel video installation titled, *In Search of Four Horses*.

In the first iteration of *The Four Horsemen of the Apocalypse*, Piper offered a crudely rendered but harrowingly depicted reflection on some of the current affairs of the time, using a combination of pigment, wax and flour, painted on cotton bedsheets. Like other works from this period, such as *Black Assassin Saints* (1982); *Most Wanted Persons* (1984); *The Seven Rages of Man* (1984); and *Go West Young Man* (1987), it presented multiple (in this case, four) interrelated rectangular panels, which he demarcated with a thick black border. Each panel included a figure with thin, contorted necks and horse-shaped heads shown in profile, combined with humanistic features facing the viewer. Each panel also included three, hand-rendered textual elements: a title; a short paragraph of explanatory text written in the third-person; and a two-word concluding statement. The first panel had a bright yellow background and featured a figure dressed in a blue and white striped shirt with a thin, black tie. At its top were the words, 'The First Horse-man of the Apocalypse', scrawled in Piper's characteristic handwriting, and at the bottom, 'Apocalypse soon'. Just above the figure was the explanatory text stating that the he 'was a newlywed mortgage burdened boy from Bath who listened when the men with all the wealth & power told him that communists, n[*]ggers and dykes were set to seize all the wealth and power → Seems he threw in his lot (although it wasn't much) with the boys from Barclay's Bank and his electoral X upside the name of his local Tory candidate. The panel speculated about the mind-set of young, white, middle-class, Tory-voting men and how their fear of 'the other' had enabled the Margaret Thatcher-led Conservative party to win two successive general elections in 1979 and 1983. The second panel had a blue background and featured a figure dressed in a black suit and bowler hat, signifying the character's employment in banking. At its top were the words 'The Second Horse-man', and at the bottom, 'Apocalypse sooner'. The explanatory text stated that the figure 'was a Middle aged Wiz-Kid from Surbiton who invested his hard earned pennies in stocks and shares from Rentokil, BP, ICI & Anglo-American → Seems he bought himself a chunk of Tanzania & a vested interest in "'the West is Best → → so oppress the rest'". This panel highlighted the complicity of financially savvy individuals in the exploitation of African countries, through their investment in multinational corporations. Stocks and shares purchased by British people enabled pesticide, oil and gas, chemical and mining companies to explore vast areas of East Africa during the mid to late twentieth century, which in countries such as Tanzania, led to the loss of land, the displacement of people and the disruption of livelihoods.[42] Revenues went primarily to these corporations and their investors, who, the panel text insinuates, were not concerned about how their profits had been generated.

The third panel had a yellow-green background and featured a figure wearing military regalia. At its top were the words 'the Third Horse-man', and at the bottom 'Apocalypse soonest'. The explanatory text stated that the figure 'was an ageing general from New England with a chest full of metal and a headful of first-strike tactics → Seems he flew into Greenham Common with the firm conviction that God was on his side and that the only good Commie is a nuked commie'. Greenham Common was a Royal Air Force station in Berkshire that was used by the US Strategic Air Command during the Cold War. In 1980, it was selected as a base for the deployment of US Air Force cruise missiles.[43] Thus, the third panel highlighted the UK's ongoing involvement in the Cold War through its allyship with the US and the troubling possibility of a nuclear war being initiated from within Britain.

The fourth, final panel had a red background and featured a figure in a black suit with black, glossy hair, clearly depicting the then US president Ronald Reagan (1911-2004). At its top were the words 'The Fourth Horse-man', and at the bottom 'Apocalypse now', perhaps referencing the 1979 Vietnam War film directed by Francis Ford Coppola (b.1939). The explanatory text stated that the figure 'used to be tall in the saddle but now was just long in the tooth. Yet another [illegible word] had put him in the world's top office job complete with a nuclear button for his itchy trigger finger. Woke up one morning, thought it was high noon. Boom, boom, boom'. Prior to Reagan's presidency, the American approach to the Cold War had sought to improve relations with the USSR and Eastern Europe's Communist nations diplomatically, often through the use of soft power. However, following his election victory in 1981,[44] Reagan increased American defences including the production of missiles, thus escalating tensions with the USSR.[45] Consequently, Reagan gained an international reputation for being 'trigger-happy', particularly within the realm of political satire.[46] This final panel encapsulated the atmosphere of anxiety that developed during Reagan's leadership, and the nuclear mushroom cloud billowing up between the closing words 'Apocalypse now' brought the four segments to an alarmingly fateful end.

Although Piper took Malcolm Poynter's sculptures as a point of departure for his production of this artwork, the painting bears more stylistic relation to the work of Basquiat. Indeed, Piper has cited Basquiat's 'aggressively hand drawn diagrammatic and cartoon-like imagery in combination with graffiti-like texts' as an influence in his making of the

[42] On neocolonialism in Africa, see Mark Langan, *Neo-Colonialism and the Poverty of 'Development' in Africa*, (London: Palgrave Macmillan, 2017).
[43] For more on the history of Greenham Common, see David Fairhall, *Common Ground: The Story of Greenham* (London: I.B. Tauris, 2006).
[44] Ronald Reagan's presidency lasted for two terms spanning 1981 to 1989.
[45] See 'Ronald Reagan: relations with the Soviet Union', *Encyclopaedia Britannica*, available at https://www.britannica.com/biography/Ronald-Reagan/Relations-with-the-Soviet-Union (accessed 2 March 2022).
[46] A notable example in the British context was the ITV television programme, *Spitting Image*, discussed below.

The Black Assassin Saints
1984

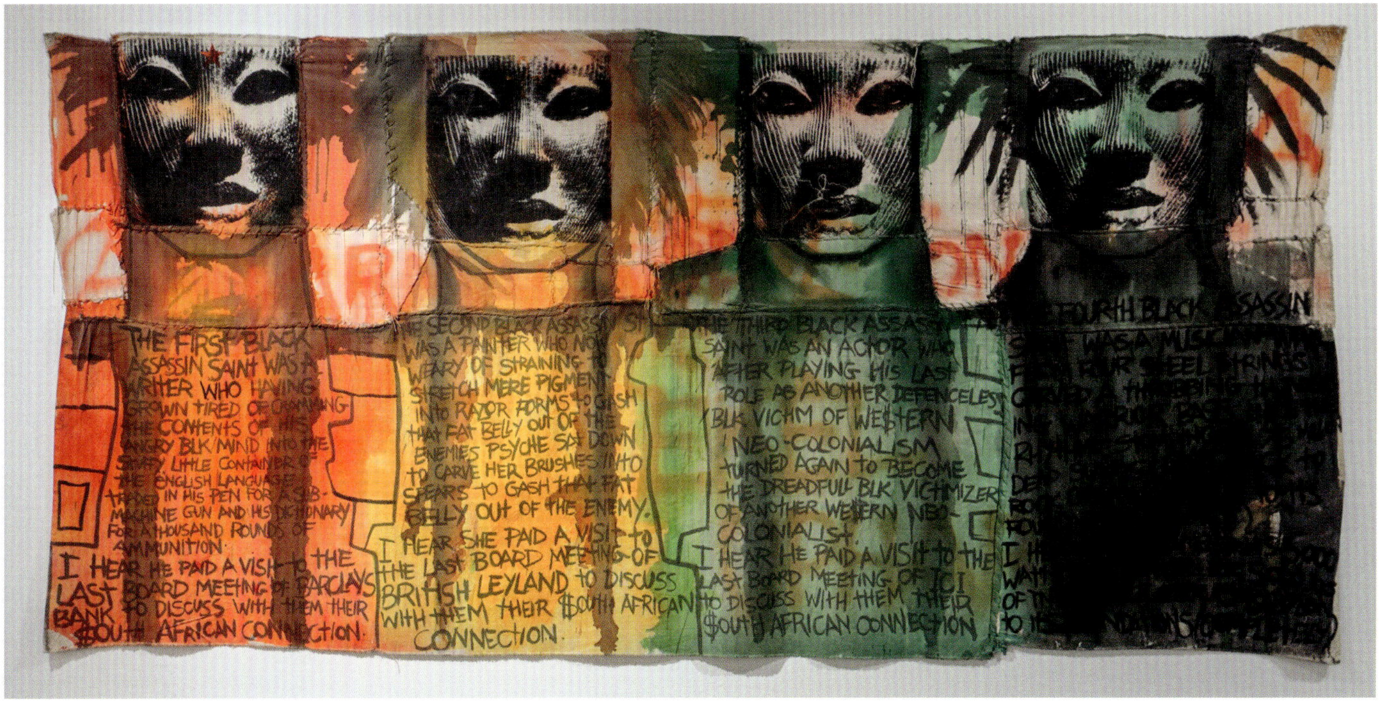

more recent *In Search of Four Horses* (2021-22).[47] Although Piper has not explicitly identified Basquiat as a reference in his production of *The Four Horsemen of the Apocalypse* in 1984, he has acknowledged some stylistic similarities, such as the graffiti-inspired text, rendered by hand to evoke a sense of raw desperation, and the haunting, therianthropic figures that also feature in many of Basquiat's paintings.[48] However, when compared to Basquiat's work, there is an altogether more methodical and structured approach within Piper's painting, which was symptomatic of the fact that he was developing a replicable format for investigating the possibilities of narrative within his practice.

This structured format first appeared in his 1982 work, *The Black Assassin Saints*, which, like *The Four Horsemen of the Apocalypse*, is a large scale, wall-based painting, comprising four similar, rectangular panels, within which Piper presents a figure that is distinguished from those in the other panels through an accompanying textual element. In *The Four Horsemen of the Apocalypse*, Piper's use of text elucidates the identity, characteristics and backstory of each figure. The texts also insert pace and rhythm, steadily guiding the viewer down each panel and onto the next. While they vary slightly in style and do not have a formal poetic structure, Piper's texts employ several literary devices including alliteration, internal rhyme, and echoes of the form of a limerick, which offer a heightened, if not poetic, quality when read.[49] In conversation, Piper commented that these texts were written with story-telling in mind, and that the repetitive,

[47] Keith Piper, 'Working Drawings Towards Four Horsemen', *Keith Piper's website*, 2020, available at http://www.keithpiper.info/jbf_working_drawings.html (accessed 19 February 2022).
[48] See for example Basquiat's painting, *The Dingoes that Park their Brains with their Gum* (1988).
[49] In the first panel of *The Four Horsemen of the Apocalypse*, the form arguably sets up a rhyming pattern that subconsciously triggers the expectation of a limerick – a poetic format that is typically funny, silly, and light. Piper then subverts this expectation by breaking the limerick-like format and continuing with a much longer, dragged out pattern of syllables that in both form and content pulls the reader through a series of images and ideas that are anything but funny, silly or light. However, this idea does not hold as clearly in the third or fourth panel.
[50] Keith Piper, unrecorded conversation with Anjalie Dalal-Clayton, 14 January 2022.

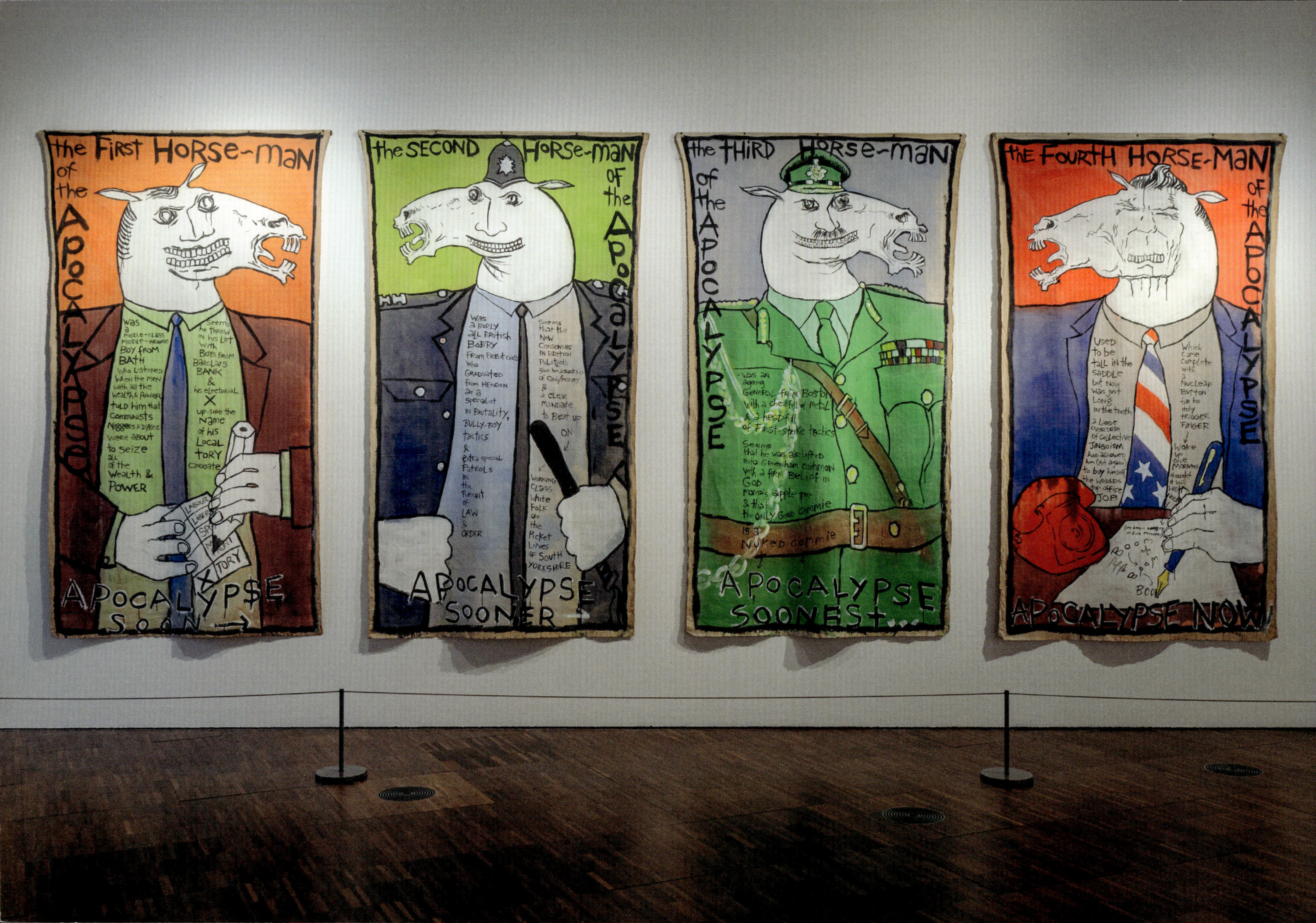
the First HORSE-MAN of the APOCALYPSE
APOCALYP$E SOON →
the SECOND HORSE-MAN OF the APOCALYPSE
APOCALYPSE SOONER
the THIRD HORSE-MAN of the APOCALYPSE
APOCALYPSE SOONEST...
the FOURTH HORSE-MAN of the APOCALYPSE
APOCALYPSE NOW!

The Four Horsemen of the Apocalypse
1984

somewhat poetic structure is, for him, more akin to the verses of a song than the stanzas of a poem.[50]
The first iteration of *The Four Horsemen of the Apocalypse* was displayed at the Blk Art Group's final exhibition, *An Exhibition of Radical Black Art*, staged at Battersea Arts Centre, London, 1 to 26 February 1984, and offered a deeply critical reflection on the relationship between British politics, banking, colonialism and the global economy, as well as the possibility of nuclear annihilation. However, the material composition of the painting rendered it difficult to conserve and display again. Thus, later in 1984, when Piper was invited by artist and book illustrator Joseph Olubu (1953 –1990) to provide an artwork for an exhibition he was devising for the Royal Festival Hall, titled *New Horizons: An Exhibition of Arts*, Piper took it as an opportunity to both reconceive and recreate this artwork.

By the autumn of 1984, Piper had relocated from Nottingham to London to undertake a master's degree in Environmental Media at the Royal College of Art. His studio there had a high ceiling, providing him with the space to produce large work. However, as he continued to face the financial limitations of being a student, some of his materials necessarily remained affordable and unconventional. Thus, when making a second version of *The Four Horsemen of the Apocalypse*, he purchased four large canvases (each 152.5 x 275 cm) but painted them with a variety of cheap children's poster paints. The paint had a particularly flat quality that, in the tradition of Pop Art, enabled him to create a uniform surface of solid colour, reminiscent of work by Patrick Caulfield (1936-2005) or Andy Warhol (1928-1987). Additionally, the four separate canvases offered a clearer distinction between each of the four panels than was achieved in his use of connected bedsheets in the first version. Positioning each canvas at a slight distance from the next enabled the viewer to consider the discreteness of each panel - its figure and socio-political moment - before reflecting on their relationship with each other and combined impact.

In addition to changing his materials and mode of display, Piper also revised the composition. The figures in the second iteration are more imposing, each occupying around two thirds of their respective canvas. While in the first iteration the figures' heads were balanced precariously on thin, distorted and disturbingly withered necks, the heads in the second version rest firmly upon thick, sturdy necks and broad humanistic torsos. Painted in bold white prime, the heads contrast starkly against the background colours orange, green, grey and red. This new composition not only provides an alternative space for the positioning of the explanatory text, but also gives each figure an altogether more imperious presence than in the first iteration. That is not to say that the figures are any less sinister than their first-iteration counterparts - Piper retained the grotesque-cum-Cubist facial and cephalic features - but their altogether more robust and substantial physiognomy aids in conveying the dangerously brutish machismo of the four archetypes represented.

A final key distinction between the two versions of the painting lies in the content and references in the second canvas. In the first iteration, the second figure depicted a banker and the accompanying text referred to the exploitation of African countries by multinational corporations thanks to investment by capitalistic individuals. However, in 2020, Piper explained that it made sense to him to combine the young Tory-voter and the banker from the first iteration of the painting into one character in the second, to enable him to introduce a new character. In the second version the figure in canvas 2 has become a police officer with an accompanying text explaining that he 'was a burly all British bobby from Brent Cross who graduated from Hendon as a specialist in brutality, bully-boy tactics & extra-special patrols in the pursuit of law and order. Seems that the new consensus in British polit(r)icks gave him a sack full of cash/money & a clear mandate to beat up on working class white folk on the picket lines of South Yorkshire'. In his text Piper is referring to the contemporaneous miners' strike of 1984, and in particular the events of 18 June 1984, which saw violent clashes between officers from the South Yorkshire and Metropolitan Police forces and striking workers at a British Steel Corporation coking plant in Orgreave, South Yorkshire. The confrontation involved excessive violence by the police and became known as 'The Battle of Orgreave'. Not only was the violence at Orgreave widely reported in the news at the time, but news reports were themselves accused of political bias; it is hardly surprising, therefore, that Piper chose to include commentary on it in the second iteration.[51]

As mentioned, Piper's separation of the four canvases of his second version of *The Four Horsemen of the Apocalypse* enables viewers to consider each figure individually. Understood as broadly representing a Conservative Party voter; the Police and in particular its relationship with Britain's working classes; the presence of US military and nuclear missiles at Greenham Common; and finally Ronald Reagan's presidency and his approach to global relations, a sequential or chronological progression is not immediately apparent when looking at the enframed figures separately. It is only when one reads the textual elements that a narrative develops, and a relationship between the individual and state power emerges as a decisive link between the four figures. Reading the work from left to right, the viewer is encouraged to see how the ethos of an 'ordinary' man can evolve with increased access to power, to the detriment of all. This is underlined by Piper's final words on each canvas: 'Apocalypse Soon'; 'Apocalypse Sooner'; 'Apocalypse Soonest'; 'Apocalypse Now'. Across the four canvases the Apocalypse of the future comes ever closer until it arrives in the now.[52]

There are multiple art historical lenses through which we might read *The Four Horsemen of the Apocalypse*, including comic strip art, Pop Art, political satire, and history painting. The comic strip, as typically found in newspapers and magazines, is constituted by a sequence of drawings arranged in interrelated panels that, together, portray a humorous situation or communicate a narrative.[53] Such drawings are presented within panels, frames or boxes, which depict a segment of action, and are frequently accompanied by text, either in the form of dialogue presented in speech bubbles, or, in the form of explanatory captions situated at the top or bottom of the panel. When considering *The Four Horsemen of the Apocalypse* in relation to the comic strip, one might be tempted to draw connections between Piper and other artists who have utilised this graphic genre within a fine art practice, particularly the American Pop artist Roy Lichtenstein (1923-1997). However, to consider Piper in relation to Lichtenstein would be to simplify and underestimate the complexity of Piper's visual strategies and conceptual goals. Lichtenstein simply replicated and enlarged frames from existing comic strips and magnified the ben-day dots to highlight how images are reproduced in the mechanical printing process. Piper, on the other hand, created a set of entirely original images and texts, and compiled them within the multi-frame format to document history as constituted by concurrent, multiplicitous occurrences and contexts. As such, Piper's segmented painting shares some of the formal and stylistic qualities of the comic strip, and its social and political commentary is also related to the satirical cartoons found in magazines such

[51] For more on the 1984 Miners Strike and the battle of Orgreave, see Dan Johnson, 'Background: "The Battle of Orgreave"', BBC, 12 June 2015, available at https://www.bbc.co.uk/news/uk-england-south-yorkshire-33107090 (accessed 2 February 2022).
[52] My thanks to Alice Correia for bringing this interpretation to my attention.
[53] The word 'comic' as an adjective denotes something humorous, and because not all comic strips are humorous, some authors and artists prefer to use the more genre-neutral term 'sequential art'.

***The Four Horsemen of the Apocalypse* (detail)**
1984

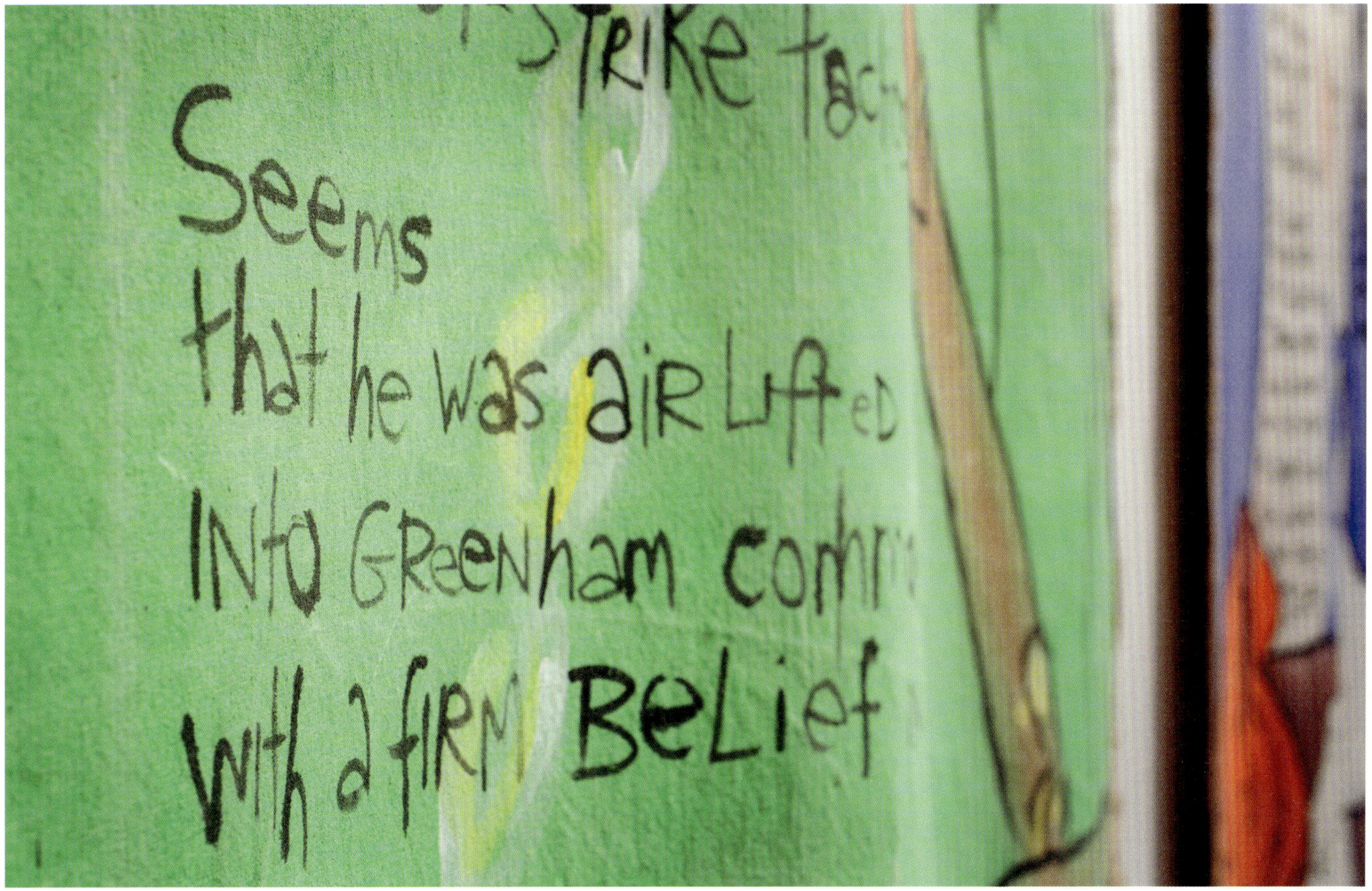

[54] Keith Piper, unpublished interview by Anjalie Dalal-Clayton, 29 May 2020.
[55] This type of imagery has a long history within British visual culture. For example, see the exhibitions: *Icons of British Satire*, Tate Britain, 15 September to 12 October 2003, available at https://www.tate.org.uk/whats-on/tate-britain/icons-british-satire (accessed 16 May 2022); and *Rude Britannia: British Comic Art*, Tate Britain, 9 June to 5 September 2010, available at https://www.tate.org.uk/whats-on/tate-britain/exhibition/rude-britannia-british-comic-art (both accessed 2 February 2022).
[56] *Spitting Image* featured puppet caricatures of contemporary celebrities and public figures and was created by Peter Fluck, Roger Law and Martin Lambie-Nairne. It aired between 1984 and 1996 on the ITV network, and was revived in 2020 on the online digital video subscription platform, BritBox. See Anthony Broxton, 'What Spitting Image did to British Politics', *The Critic Magazine*, 3 October 2020, available at https://thecritic.co.uk/what-spitting-image-did-to-british-politics/ (accessed 4 March 2022).
[57] Anthropomorphism is not an unusual visual strategy for political cartoonists and comic strip artists. A significant example is the *Pogo* comic strip created by American cartoonist Walt Kelly (1913-1973), which featured in American newspapers between the 1940s and 1970s. Kelly created a variety of anthropomorphic characters to caricature political figures, most notably, his character Simple J. Malarkey – a megalomaniac bobcat that was a caricature of an anti-communist US senator Joseph McCarthy (1908-1957).

as *Private Eye*. Indeed, Piper has cited the British political cartoonists Gerald Scarfe, Ralph Steadman and Steve Bell as influences in his making of this artwork.[54] These cartoonists, and others, offer biting social or political commentary, producing images strongly satirical in tone and containing elements of caricature and the grotesque in their depiction of political figures and celebrities.[55] It is perhaps significant that in early 1984, political satire and caricature stepped out of the newspapers and onto British television screens in the British puppet show *Spitting Image*. Satirising contemporary popular culture and politics, it was one of the most-watched television shows of the 1980s, and one of its most memorable political characters, alongside those of Margaret Thatcher and Mikhail Gorbachev, was Ronald Reagan, whom it presented as a blundering buffoon fixated with nuclear weapons.[56] Thus, in terms of its political subject matter, its caricaturistic depiction of Reagan, and its presentation of the four figures as grotesque, anthropomorphic creatures, each with two noses and two sets of menacing, gnashing teeth, Piper's *The Four Horsemen*

of the Apocalypse is as much a reflection of popular culture and opinion as it is about political commentary.[57]
In its presentation of significant people and moments in British life, Piper's work can also be understood as a form of history painting. During the nineteenth century, subjects deemed appropriate to painting expanded from portraiture and allegorical and religious narratives to include scenes from secular history and the documentation of what was then recent and contemporary history. With an emphasis on the visualisation of monumental events and exemplary deeds, and characterised by a large scale format that could impact the communal consciousness, history painting was considered one of the highest forms of visual art until the advent of modernism.[58] Despite its diminishing popularity, the genre of history painting continued to pepper developments in twentieth century art, with works such as Pablo Picasso's (1881-1973) *Guernica* (1937) and *Lot's Wife* (1989) by Anselm Kiefer (b.1945) being notable examples. In the twenty-first century, contemporary artists including K.P. Reji (b.1972), Daniel Boyd (b.1982) and Michael Armitage (b.1984) are now engaging with history painting as a means for portraying contemporary scenes from a globalised perspective.[59] As Kobena Mercer briefly noted in his 1997 essay 'Witness at the Crossroads', Piper's use of biblical allegory and documentation of several related socio-political moments and situations in the 1980s, unequivocally places *The Four Horsemen of the Apocalypse* within the wide-ranging canon of history painting.[60] Viewed today, almost forty years after the events that it depicts took place, this reading seems particularly apposite. In 1984, Piper's work served as a critically reflective contemporary document of the socio-political moment, utilising the visual style of the political cartoon to evoke the cultural zeitgeist of the time, whilst also enabling viewers to consider recent events and current affairs, their relationship to each other and what their culmination might mean for the future of humanity. Evidently, the Cold War did not conclude with nuclear annihilation as anticipated by the painting, so now, it functions as history paintings do, by portraying key historical events, acting as an expression of the atmosphere of the time, and as a document of Piper's own concerns about a potential apocalypse.

As mentioned, the 'apocalypse' is a recurrent theme in the history of art, and features regularly in Piper's work. In addition to *The Four Horsemen of the Apocalypse*, concerns about nuclear annihilation can be seen in his large-scale mural *Nanny of the Nation Gathers her Flock* (1987), and his more recent three-channel video installation *Unearthing the Banker's Bones* (2015) presents a post-apocalyptic landscape. Historically artists addressing apocalyptic notions and visions did so within a religious context, as seen in Dürer's *The Four Horsemen* (1498) and *A Vision of the Last Judgement* (1808) by William Blake (1757-1827). More recently, artists have addressed apocalyptic themes to address the very real threats to human existence that have been posed by social, political and environmental circumstances. In 2008, Dominique Gonzalez-Foerster (b.1965) installed *TH2058* (2008) in Tate Modern's Turbine Hall, presenting that space as a bunk-bed filled shelter during an unspecified future crisis; while Gordon Cheung (b.1975) presents '"techno-sublime" dystopic vistas' in his paintings.[61] In his painterly meditations on the factors that could contribute towards an apocalypse, Ricky Allman (b.1978) depicts futuristic church-like constructions set against backgrounds of looming peaks and leaden skies, and allude to human greed, environmental destruction and religious fundamentalism. Despite such minatory reference points, Allman's work vacillates between pessimism and optimism so that the notion of the apocalypse is presented as a possibility rather than an eventuality. For example, the angular, floating cityscapes in works such as *Unravel Redux* (2005-2015)

[58] For a thorough and varied overview of history painting, see Mark Salber Phillips and Jordan Bear (ed.), *What was History Painting and What is it Now?* (Montreal: McGill-Queen's University Press, 2019).
[59] For more on Reji, Boyd and Armitage, see Ellen Mara De Wachter, Zehra Jumabhoy, and Stella Rosa McDonald, 'The New Future of History Painting: 3 International Artists Reclaiming the Genre', ArtSpace, 9 December 2016, available at https://www.artspace.com/magazine/art_101/book_report/phaidon-p3-history-painting-54452 (accessed 19 February 2022).
[60] Kobena Mercer, 'Witness at the Crossroads: An Artist's Journey in Postcolonial Space', *Keith Piper: Relocating the Remains*, 15 and 19.
[61] Paul Hobson, 'Hacking into the present: the Apocalyptic imaginings of Gordon Cheung' in *The Four Horsemen of the Apocalypse: Gordon Cheung* (The New Art Gallery Walsall, 2009), v-viii.

and *Neighborhoods* (2014) are as much utopian as they are dystopian in their imaginings of the future. Indeed, as Allman has commented, 'I don't believe in the apocalypse of humanity; despite all our problems, we're definitely going to figure out our way'.[62] Keith Piper's *The Four Horsemen of the Apocalypse* (1984) has nothing of the hope that is found in Allman and even Gonzalez-Foerster's work. However, its critical reflection of contemporary socio-political moments and circumstances, its suggestion of impending doom, and its invocation of the four horsemen of the apocalypse motif, firmly situate the work within the canon of apocalyptic art.[63]

The second version of *The Four Horsemen of the Apocalypse* was first displayed in *New Horizons* at Royal Festival Hall, London, 18 January to 5 February 1985, followed by *New Contemporaries* staged at Institute of Contemporary Art, London, 11 March to 6 April 1986. It was then placed in Piper's attic, becoming long-forgotten in his mind until he was approached by Middlesbrough Institute of Modern Art (MIMA) with a request to include the painting in its exhibition *Wilderness Way* (17 June to 8 October 2017).[64] When MIMA acquired the artwork that same year, it became an important part of the Institute's collection, serving as a record of some of the defining moments of early-1980s Britain and Piper's own anxieties at the time.

In the thirty-eight years since Piper created the *The Four Horsemen of the Apocalypse* paintings, his speculations about the future, like Allman's, have become more ambivalent and nuanced. Produced for his solo exhibition *Jet Black Futures*, Piper's new four channel video installation, *In Search of Four Horses* (2021-22) takes the two 1984 iterations of *The Four Horsemen of the Apocalypse* as a point of departure for exploring contemporary perspectives on the socio-political and ecological conditions of the early twenty-first century. To insert contemporary relevance into the artwork, Piper could easily have exchanged Reagan for Donald Trump, swapped the brutish 'British Bobby' for a murderous American police officer, or replaced the 1980s Tory-voter with a 2010s Brexit-voter. However, creating an updated version of the 1984 paintings that would centre his personal political views and concerns was not Piper's objective. Instead, he sought to 'return to the strange narrative around the four horsemen of the apocalypse as a way of articulating how very particular anxieties around the future and politics can be reframed through the metaphor'.[65] Thus, taking a more research-driven approach, he returned to the biblical allegory of the four horsemen of the apocalypse with greater focus. His research led him to explore first century Greek writing about John of Patmos, who is widely understood as the author of the Book of Revelation, and from there, Greek mythology – specifically the figure of Cassandra, who was granted the gift of prophecy but would never be believed.[66] Recognising the parallels between these two figures and present-day scientists, whose warnings about climate change and the increase and spread of disease are not always taken seriously, Piper sought to invoke both characters in his new video installation, as part of his 'ongoing fascination with the way various narratives can be used to frame history'.[67]

Projected across the 26m wall of one of The New Art Gallery Walsall spaces, the 30 minute video begins with flickers of grey, white, black and yellow, echoing three of the four colours from the biblical allegory. A bleak, animated landscape reminiscent of that in *Unearthing the Banker's Bones* then fades into view. As discussed, despite Piper's engagement with digital media since the 1990s, he has sought different ways to retain the tactility of his earlier work, particularly in terms of mark-making. This new video is no exception. Grass-like scratches dominate the foreground of the landscape, animated white marks

[62] Allman cited in Alice Thorson, 'Ricky Allman: Science Fiction Solutions', *KC Studio*, 19 January 2016, available at https://kcstudio.org/ricky-allman-science-fiction-solutions/ (accessed 19 February 2022).
[63] For more on modern and contemporary apocalyptic art see: Norman Rosenthal, *Apocalypse: Beauty and Horror in Contemporary Art* (London: Royal Academy of Arts, 2000); Natasha O'Hear and Anthony O'Hear, *Picturing the Apocalypse: The Book of Revelation in the Arts over Two Millennia* (Oxford: Oxford University Press, 2015) 235-283; and Eleanor Heartney, *Doomsday Dreams: The Apocalyptic Imagination in Contemporary Art*, (Paris: Silver Hollow Press, 2019).
[64] For more information on the exhibition *Wilderness Way*, see *MIMA's website* available at https://mima.art/exhibition/wilderness-way/ (accessed 19 February 2022].
[65] Keith Piper, unpublished interview by Anjalie Dalal-Clayton, 7 October 2021.
[66] For an account of Piper's research on John of Patmos and Kassandra, see Keith Piper, 'In Search of Four Horses: Notes on the Research and Development of a multi-channel video project, as part of Jet-Black Futures', *Keith Piper's website*, April 2020, available at http://www.keithpiper.info/jbf_fourhorses.html (accessed 19 February 2022).
[67] Keith Piper, unpublished interview by Anjalie Dalal-Clayton, 7 October 2021.

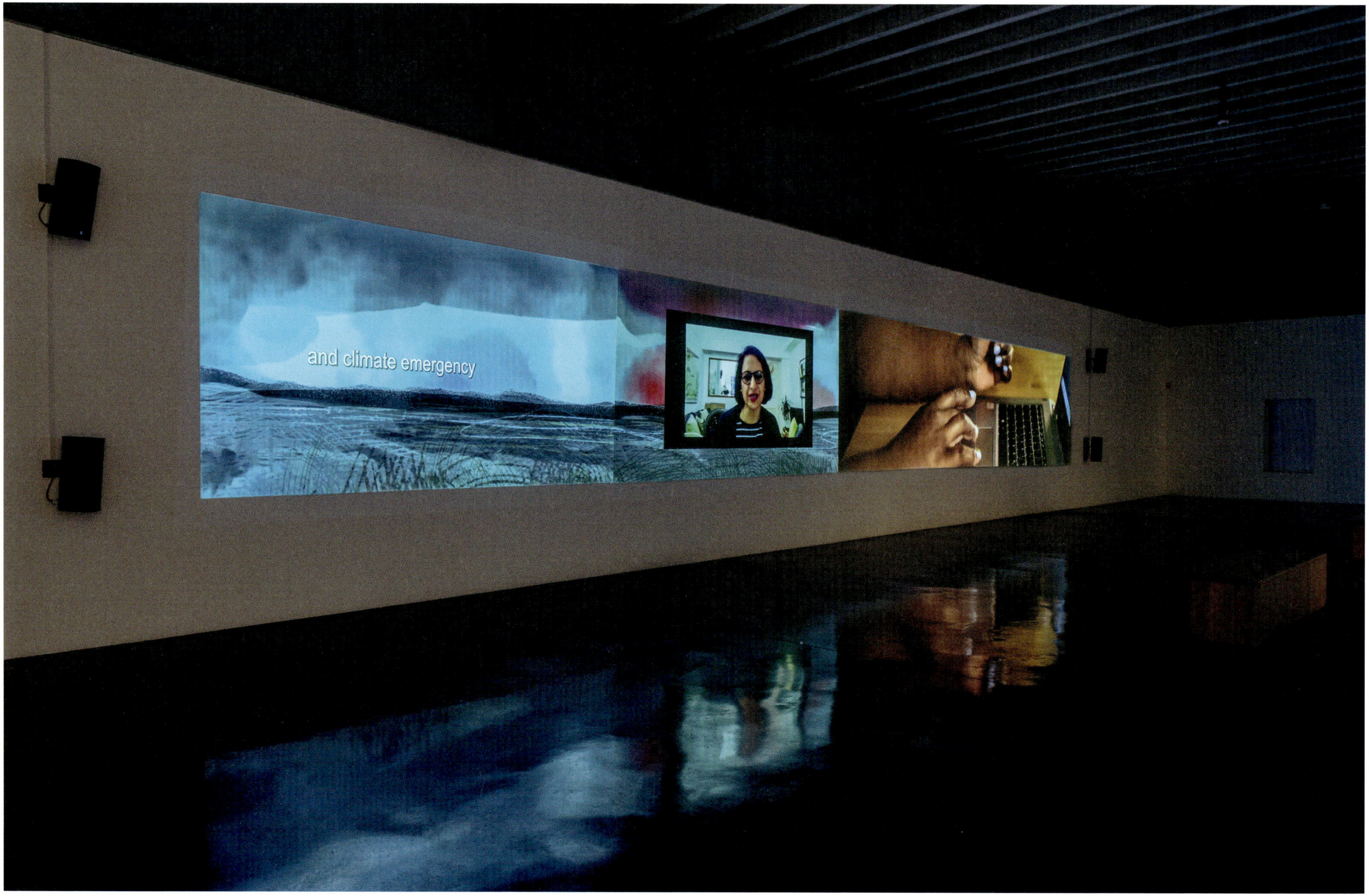
and climate emergency

In Search of Four Horses
2021-22

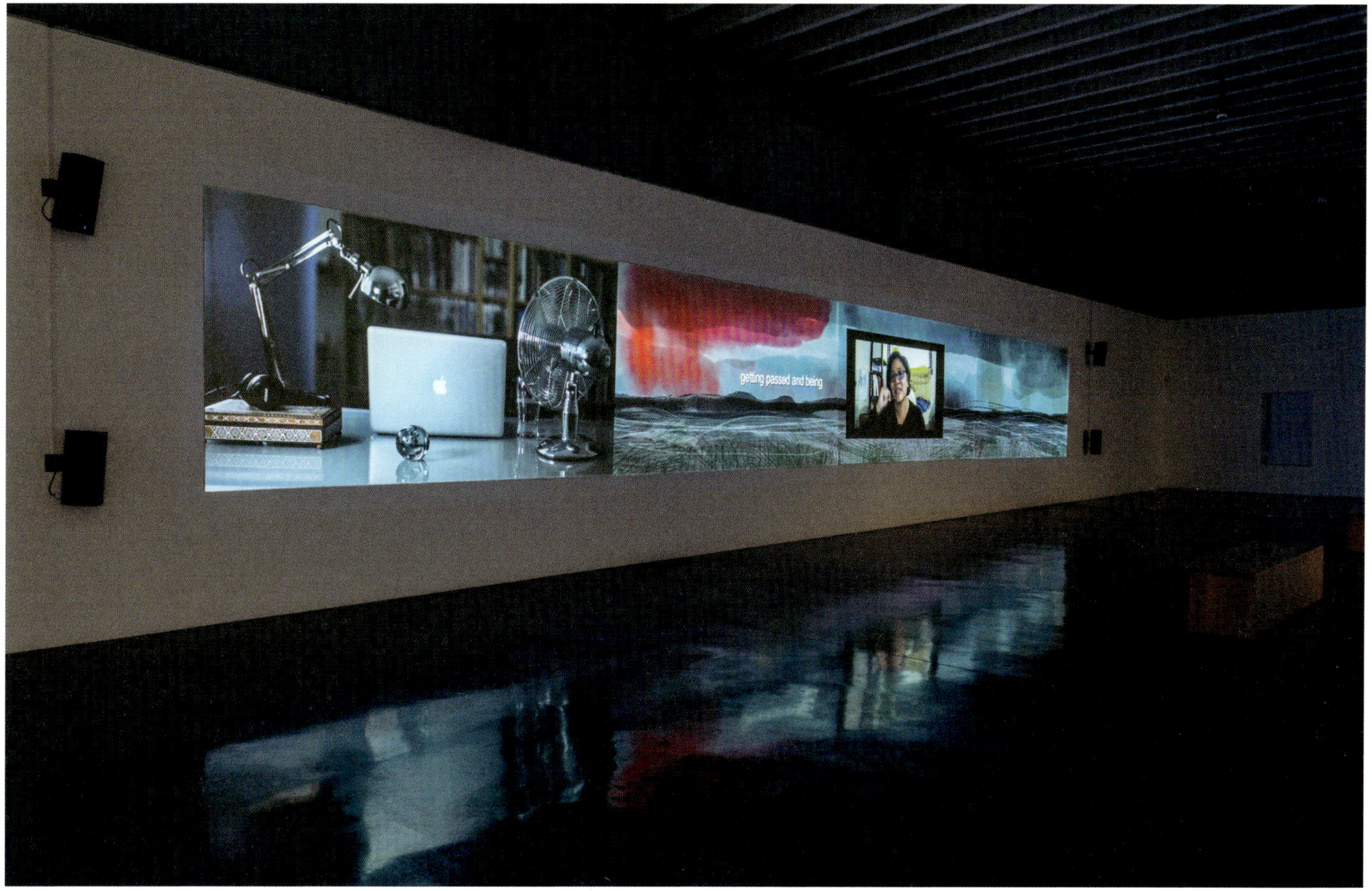

agitate its middle ground, while a gently undulating line provides a horizon that is completed by a foreboding, watercolour sky. The title for the artwork gradually emerges across the four projections, quivering momentarily, then fading to allow four roughly sketched, horse-riding figures to charge menacingly towards the viewer. Piper created these various hand drawn elements with a digital stylus, taking inspiration from the 'aesthetics of graffiti, diagrammatic, spontaneous, interspersing fragmented texts with cartoonistic drawing and mark making'[68] found in the work of Basquiat. The subtly agitative quality of these marks builds a tension within the video's opening moments, which Piper has heightened by using animation tools to make them 'tremble' against the static background.[69]

Within seconds the four galloping figures disappear from view and a woman's voice begins to describe the story of John of Patmos and his prophecy of the four horsemen of the apocalypse. While the woman recounts the story, montaged scenes of her gloved hands carefully

[68] Keith Piper, 'Working Drawings Towards Four Horsemen', 2020.
[69] Keith Piper, 'The Twanged Line Trembles: Notes on the Research and Development of a multi-channel video project as part of Jet-Black Futures', *Keith Piper's website*, May 2020, available at http://www.keithpiper.info/jbf_twangedlines.html (accessed 19 February 2022).

handling archival documents and a variety of biblical images indicate to the viewer that she is a researcher. She concludes the story and the words 'Kassandra's Journal Interview#' appear letter by letter, accompanied by the sound of typing. The woman appears, facing the viewer from behind a laptop and she introduces herself; 'Hello, my name is Kassandra and I'm doing research on people's views of the future. Would you say your view is positive, negative, or a combination of both?'[70] In the adjacent projections, a collage of alternating images evidence her surroundings – a laptop, lamp, glass of water, plant, fan, paperweight, a jar of wooden scrabble pieces, cotton gloves, and old books. Her question is directed at an interviewee, pictured in the now familiar, rectangular window of an online video conferencing application. The interviewee proceeds to describe their reflections on the current moment and their predictions for the future.

A pattern of question and answer between Kassandra and her interviewees is repeated fourteen times, with each interviewee providing a distinct response. Topics of reflection include climate change, scarcity of food and clean water, developments in technology and science, neocolonialism, Black survival strategies, and the different attitudinal approaches one might take when considering what the future holds. While some of the perspectives are devastatingly pessimistic, others are more hopeful. Perhaps coincidentally, they variously reference the four plagues brought forth by the horsemen in the biblical allegory – disease, war, famine and death. The realities of the first of the plagues are particularly resonant in the format through which the interviews take place. Indeed, the online video call has become one of the quintessential symbols of the Covid-19 pandemic (along with the surgical face covering). The physical distance between Kassandra and her research participants is especially apparent when the interview audio becomes muffled due, presumably, to unreliable internet connections and audio capture, but closed captions provide clarity whilst underscoring the gravity of the issues being discussed. However, when the Zoom windows start to slowly drift across the four projected segments of the installation, or when the captions jump unpredictably to different locations in the composition, the viewer's gaze, and sense of clarity, is unsettled, which in turn amplifies the uncertainty evoked by the interviewees' reflections. Concurrent footage of Kassandra's smiling face and gently nodding head offers a sense of calm, but this is similarly undermined by a sombre, ominous soundtrack composed by Piper and layered images of the sinister, imagined landscape. Once the fourteenth interview concludes, the video projection draws to a gradual close through a reversal of its opening: Kassandra's voice is heard although her words are now inaudible; the animated horsemen reappear momentarily; the flickering colours - grey, white, black and yellow - flash in and out of view; and finally, the credits roll.

This new video work is a marked departure from Piper's earlier *The Four Horsemen of the Apocalypse*, not simply in terms of media, but also in terms of purpose. Although the 1984 paintings encapsulated what were widely regarded as troubling conditions of the time, the selection, interpretation and depiction of those conditions were ultimately determined by Piper, and the paintings may therefore be read as a monologic expression of his own concerns and anxieties. Despite a comparable grounding in the biblical allegory of the four horsemen of the apocalypse, this new video installation is, by contrast, a genuinely dialogic exploration of different perspectives. Unlike *The Four Horsemen of the Apocalypse*, which, in the tradition of history painting, documented particular events and situations of socio-political importance, *In Search of Four Horses* is a relatively unmediated record

[70] We do not learn of Kassandra's significance within Greek mythology from the video itself nor what she might represent within it. However, her significance is discussed in the accompanying guide for the exhibition on The New Art Gallery Walsall website, available at https://thenewartgallerywalsall.org.uk/digital/keith-piper/ (accessed 20 February 2022).

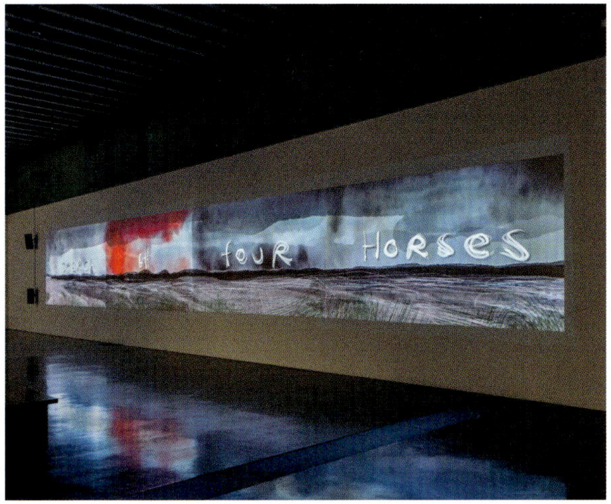

In Search of Four Horses
2021-22

of the hopes, fears and imaginings of other people, which Piper achieved through adopting what might be described as a socially-engaged approach. Whether or not socially-engaged practices will begin to feature more in Piper's work remains to be seen, but it is interesting to consider its impact within his oeuvre via this new installation, particularly in terms of his engagement with, and production of narratives. By soliciting and presenting a range of different futurological reflections and perspectives in *In Search of Four Horses*, Piper has created what might be his first multivocal narrative. That is not to say that he has relinquished his role as chief narrator – after all, he was responsible for staging and contextualising the interview recordings. Rather, by choosing not to centre his own concerns, the narrative in this new installation has multiple authors, and several concurrent strands, which does not simply expand his long-standing approach to narration and storytelling; it completely transforms it. How his cyclical, looping, but ultimately forward-facing approach to art-making will manifest next is an exciting prospect.

Δ

Thanks to Keith Piper and Deborah Robinson for inviting me to write this text, to Alice Correia for her careful edits and for generously sharing her thoughtful insights, to Amy Hailwood for supporting my analysis of the poetic aspects of the texts in Piper's work, and to Barry Dalal-Clayton for deepening my understanding of the local impacts of mid-twentieth century mining in East Africa.

Body Politics: Works from 1982-2007

WOLVERHAMPTON ART GALLERY, 10 OCTOBER – 1 DECEMBER 2019

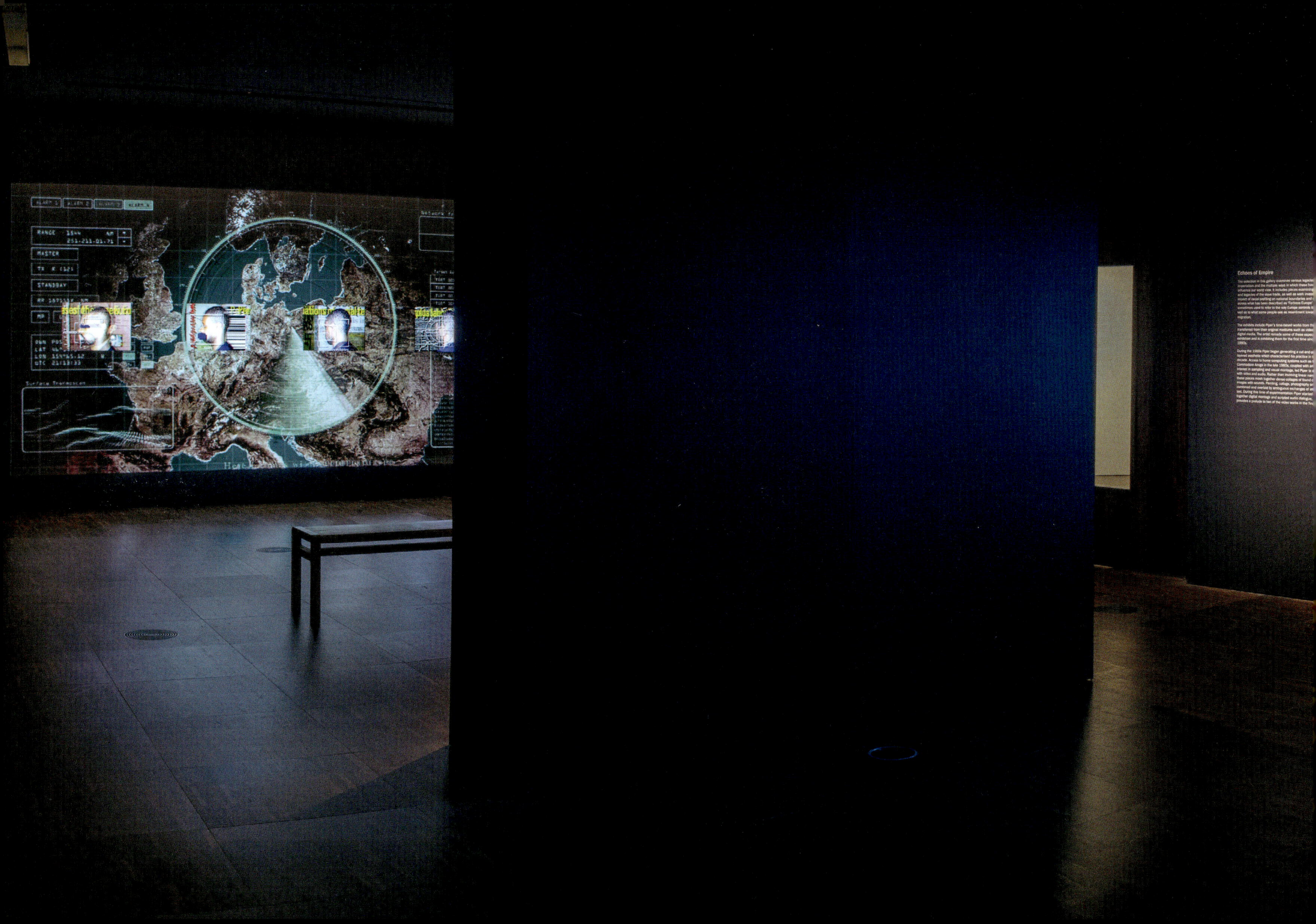
RANGE
MASTER
STANDBY
Echoes of Empire

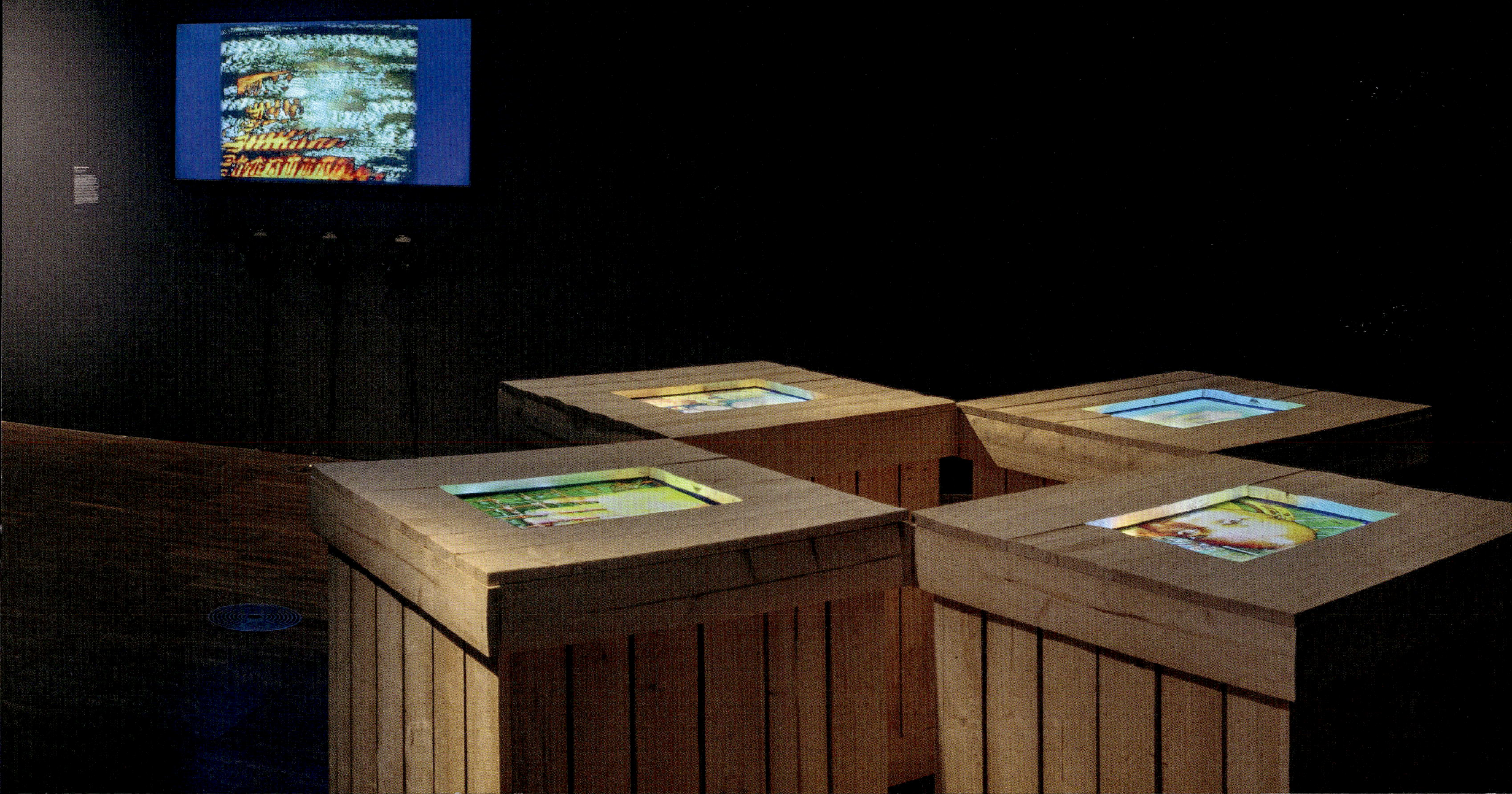

Trade Winds
1992

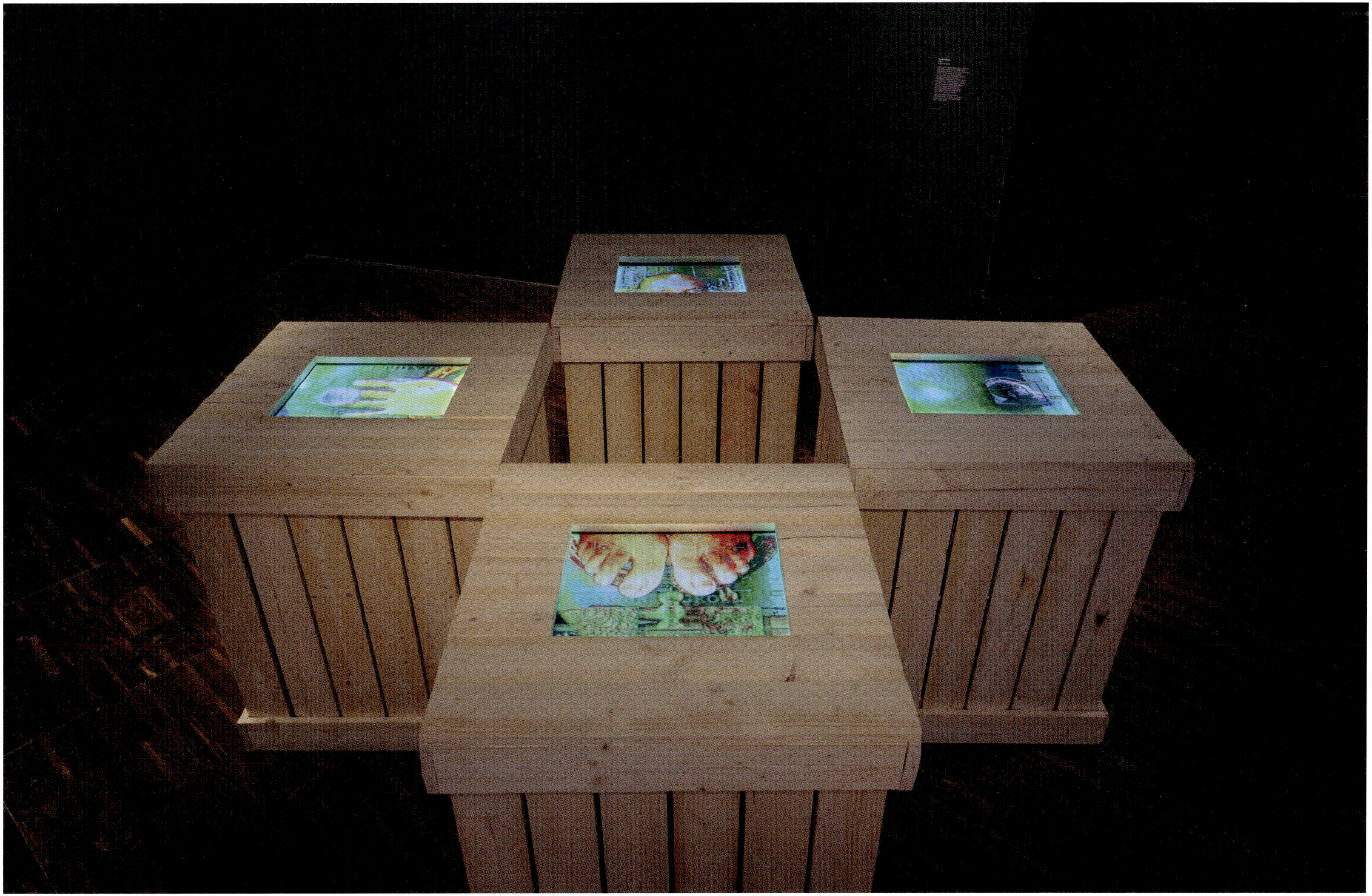

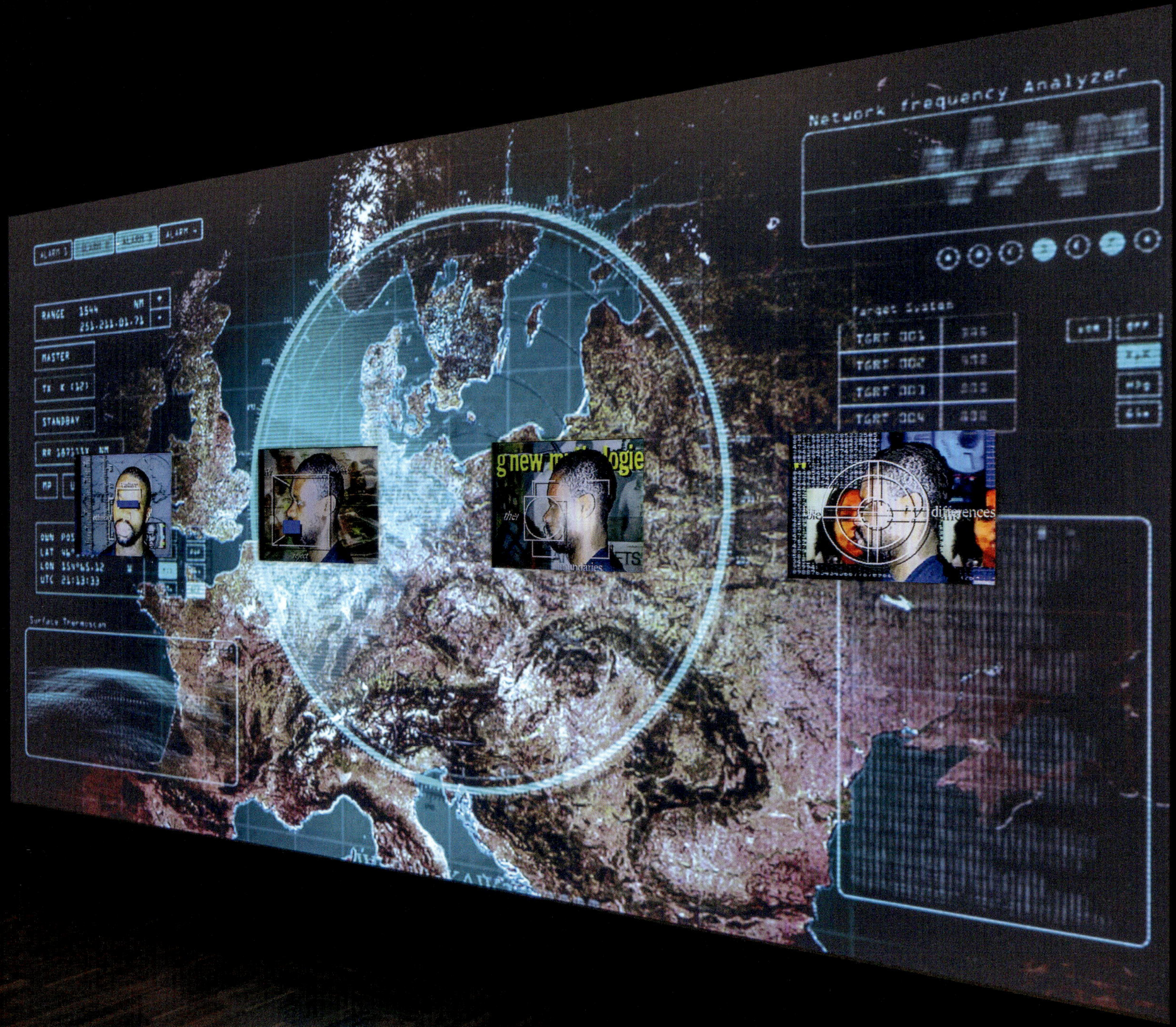

Surveillance: Tagging the Other
1992

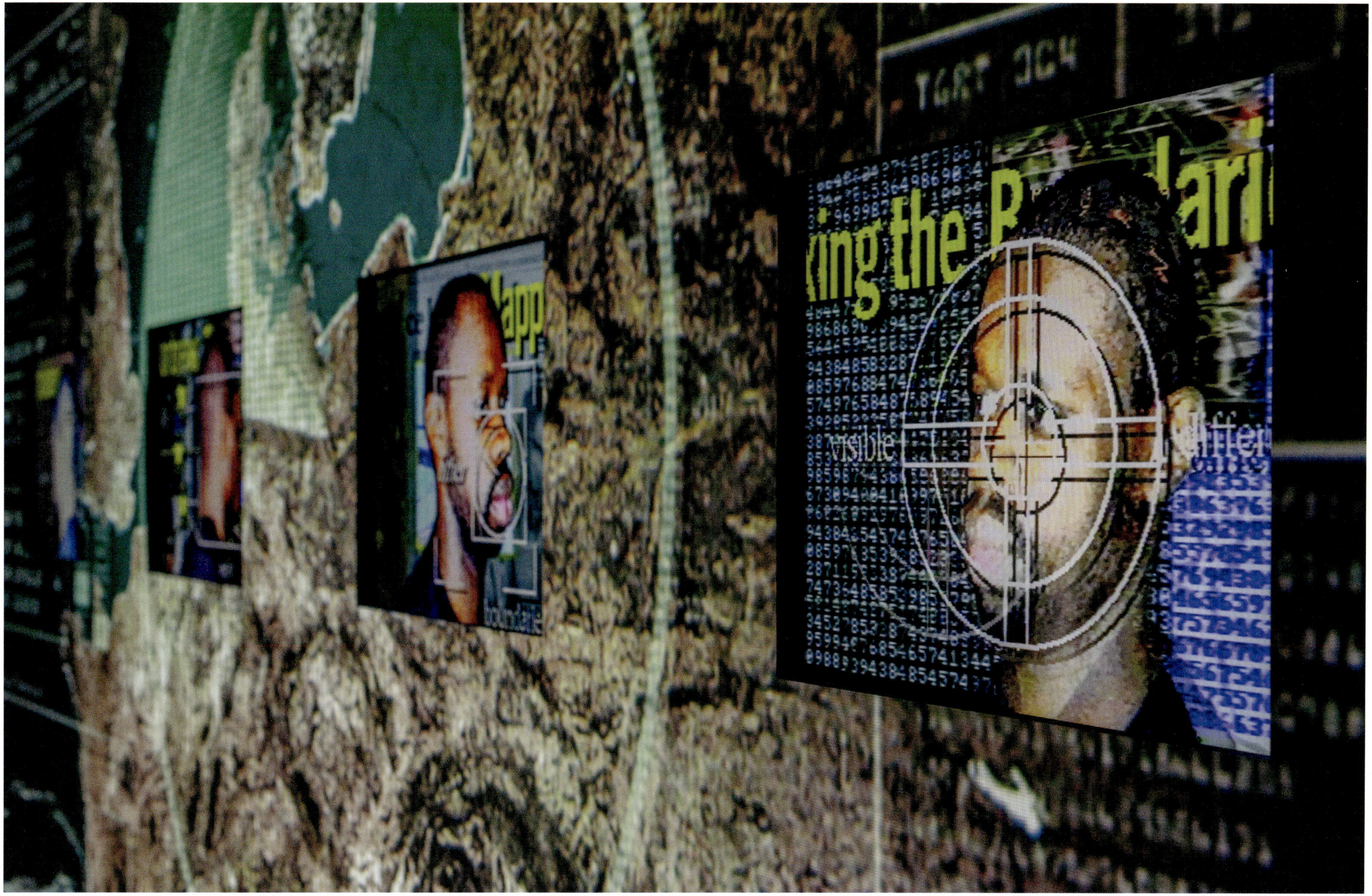

king the
visible

The Black Assassin Saints
1982

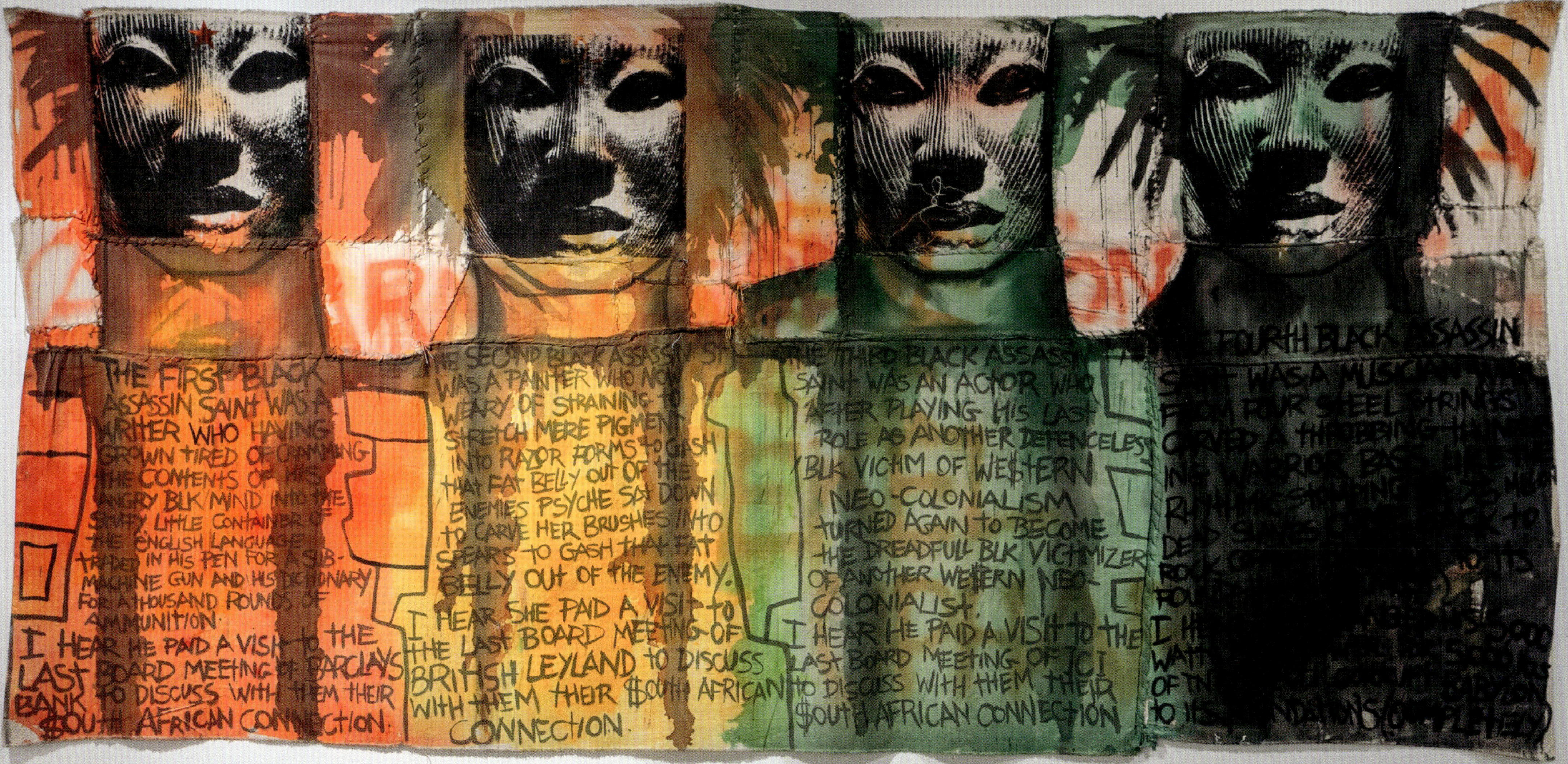
THE FIRST BLACK ASSASSIN SAINT WAS A WRITER WHO HAVING GROWN TIRED OF CRAMMING THE CONTENTS OF HIS ANGRY BLK MIND INTO THE STUFFY LITTLE CONTAINER OF THE ENGLISH LANGUAGE TRADED IN HIS PEN FOR A SUB-MACHINE GUN AND HIS DICTIONARY FOR A THOUSAND ROUNDS OF AMMUNITION.
I HEAR HE PAID A VISIT TO THE LAST BOARD MEETING OF BARCLAYS BANK TO DISCUSS WITH THEM THEIR $OUTH AFRICAN CONNECTION.
THE SECOND BLACK ASSASSIN SAINT WAS A PAINTER WHO NOW WEARY OF STRAINING TO STRETCH MERE PIGMENT INTO RAZOR FORMS TO GASH THAT FAT BELLY OUT OF THE ENEMIES PSYCHE SAT DOWN TO CARVE HER BRUSHES INTO SPEARS TO GASH THAT FAT BELLY OUT OF THE ENEMY.
I HEAR SHE PAID A VISIT TO THE LAST BOARD MEETING OF BRITISH LEYLAND TO DISCUSS WITH THEM THEIR $OUTH AFRICAN CONNECTION.
THE THIRD BLACK ASSASSIN SAINT WAS AN ACTOR WHO AFTER PLAYING HIS LAST ROLE AS ANOTHER DEFENCELESS BLK VICTIM OF WESTERN NEO-COLONIALISM TURNED AGAIN TO BECOME THE DREADFULL BLK VICTIMIZER OF ANOTHER WESTERN NEO-COLONIALIST.
I HEAR HE PAID A VISIT TO THE LAST BOARD MEETING OF ICI TO DISCUSS WITH THEM THEIR $OUTH AFRICAN CONNECTION.
THE FOURTH BLACK ASSASSIN SAINT WAS A MUSICIAN WHO FROM FOUR STEEL STRINGS CARVED A THROBBING

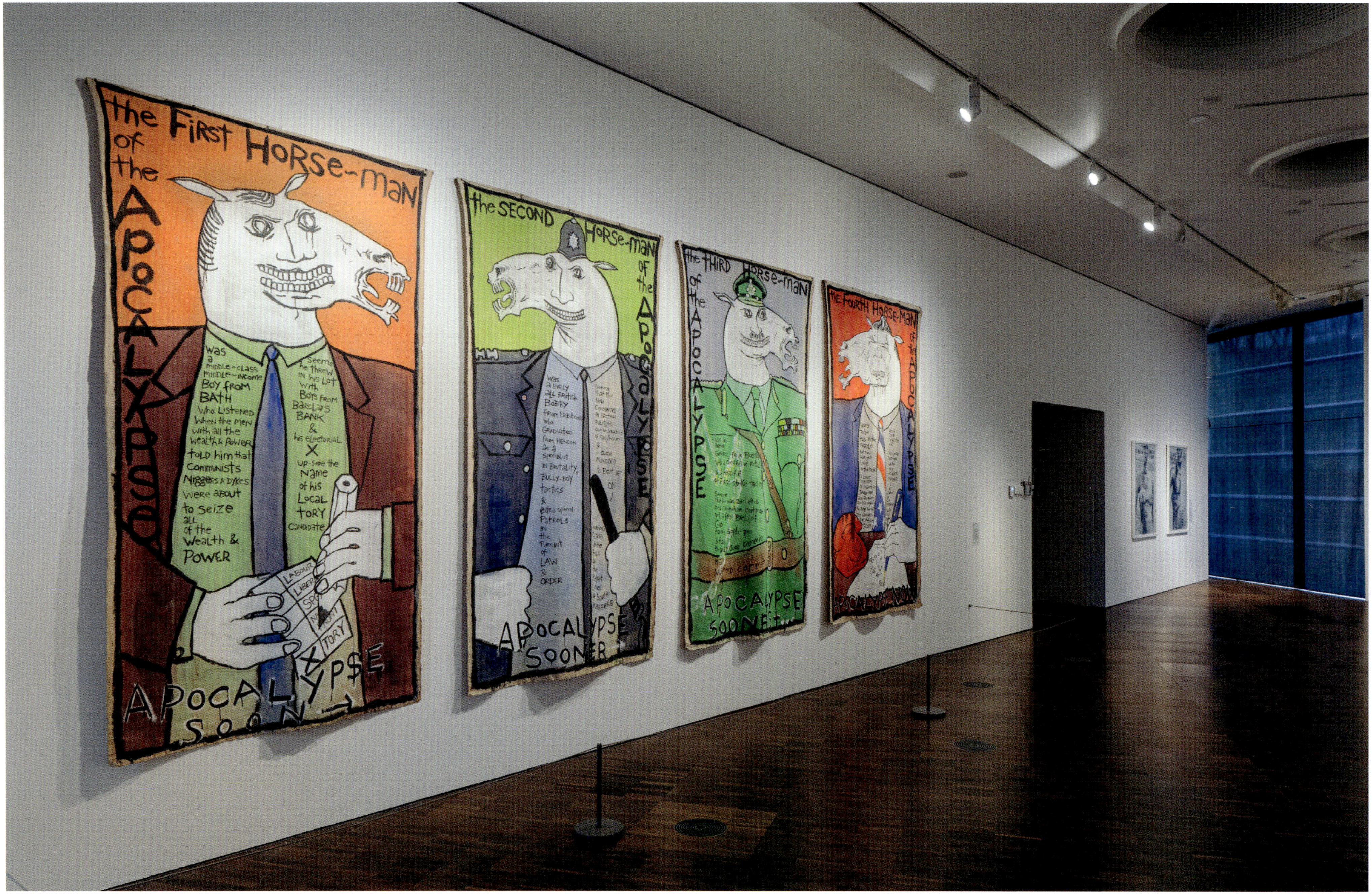

the First Horse-man of the Apocalypse
Was a middle-class middle-income Boy from Bath Who Listened When the men with all the wealth & Power told him that Communists Niggers & Dykes Were about to seize all of the Wealth & Power
Seems he threw in his lot with Boys from Barclays Bank & his electorial X up-side the Name of his Local Tory Candidate
Labour
Tory
Apocalypse Soon →
the Second Horse-man of the Apocalypse
Apocalypse Sooner
the Third Horse-man of the Apocalypse
Apocalypse Soonest
the Fourth Horse-man of the Apocalypse
Apocalypse Now

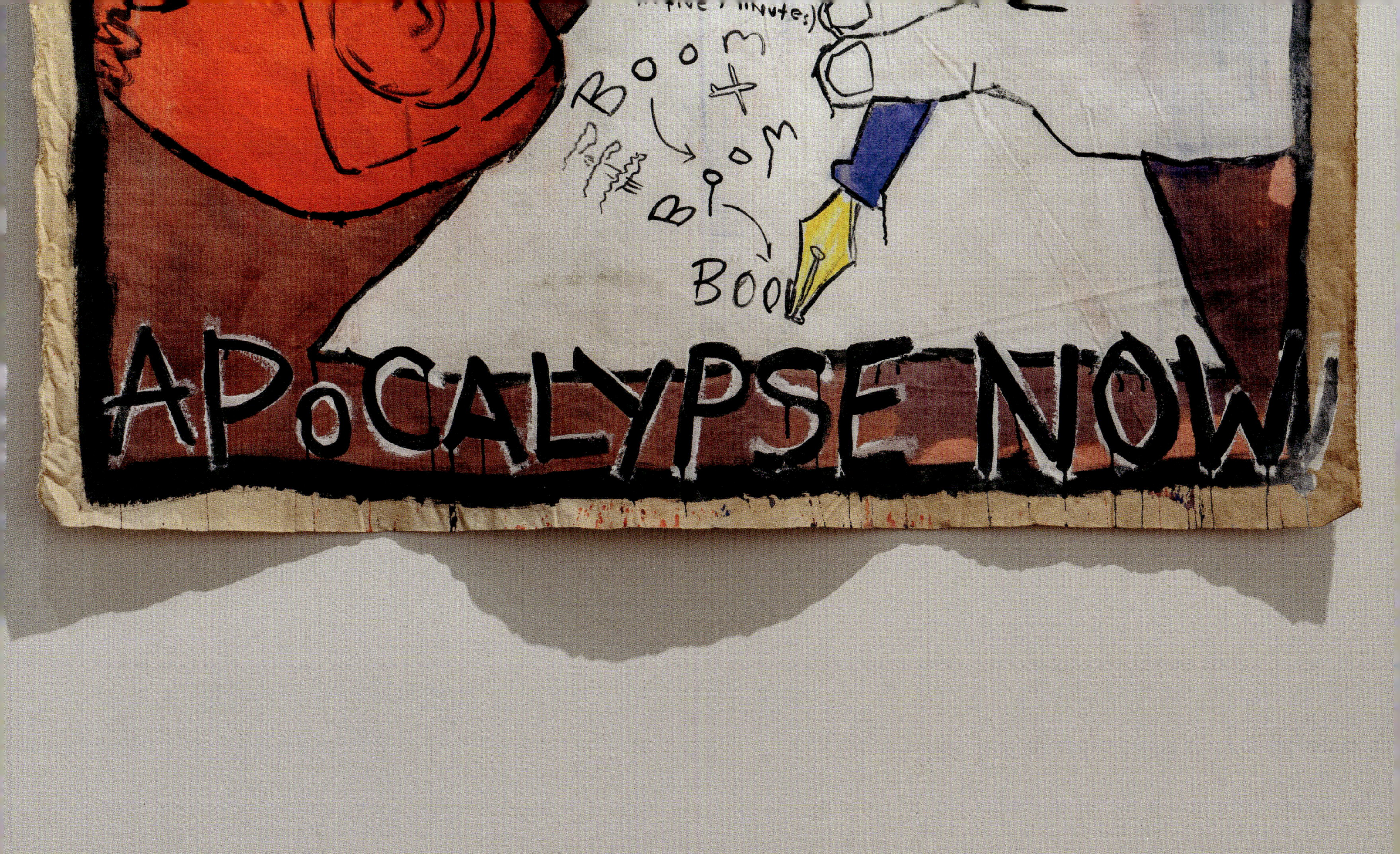

The Four Horsemen of the Apocalypse
1984

Body Type 1
1982

Body Type 2
1982

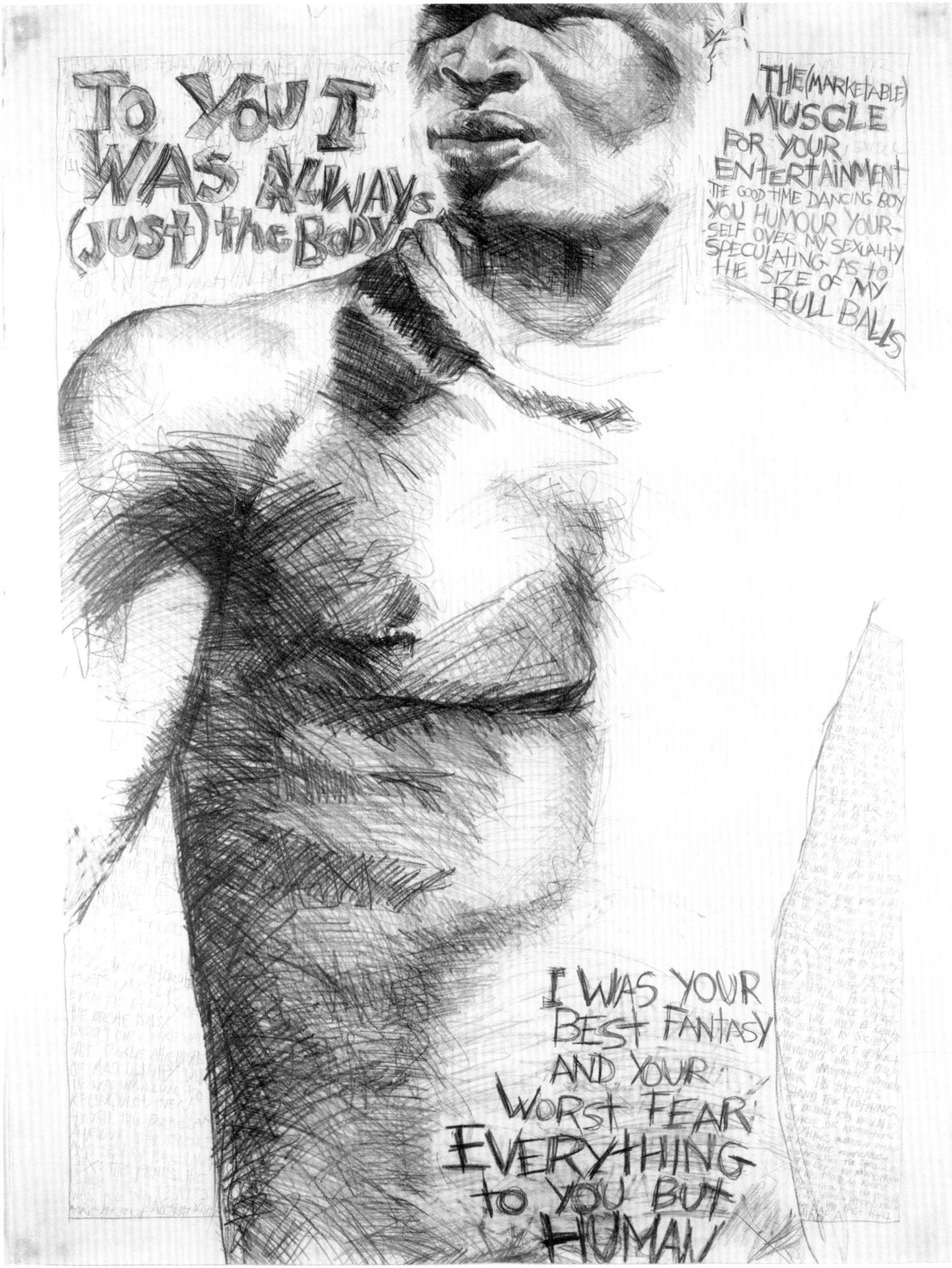
TO YOU I WAS ALWAYS (JUST) the BODY
THE (MARKETABLE) MUSCLE FOR YOUR ENTERTAINMENT
THE GOOD TIME DANCING BOY
YOU HUMOUR YOURSELF OVER MY SEXUALITY SPECULATING AS TO THE SIZE OF MY BULL BALLS
I WAS YOUR BEST FANTASY AND YOUR WORST FEAR
EVERYTHING to YOU BUT HUMAN

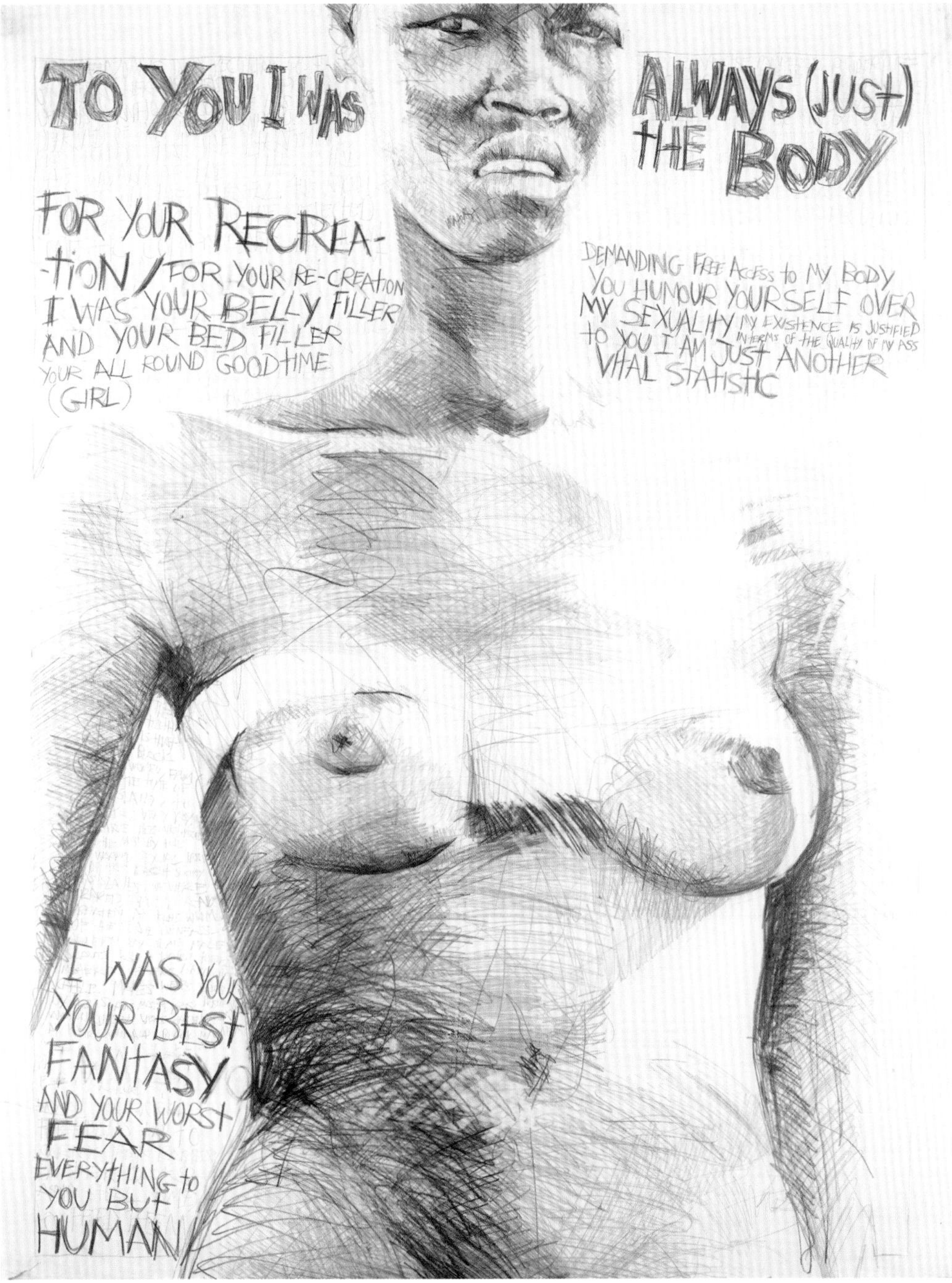
TO YOU I WAS
ALWAYS (JUST) the BODY
FOR YOUR RECREA-TION / FOR YOUR RE-CREATION
I WAS YOUR BELLY FILLER AND YOUR BED FILLER
YOUR ALL ROUND GOODTIME (GIRL)
DEMANDING FREE ACCESS to MY BODY
YOU HUMOUR YOURSELF OVER MY SEXUALITY MY EXISTENCE IS JUSTIFIED IN TERMS OF THE QUALITY OF MY ASS
to YOU I AM JUST ANOTHER VITAL STATISTIC
I WAS YOUR YOUR BEST FANTASY AND YOUR WORST FEAR
EVERYTHING to YOU BUT HUMAN

The Seven Rages of Man
2018

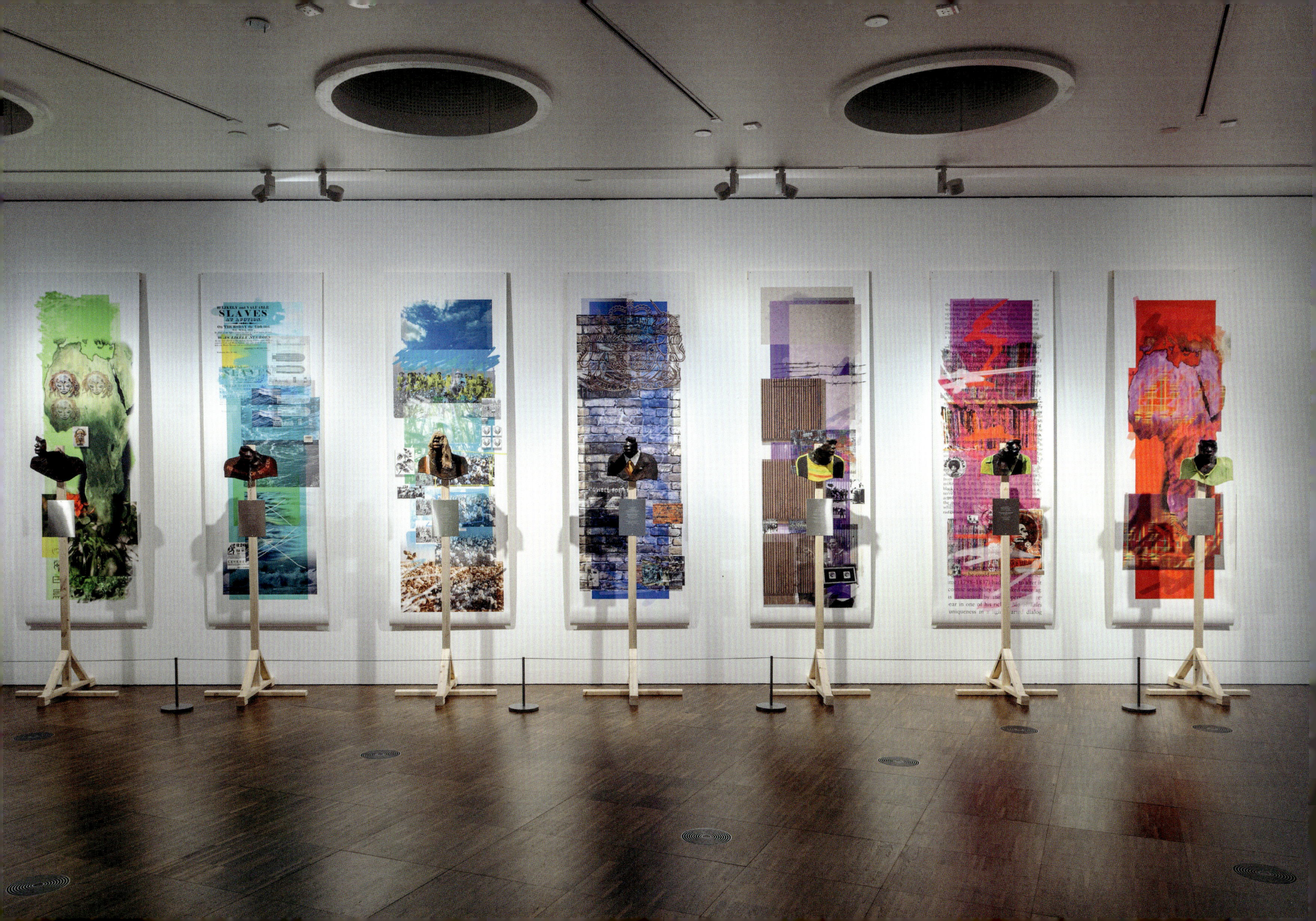
SLAVES

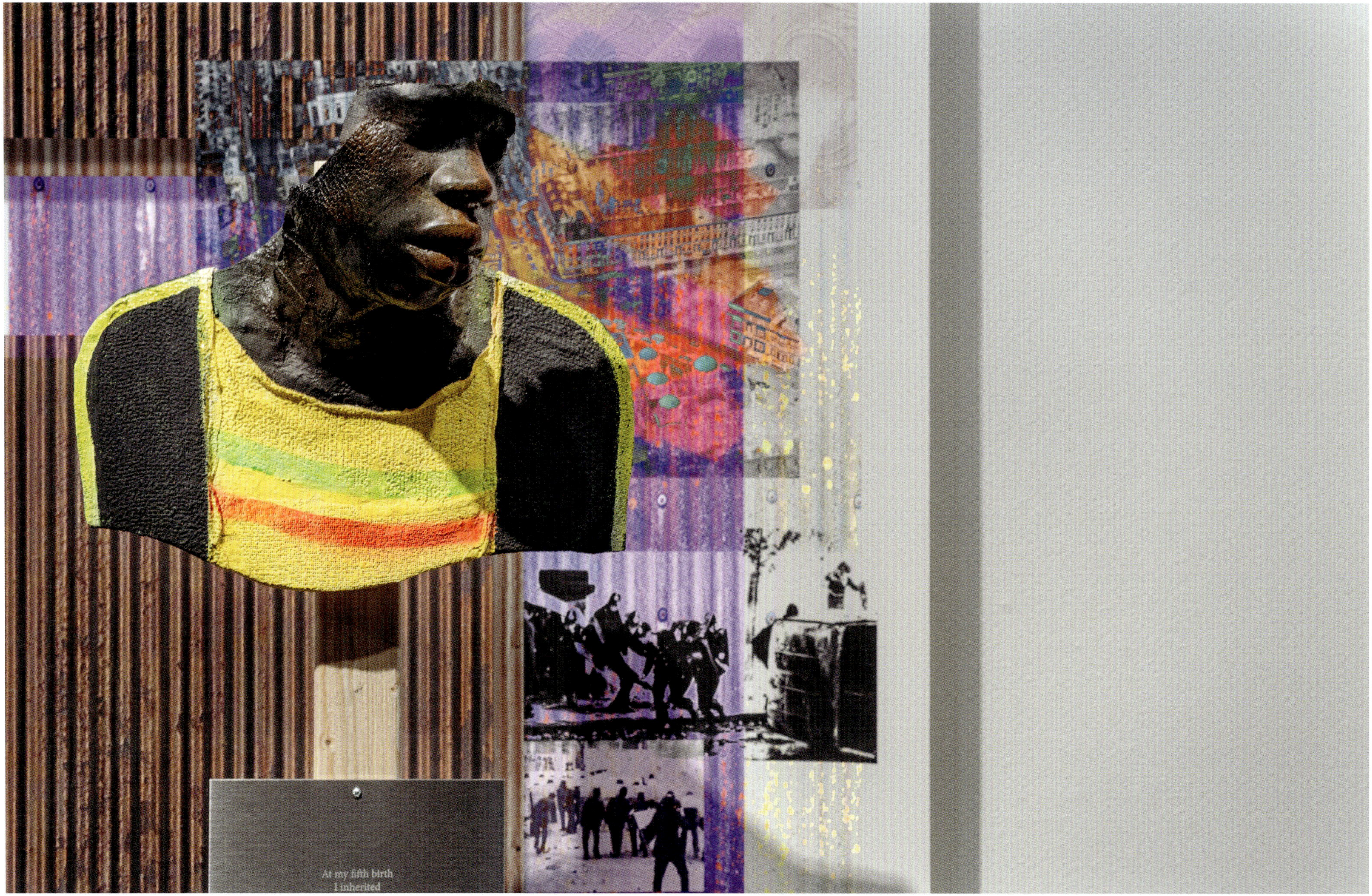
At my fifth birth
I inherited

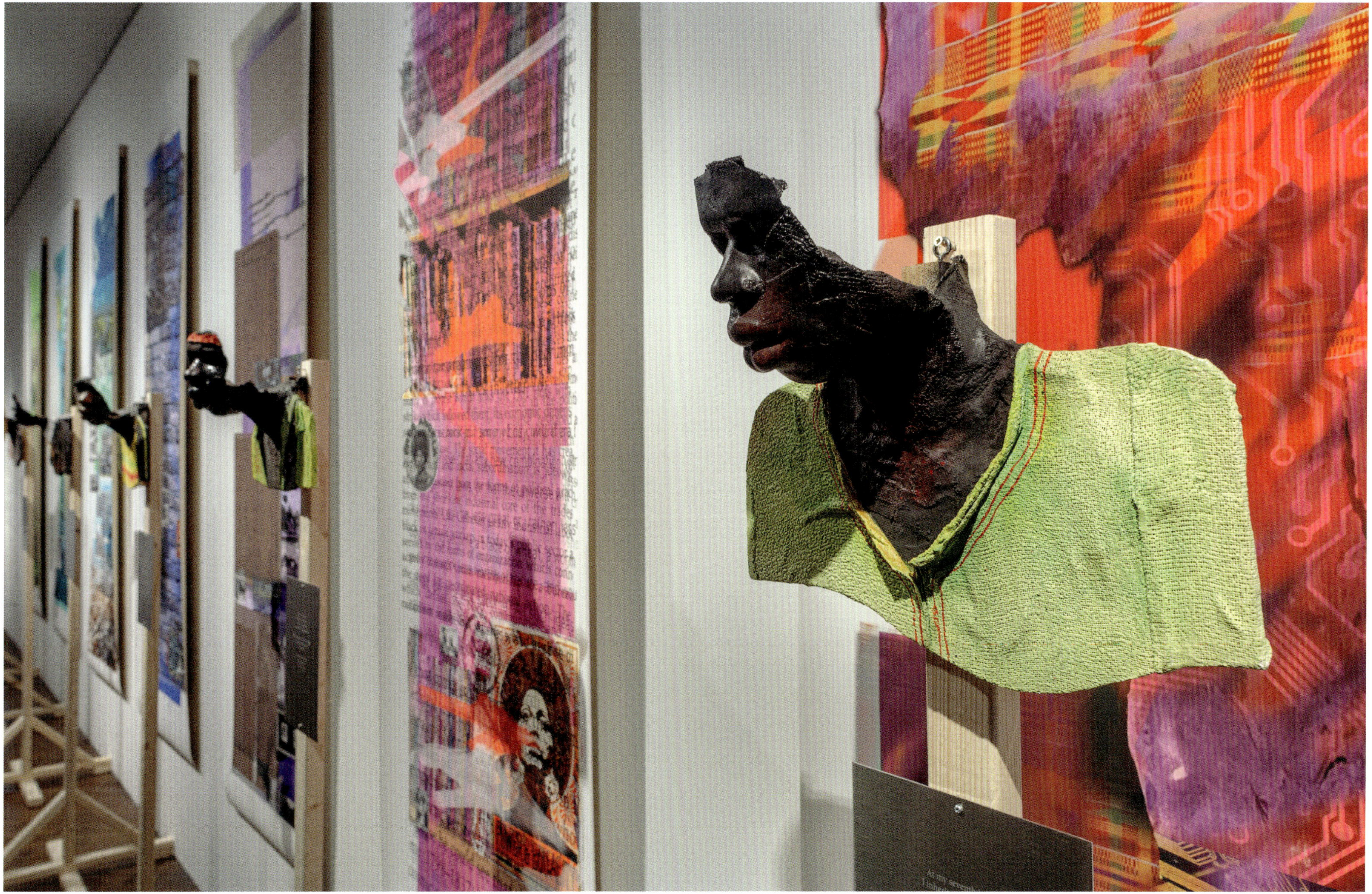

Go West Young Man
1987

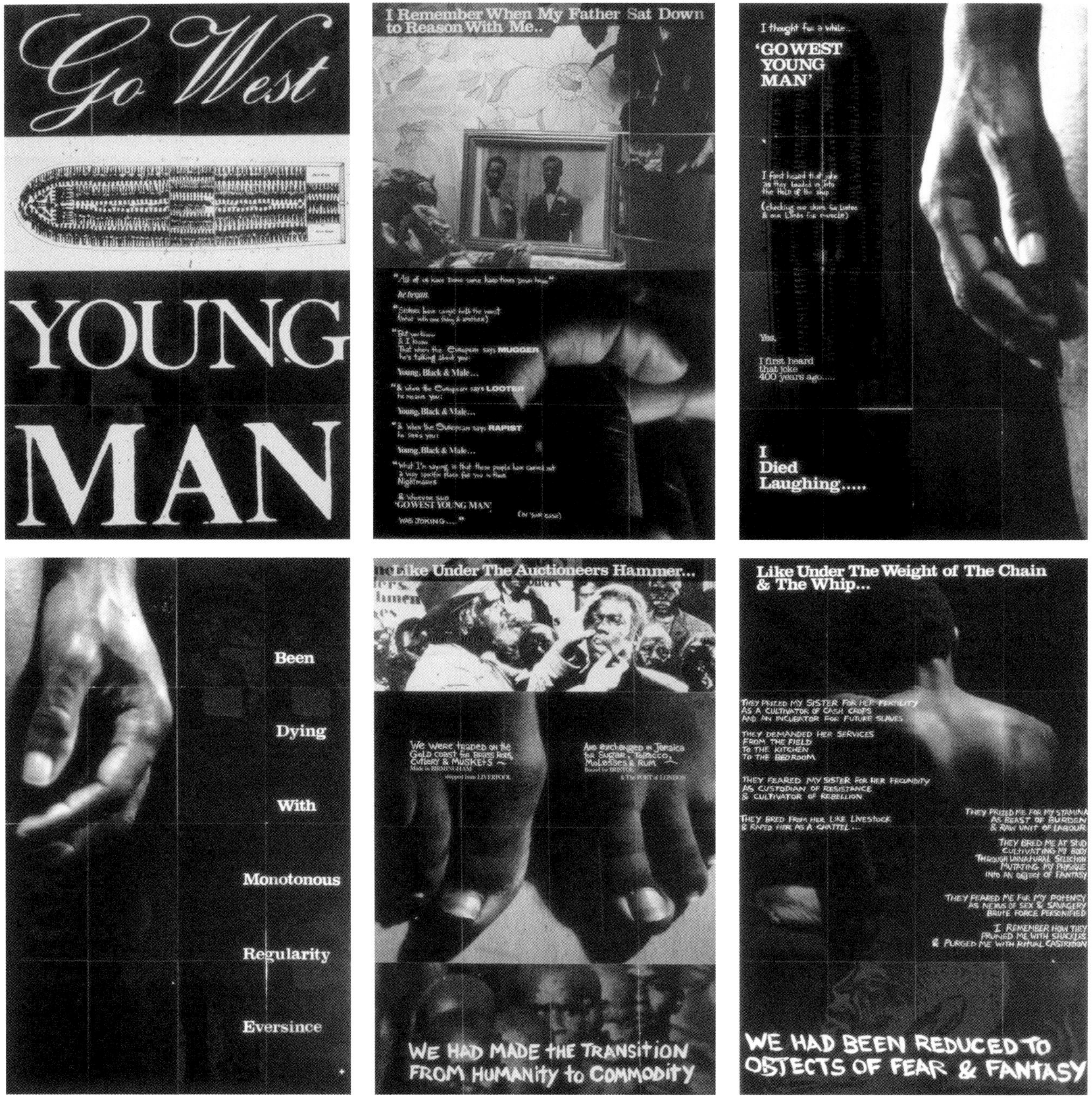

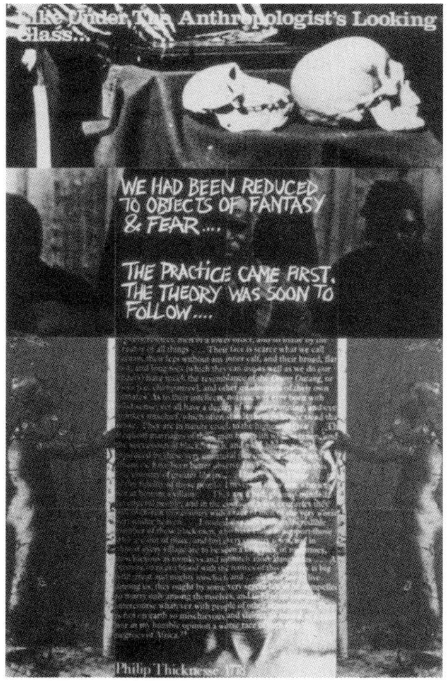
Like Under The Anthropologist's Looking Glass...
WE HAD BEEN REDUCED TO OBJECTS OF FANTASY & FEAR....
THE PRACTICE CAME FIRST. THE THEORY WAS SOON TO FOLLOW....
Philip Thicknesse

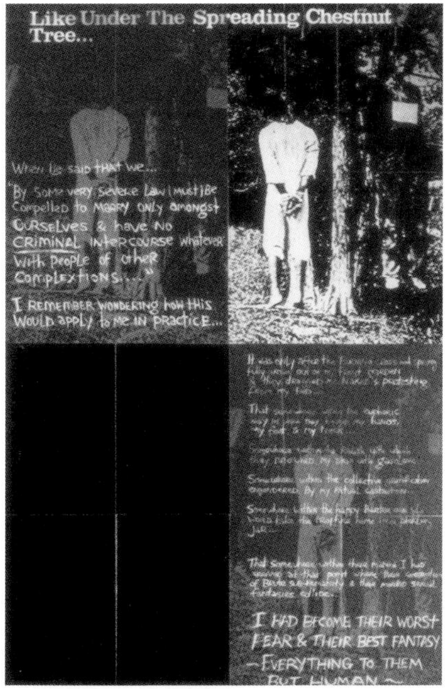
Like Under The Spreading Chestnut Tree...
"By Some very Severe Law I must Be Compelled to marry only amongst Ourselves & have No CRIMINAL intercourse whatever with People of other Complexions..."
I REMEMBER WONDERING HOW THIS WOULD APPLY TO ME IN PRACTICE...
I HAD BECOME THEIR WORST FEAR & THEIR BEST FANTASY
—EVERYTHING TO THEM

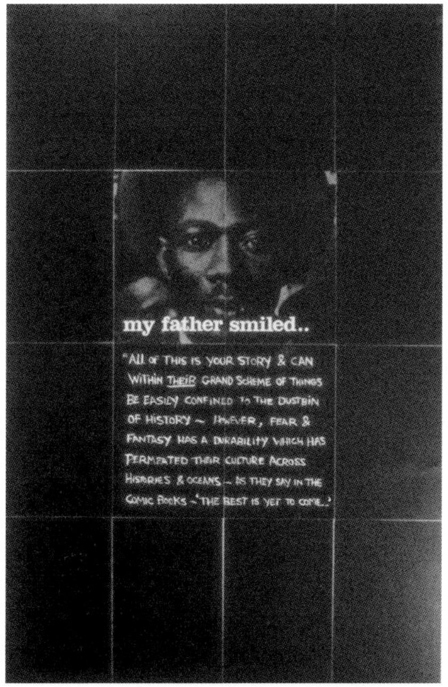
my father smiled..
"ALL OF THIS IS YOUR STORY & CAN WITHIN THEIR GRAND SCHEME OF THINGS BE EASILY CONFINED TO THE DUSTBIN OF HISTORY ~ HOWEVER, FEAR & FANTASY HAS A DURABILITY WHICH HAS PERMEATED THEIR CULTURE ACROSS HISTORIES & OCEANS... AS THEY SAY IN THE COMIC BOOKS ~ 'THE BEST IS YET TO COME..'

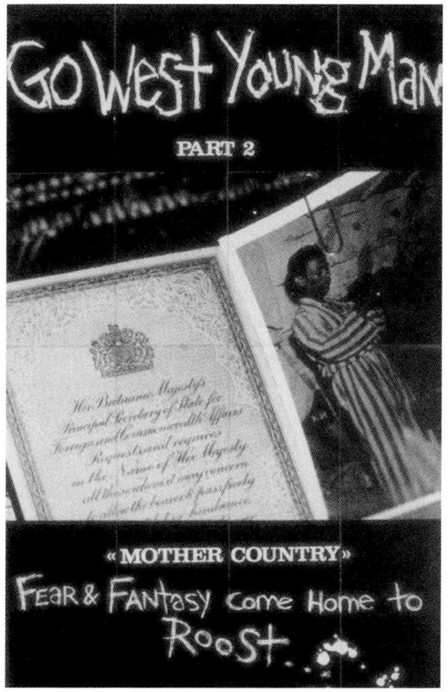
GO WEST YOUNG MAN
PART 2
«MOTHER COUNTRY»
FEAR & FANTASY COME HOME TO ROOST...

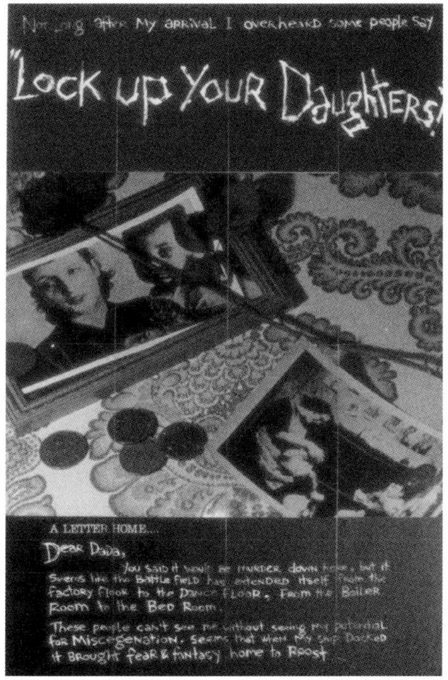
My arrival I overheard some people say
"Lock up Your Daughters!"
A LETTER HOME...
Dear Dada,
You said it would be murder down here, but it Seems like the Battle Field has extended itself from the Factory Floor to the Dance Floor, From the Boiler Room to the Bed Room.
These people can't see me without seeing my potential for Miscegenation. Seems that when my ship Docked it Brought fear & fantasy home to Roost...

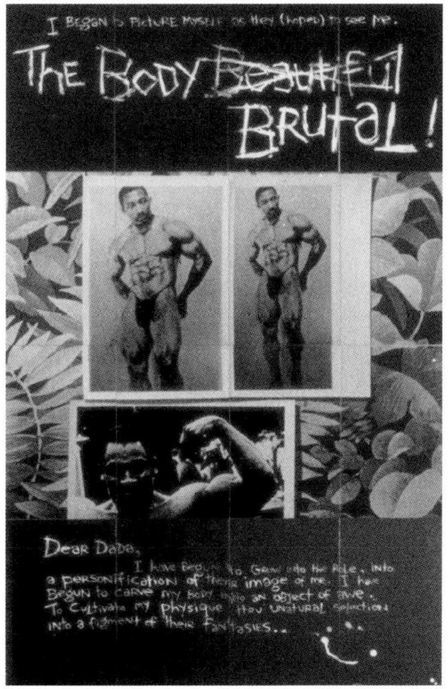
I BEGAN to PICTURE MYSELF as they (hoped) to see me.
THE BODY Beautiful BRUTAL!
Dear Dada,
a personification of their image of me. I have Begun to carve my body into an object of awe. To Cultivate my physique into a figment of their fantasies..

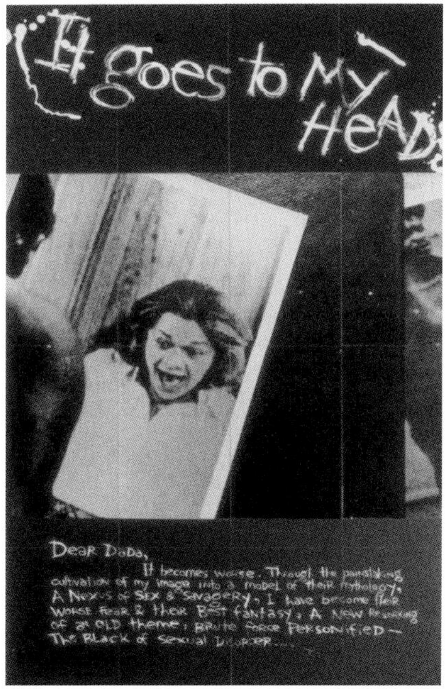
It goes to My HEAD!
Dear Dada,
It becomes worse.
A Nexus of Sex & Savagery, I have become their worse fear & their Best fantasy.
of an OLD theme; Brute force personified—
The Black of Sexual Disorder....

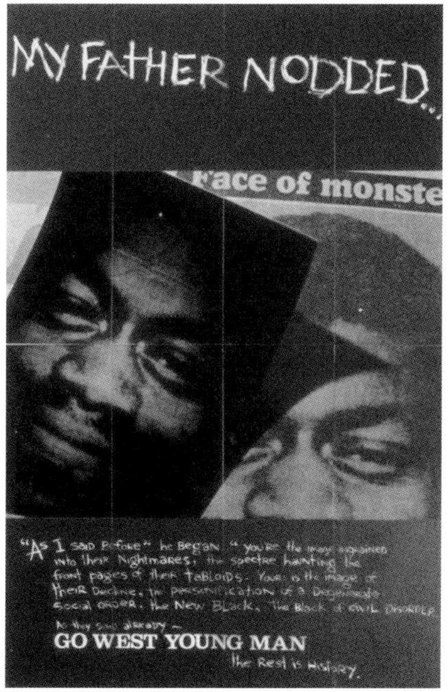
MY FATHER NODDED...
Face of monste
"As I said Before" he Began. "
into their Nightmares, the specter haunting the front pages of their TabloiDs.
Social ORDER, the New Black, the Black of Civil Disorder
GO WEST YOUNG MAN
the Rest is History.

Go West Young Man
1996

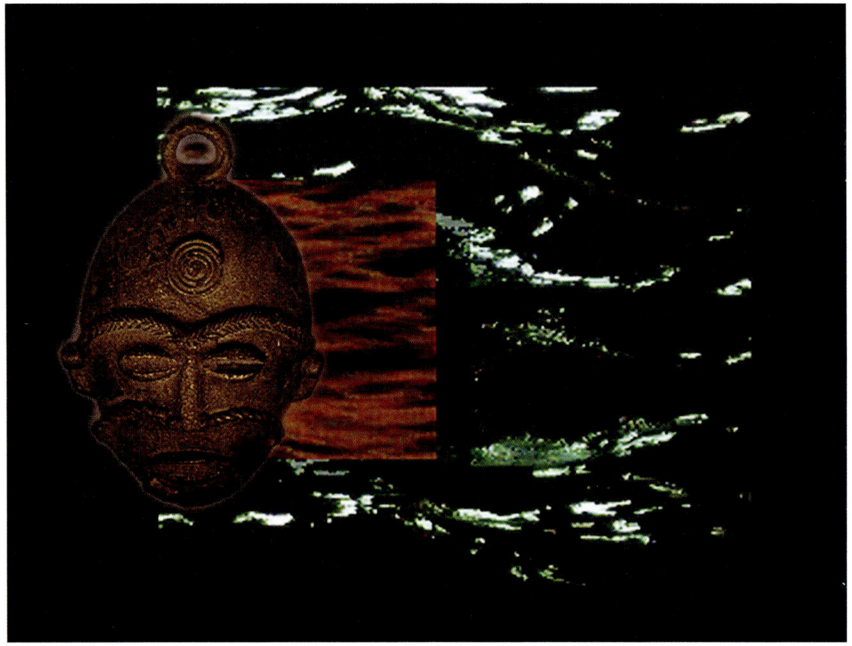

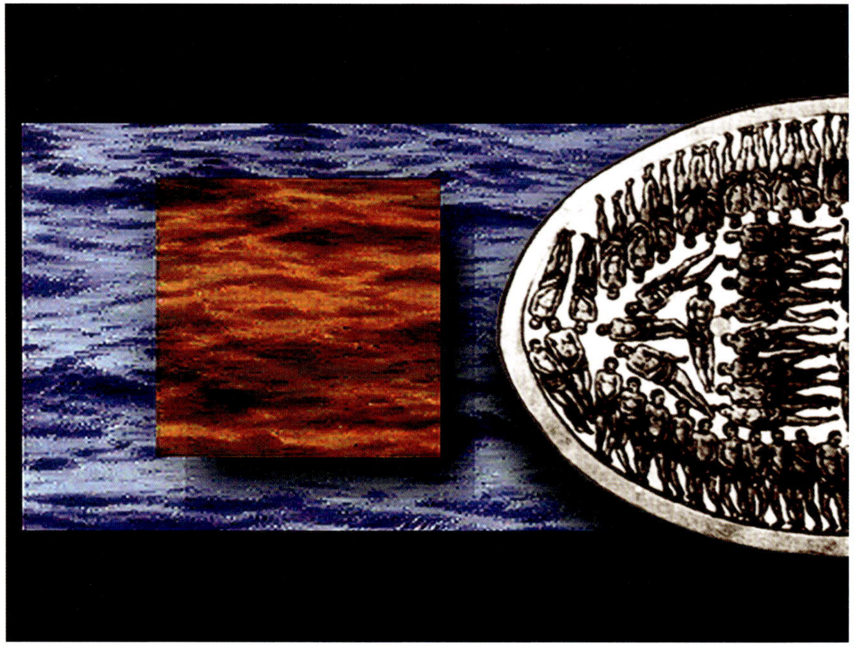

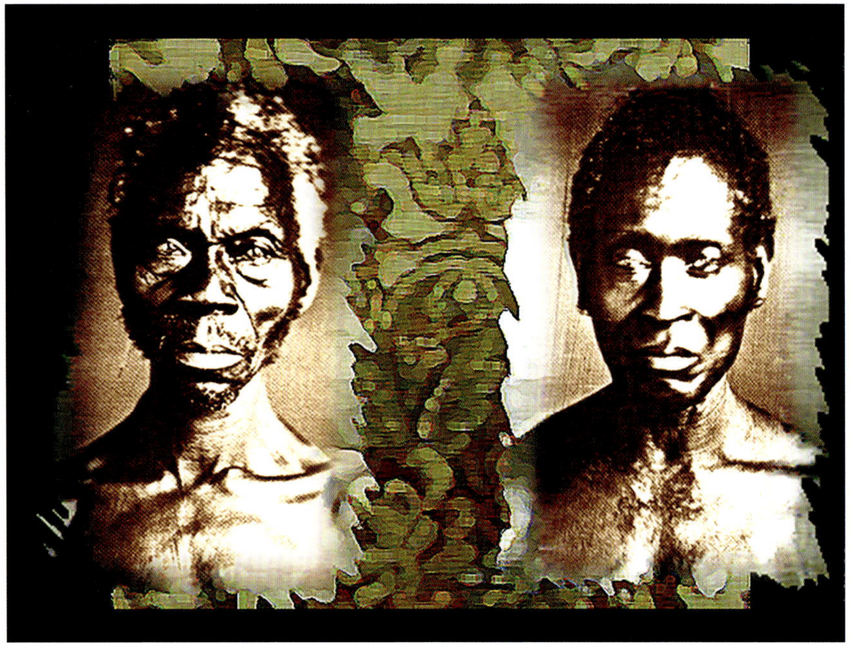

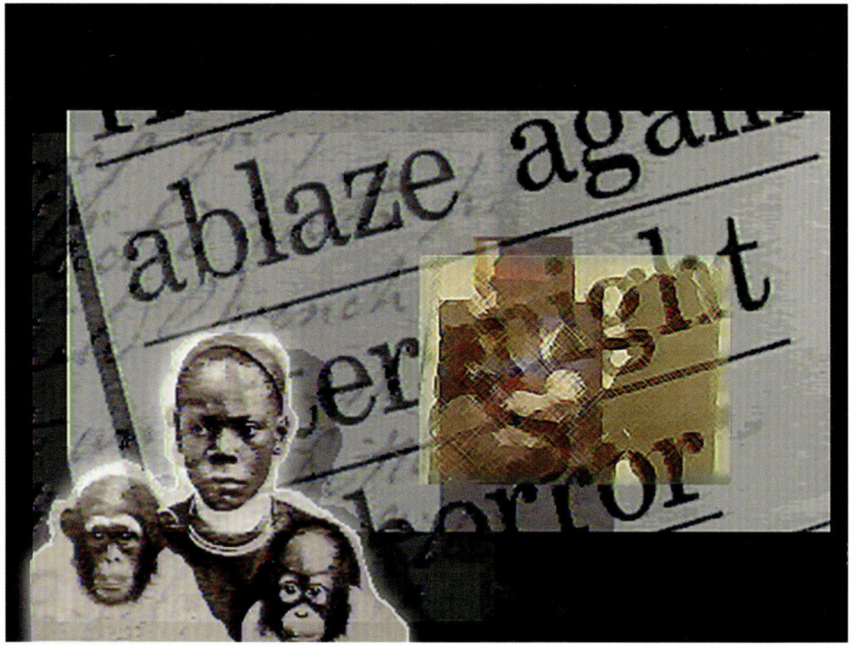

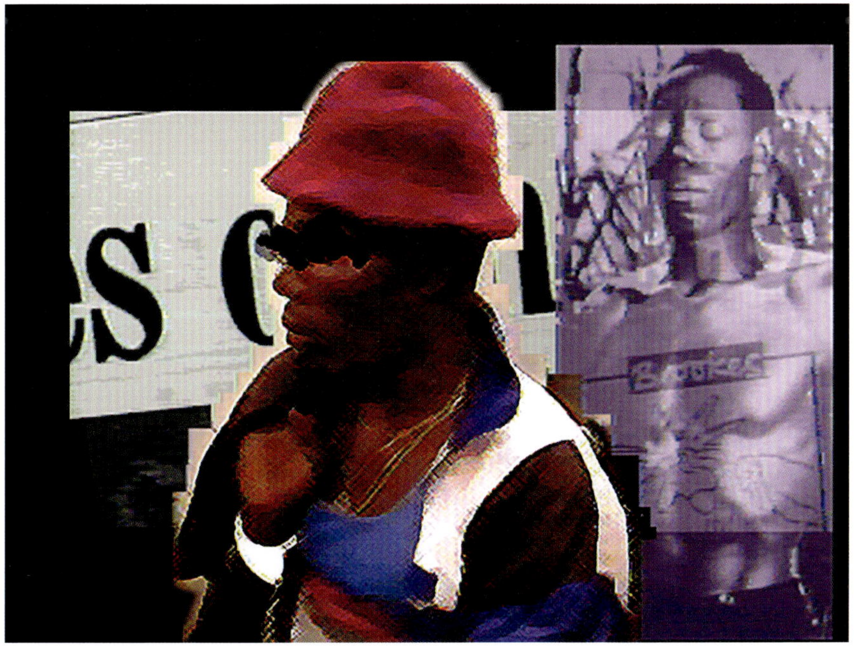

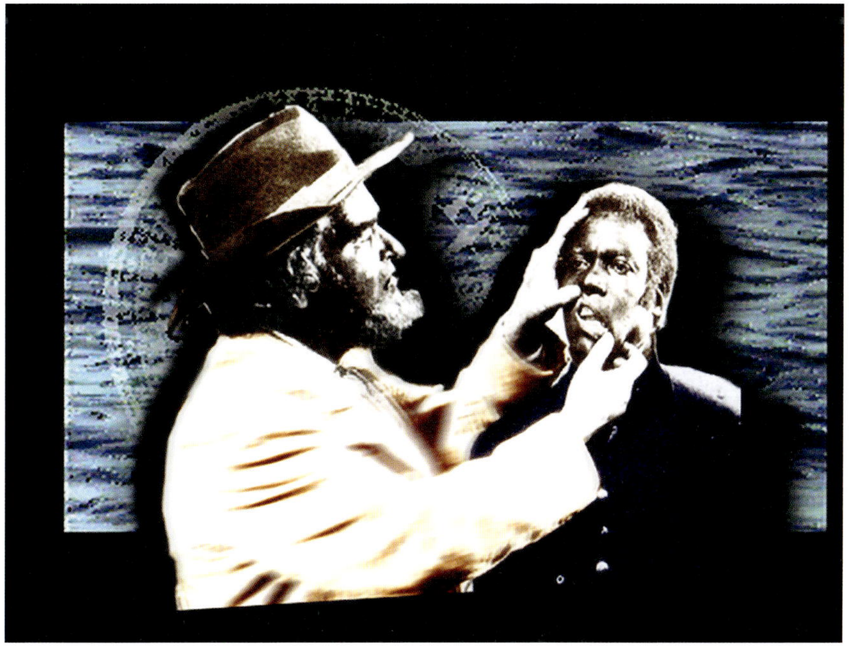

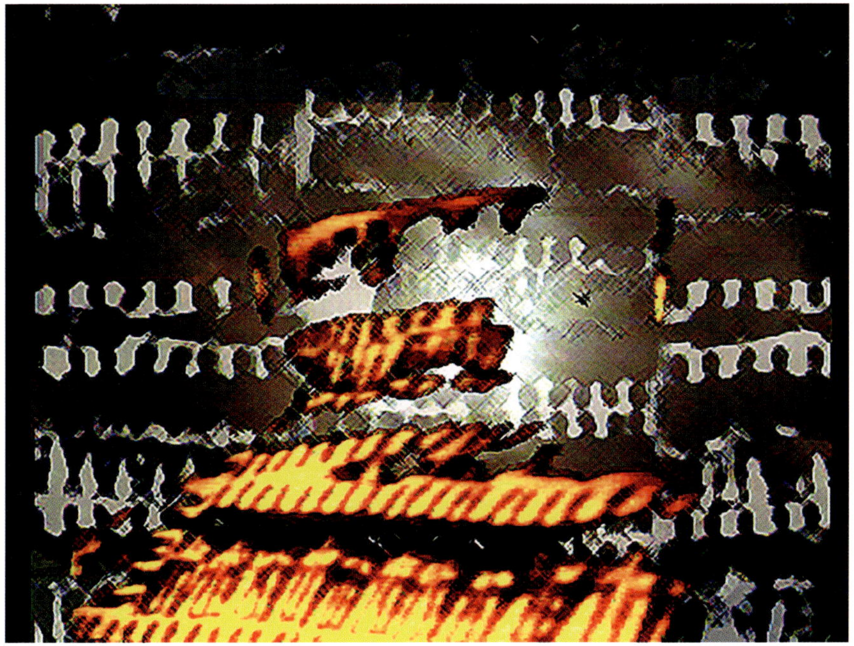

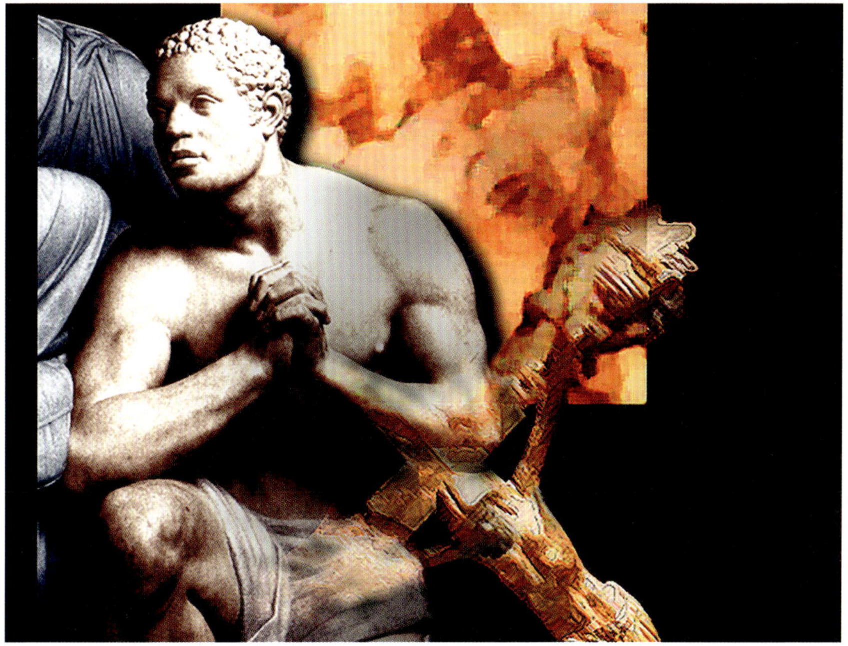

The Nation's Finest
1990

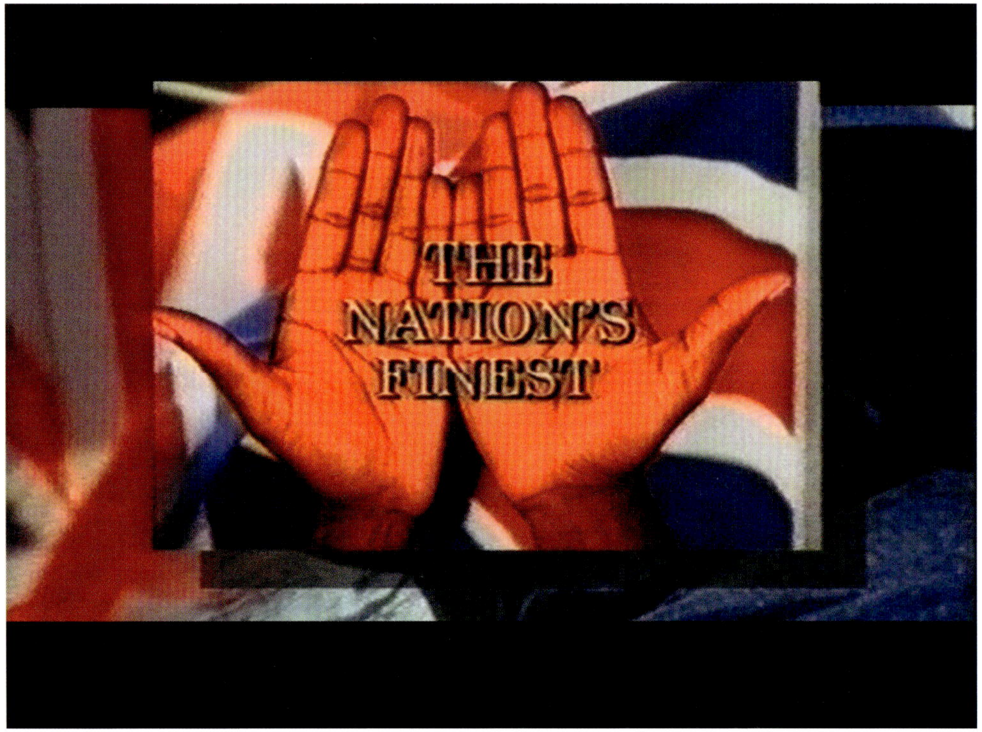

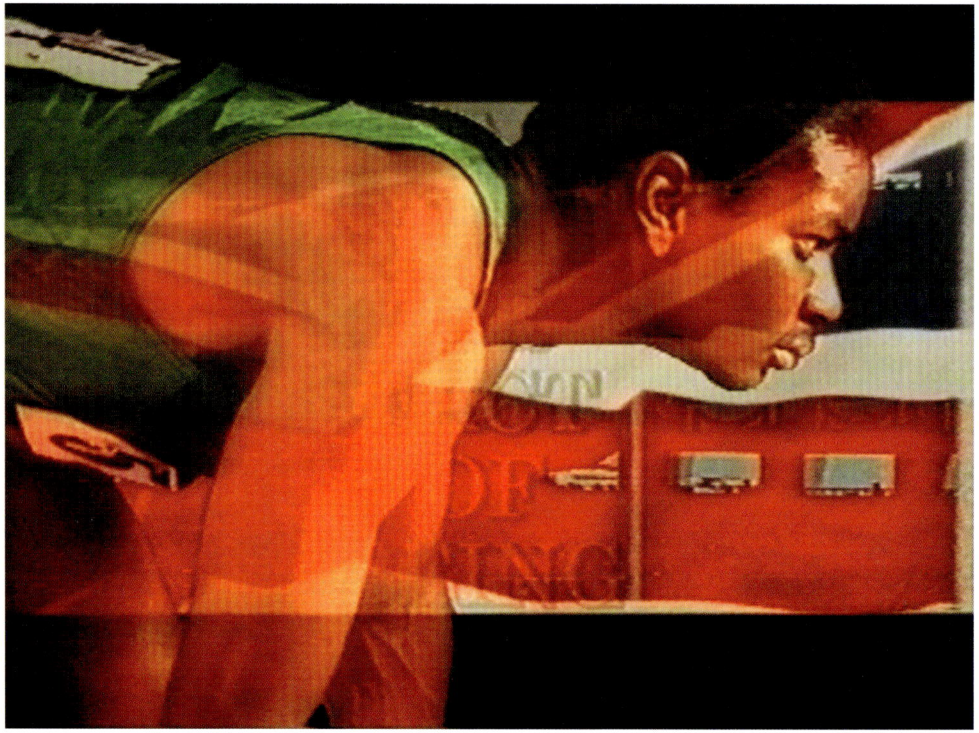

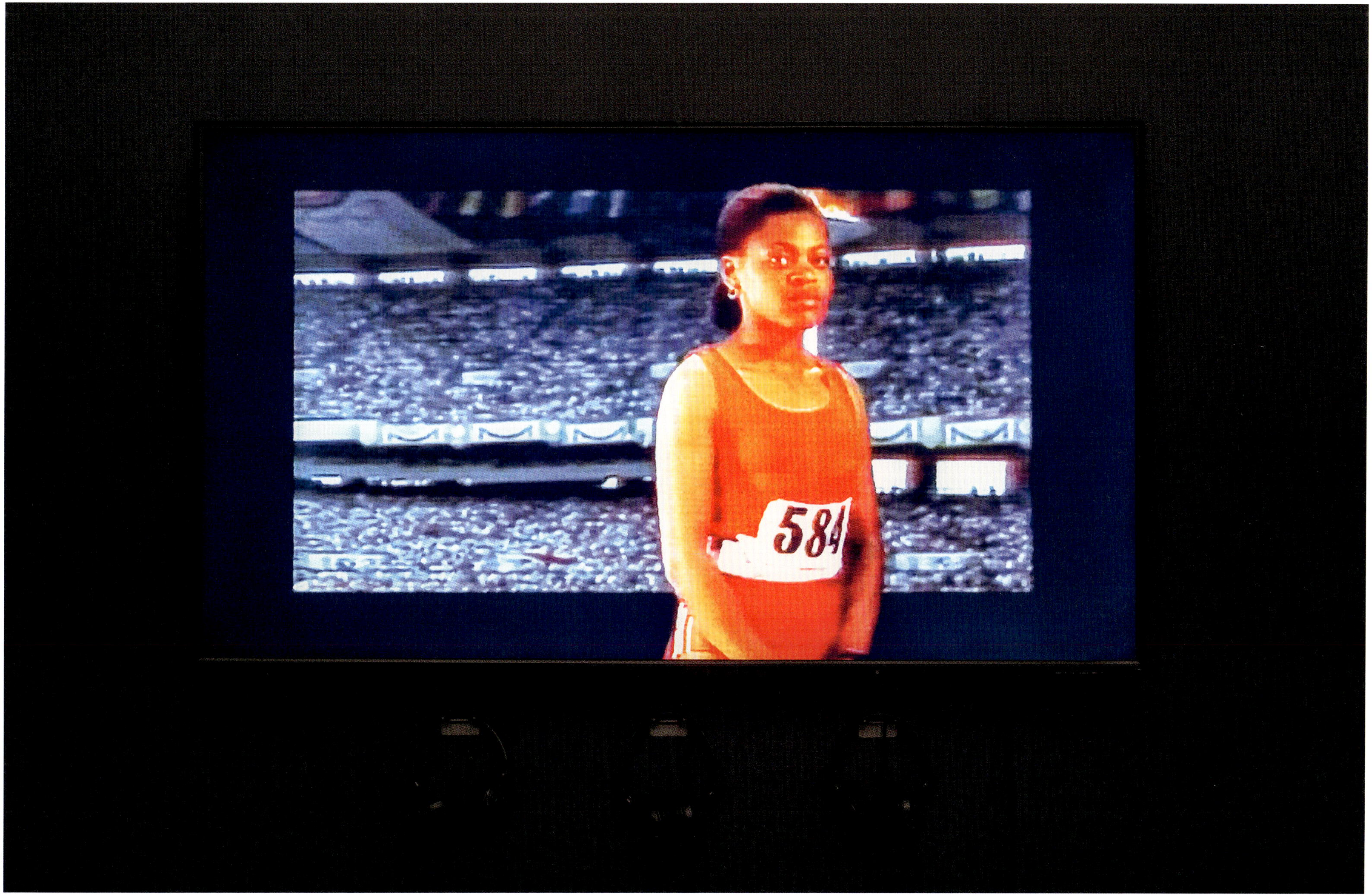
584

The Perfect City
2007

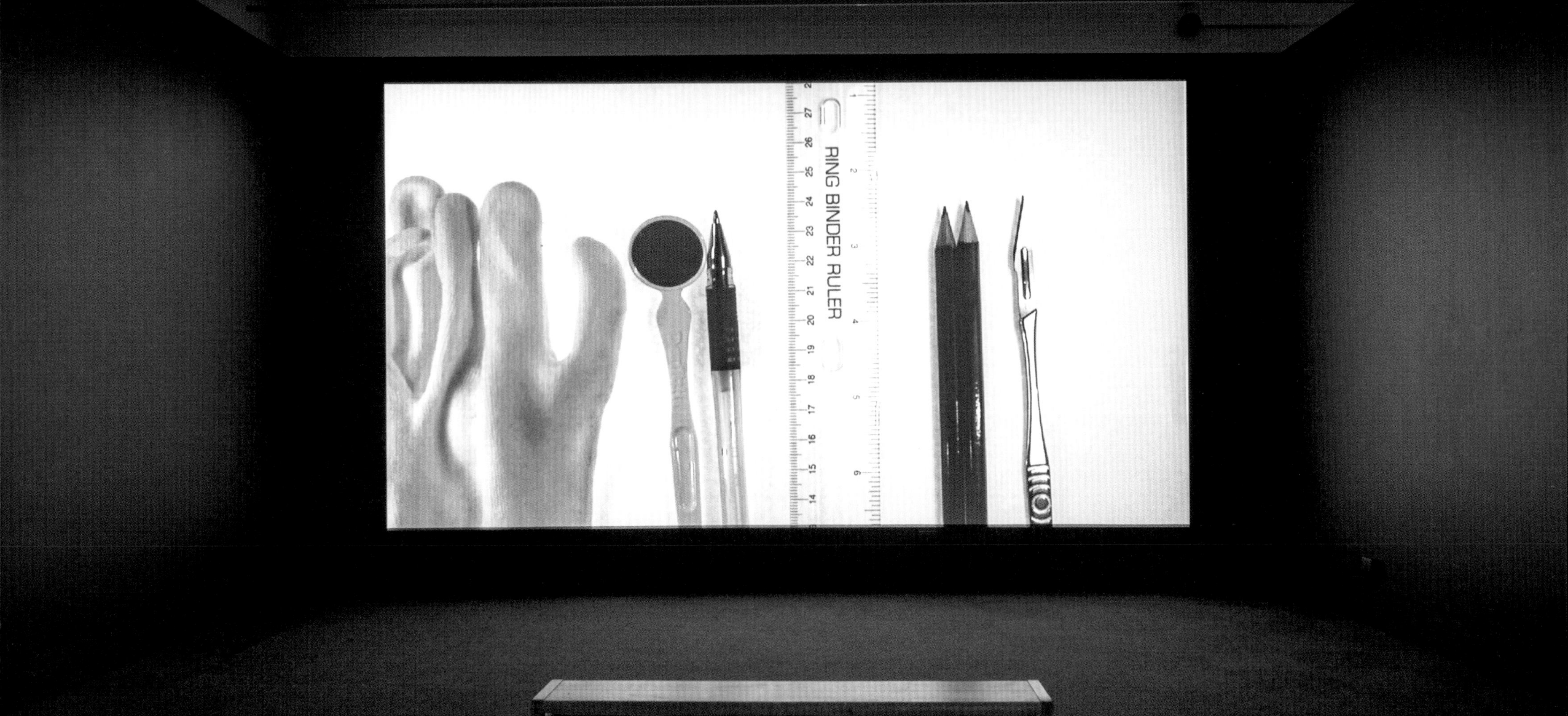
RING BINDER RULER

The Perfect City
2007

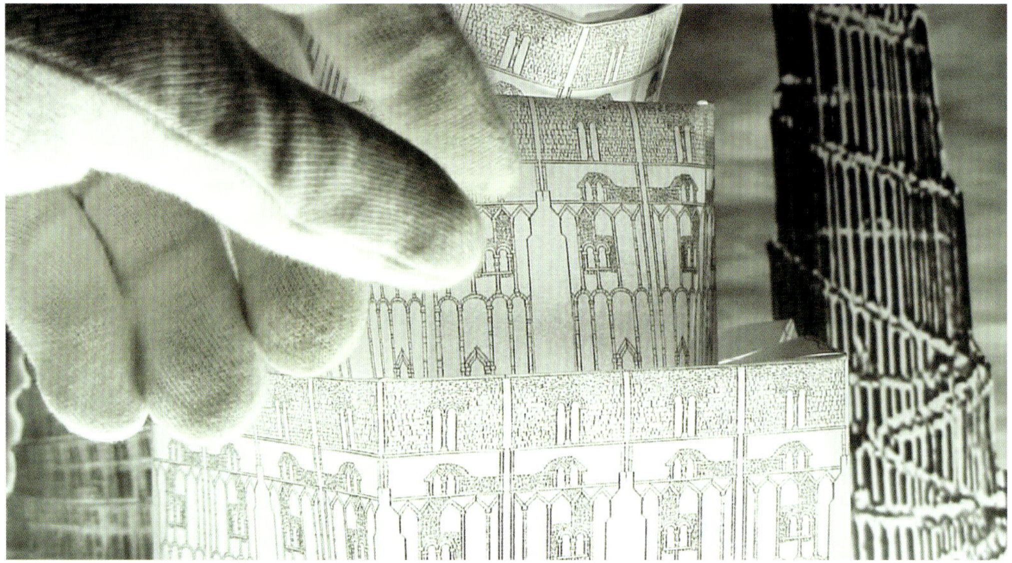

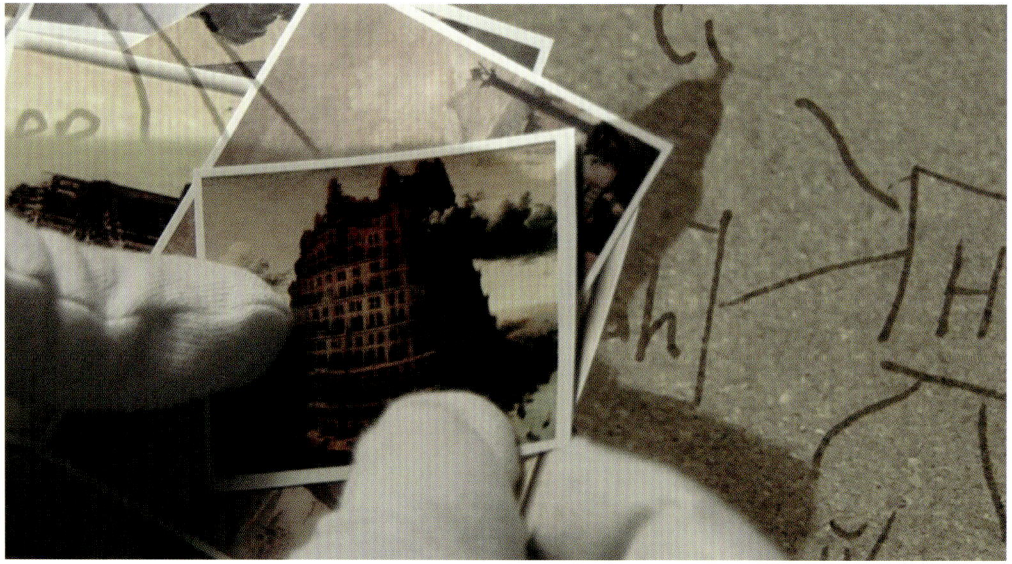

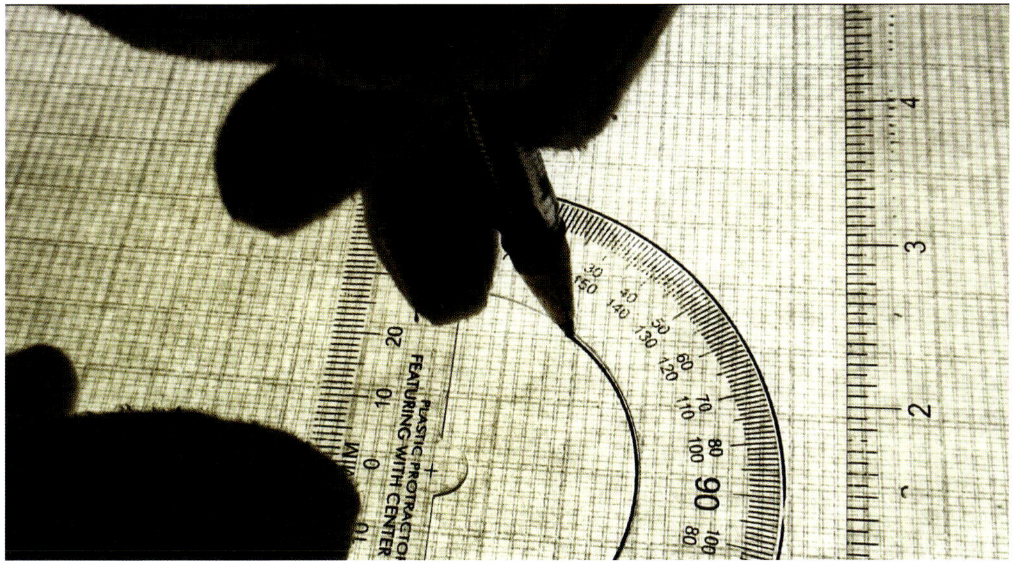
FEATURING WITH CENTER

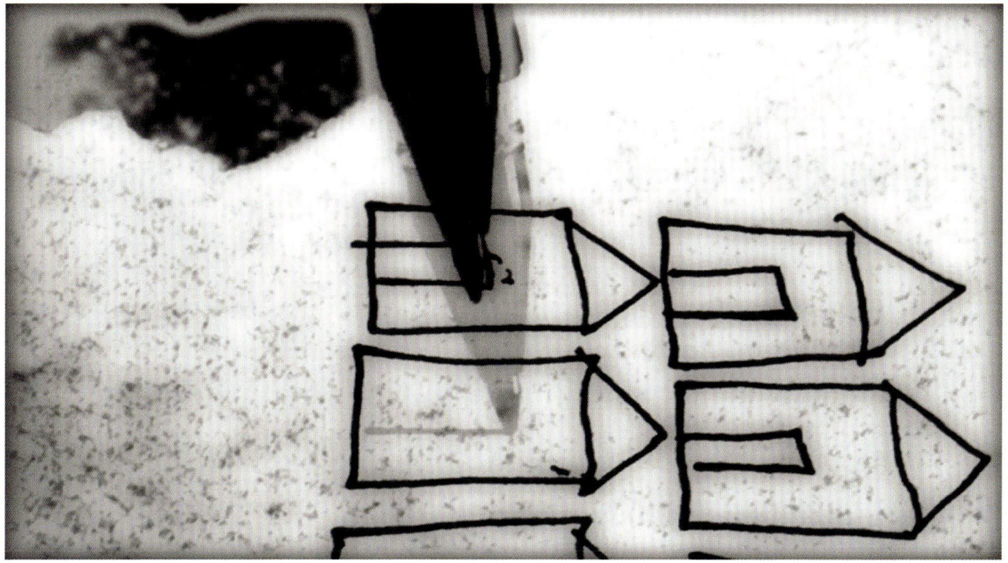

The Trophies of Empire
1985

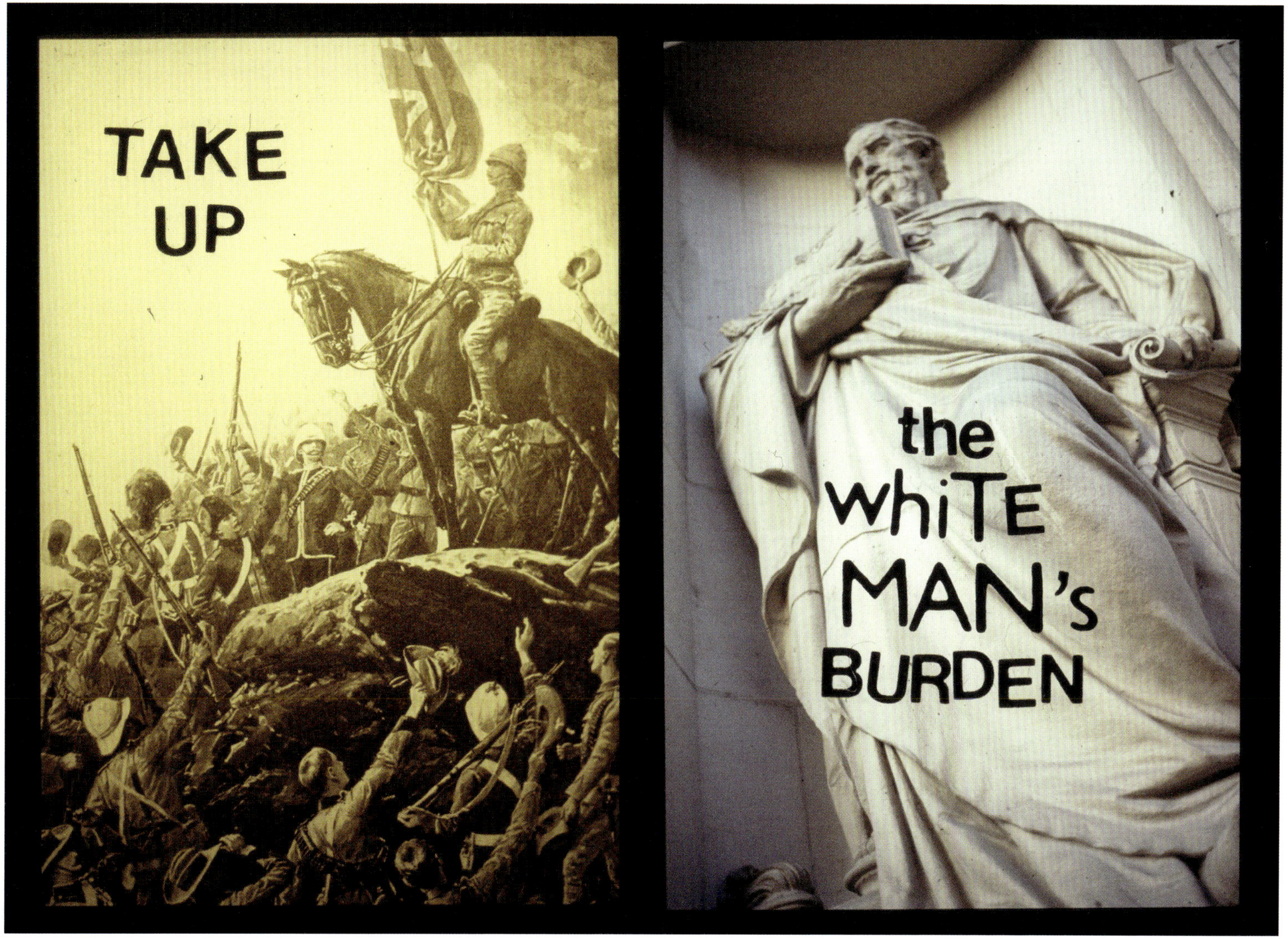
TAKE
UP
the
whiTE
MAN's
BURDEN

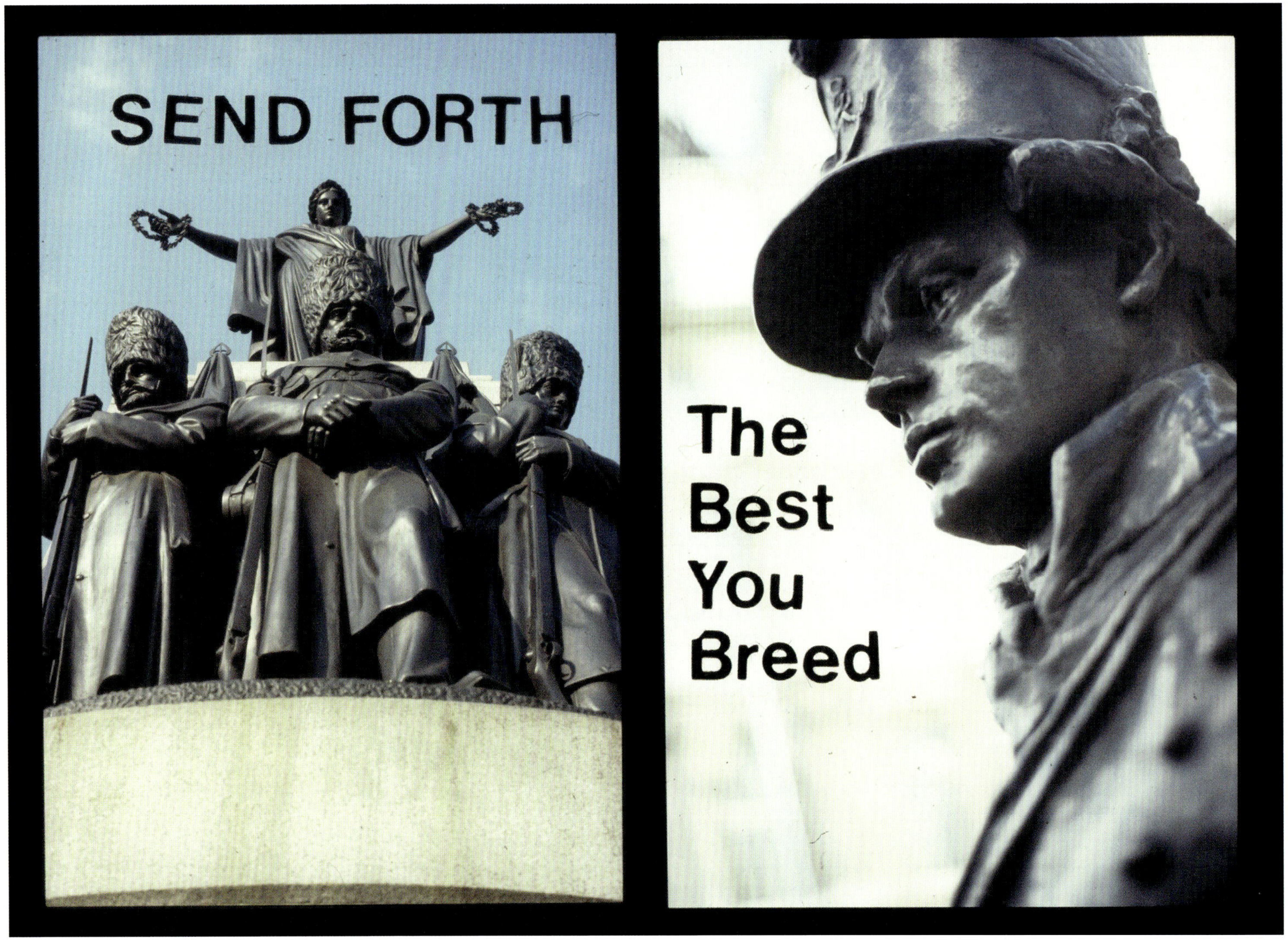
SEND FORTH
The
Best
You
Breed

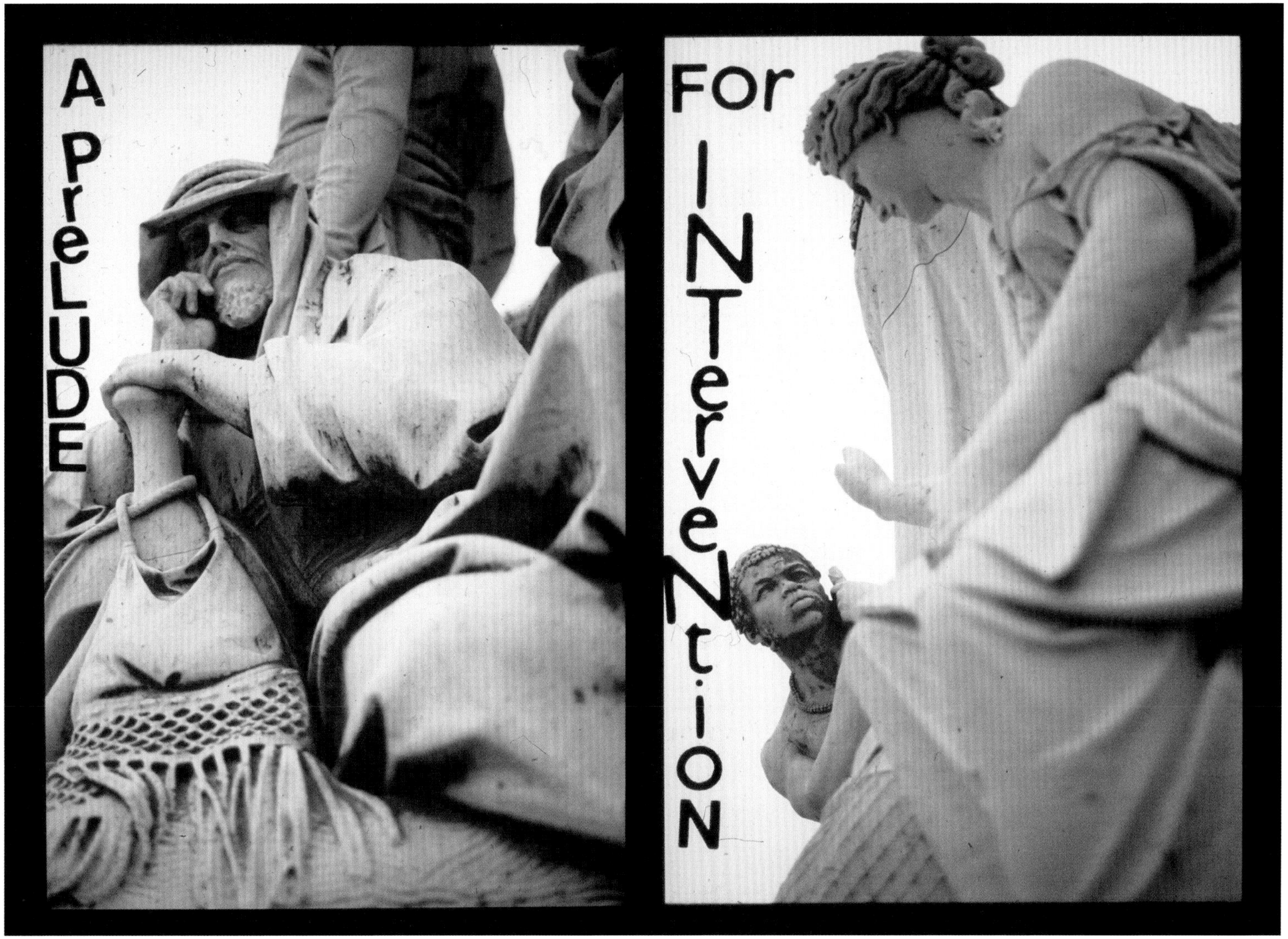
A PreLUDE
For INTerveNtion

The Trophies of Empire
1985

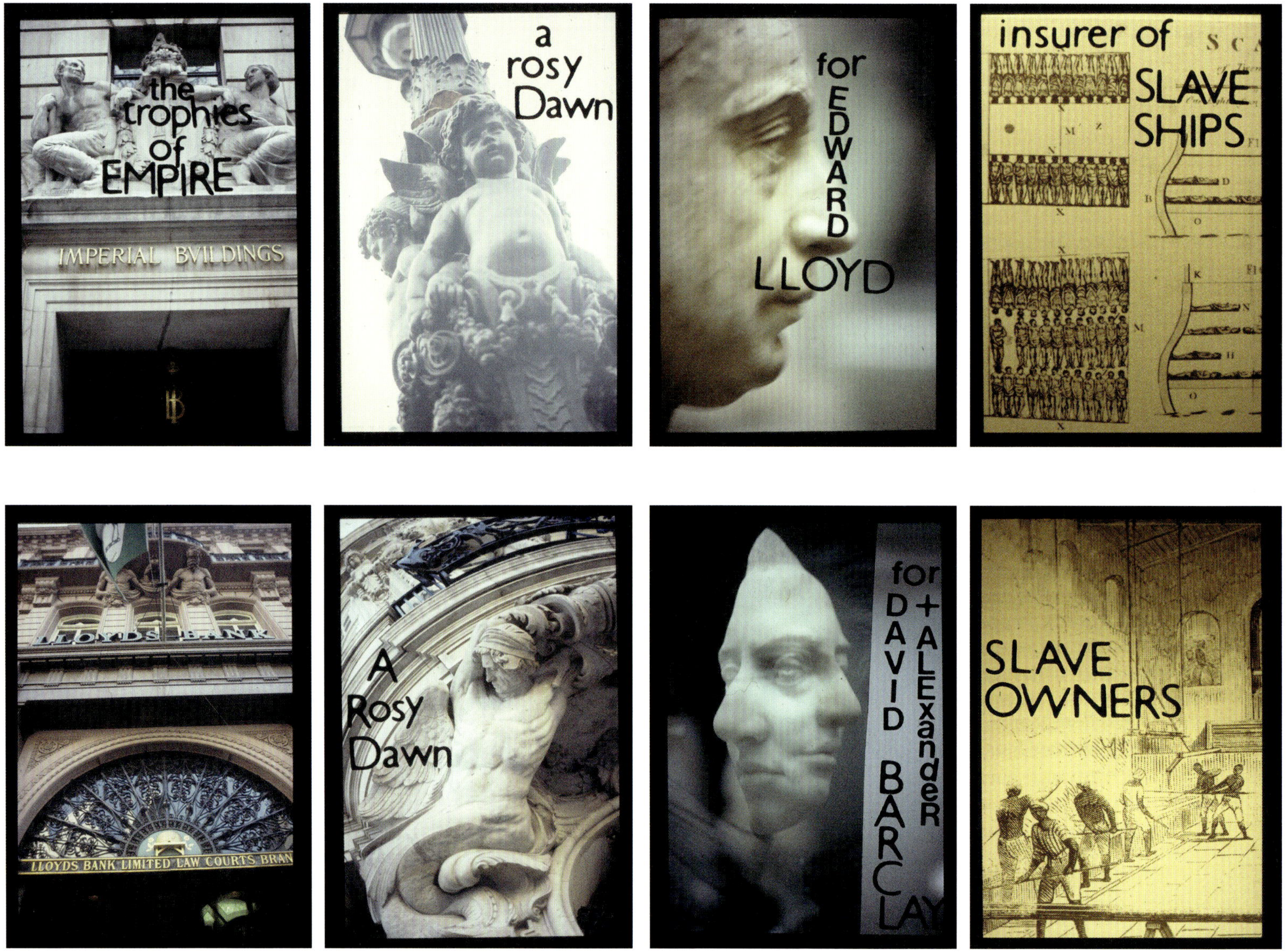

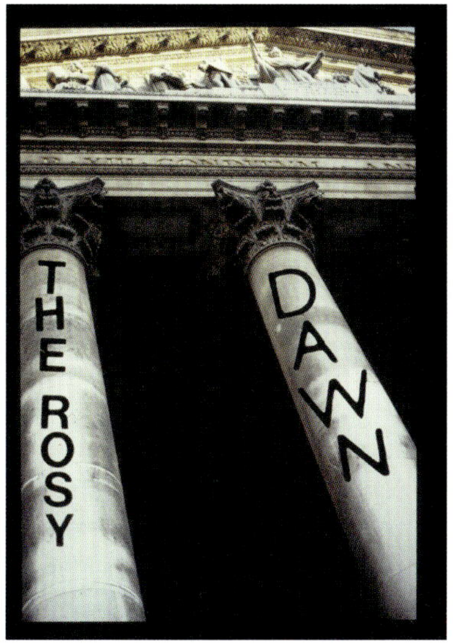
THE ROSY
DAWN

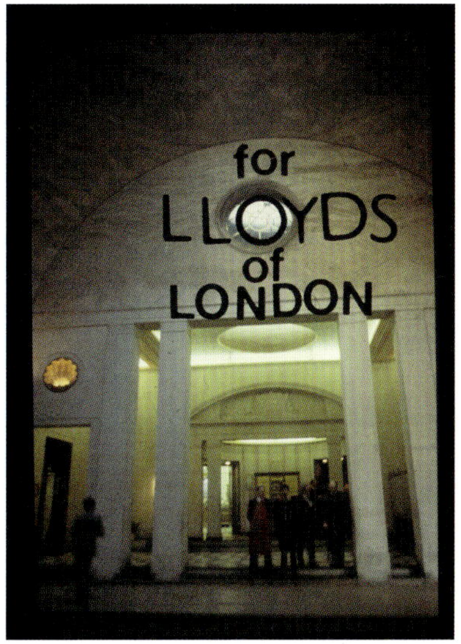
for
LLOYDS
of
LONDON

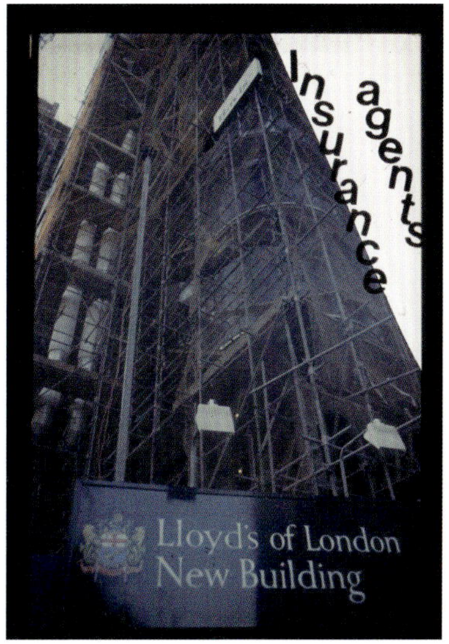
Insurance
agents
Lloyd's of London
New Building

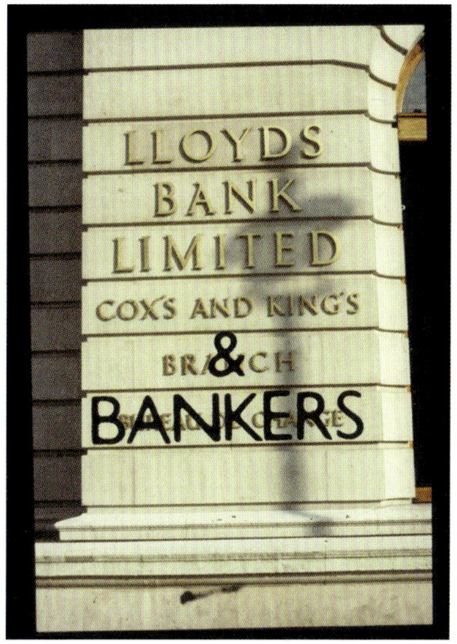
LLOYDS
BANK
LIMITED
COX'S AND KING'S
&
BANKERS

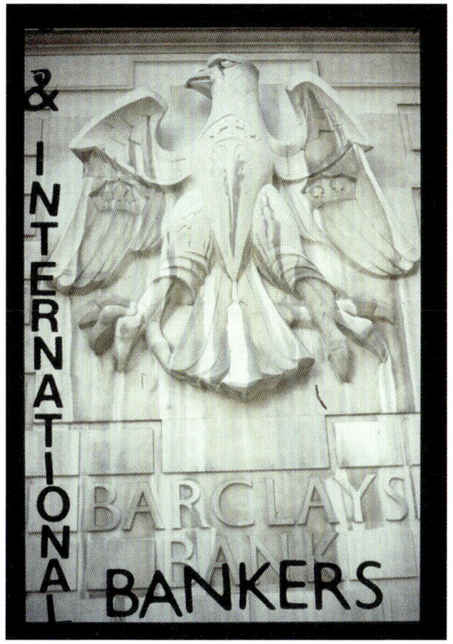
&
INTERNATIONAL
BARCLAYS
BANKERS

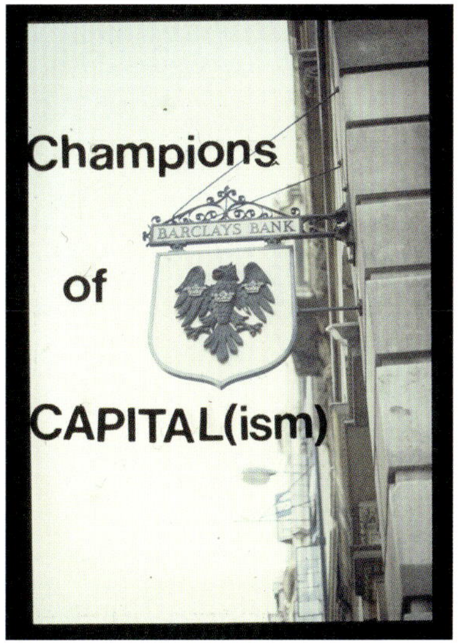
Champions
BARCLAYS BANK
of
CAPITAL(ism)

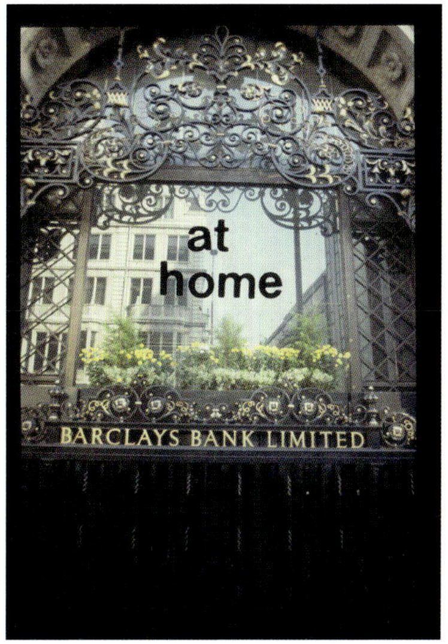
at
home
BARCLAYS BANK LIMITED

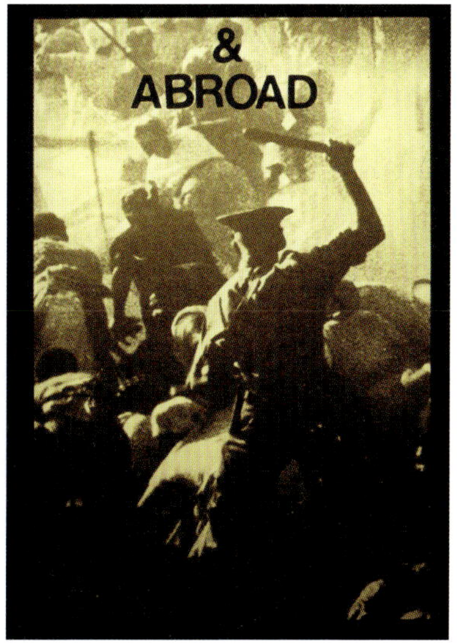
&
ABROAD

Jet Black Futures

THE NEW ART GALLERY WALSALL, 14 JANUARY – 24 APRIL 2022

Searching for a Jet Black Future
2021-22

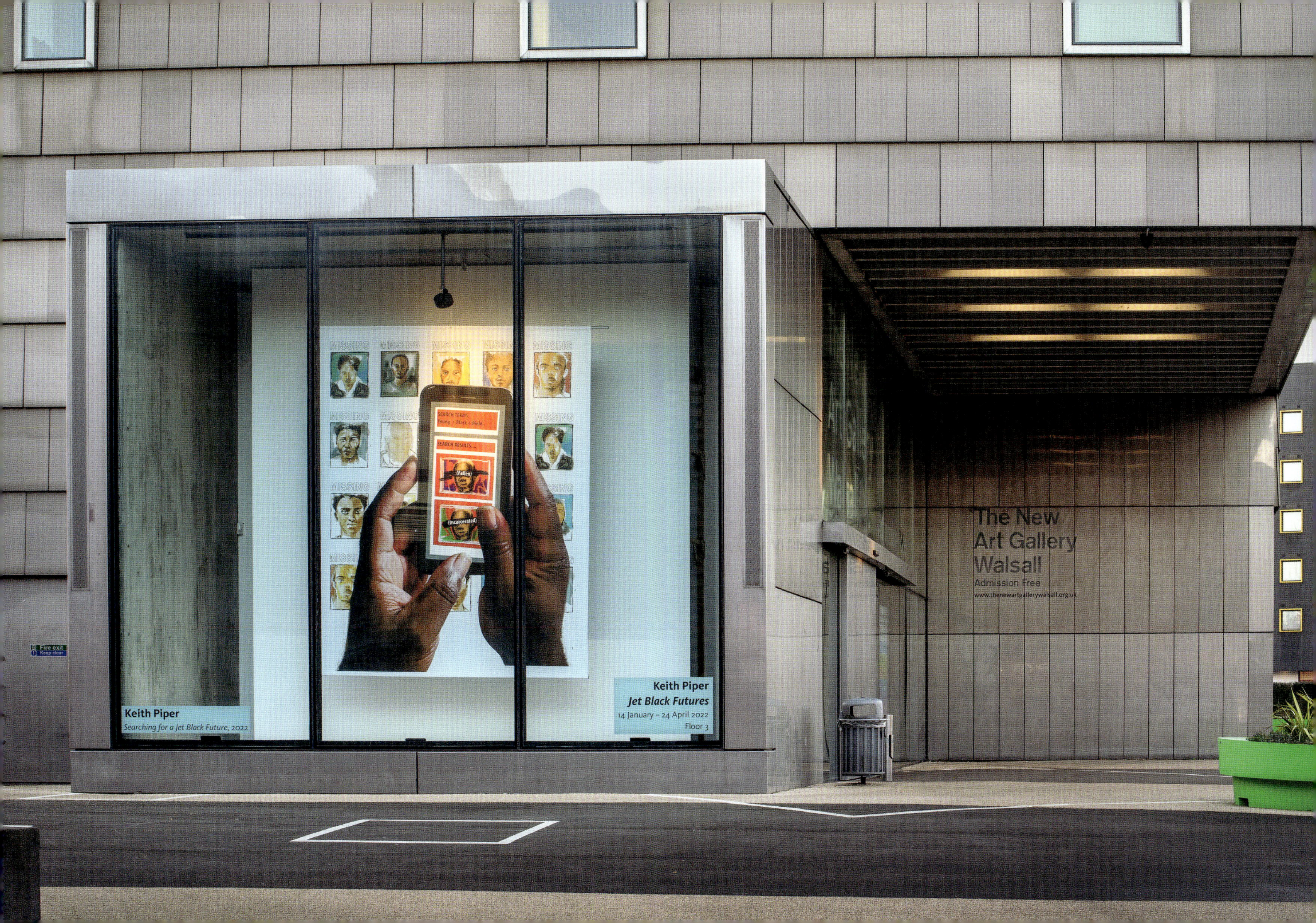

SEARCH TERMS.
Young + Black + Male..
SEARCH RESULTS....
(Fallen)
(Incarcerated)
Keith Piper
Searching for a Jet Black Future, 2022
Keith Piper
Jet Black Futures
14 January – 24 April 2022
Floor 3
The New
Art Gallery
Walsall
Admission Free
www.thenewartgallerywalsall.org.uk

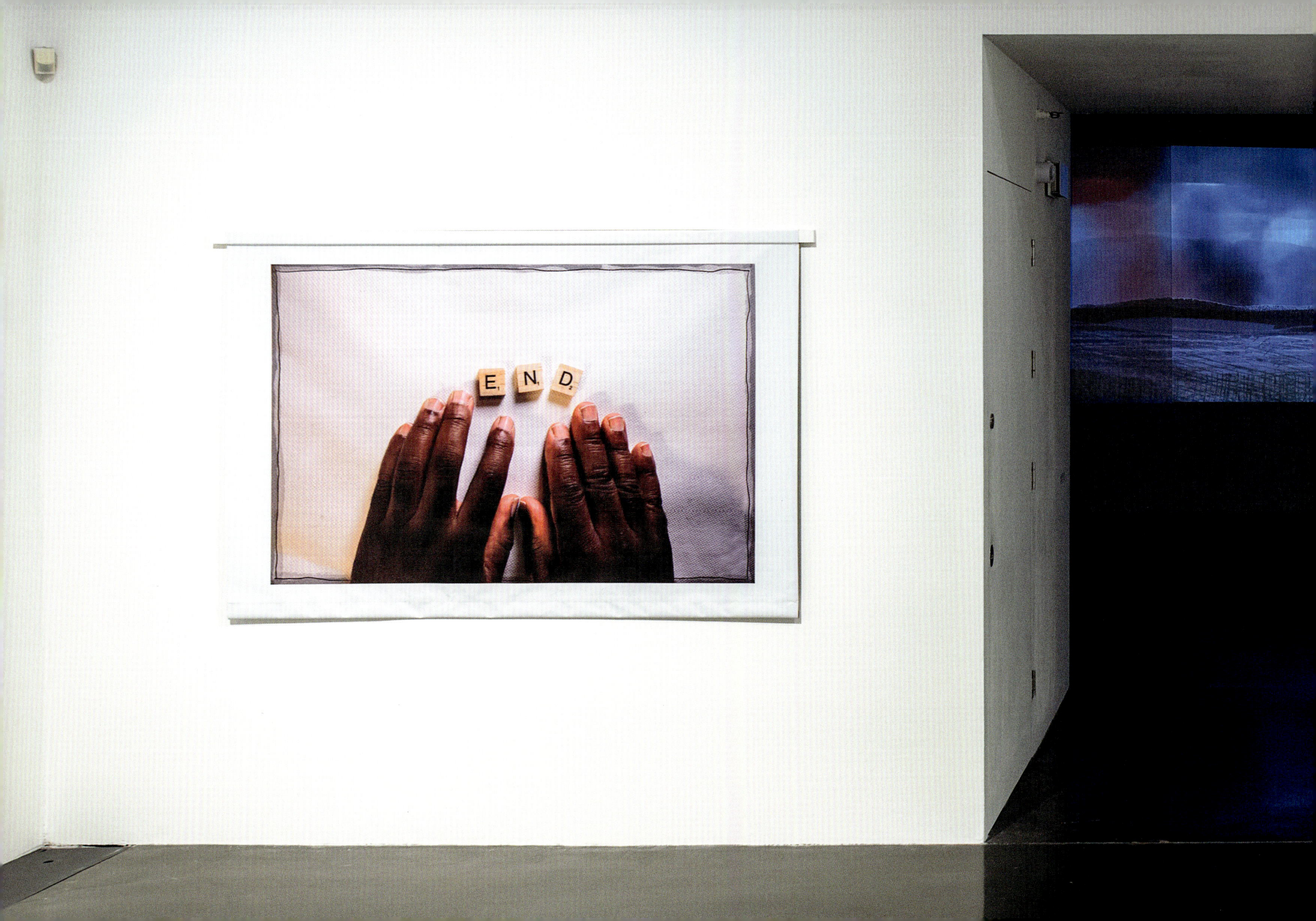
END

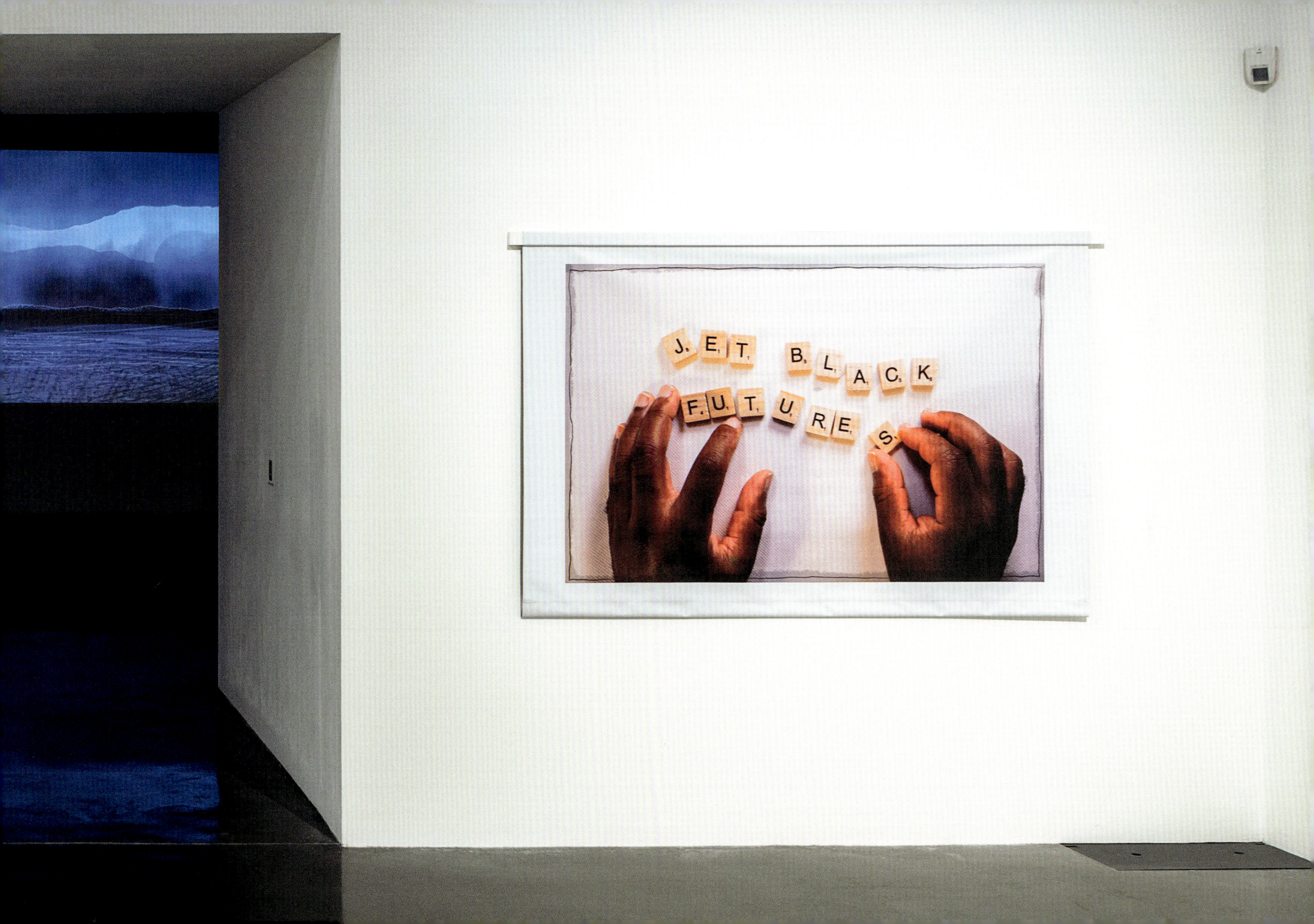
JET BLACK
FUTURES

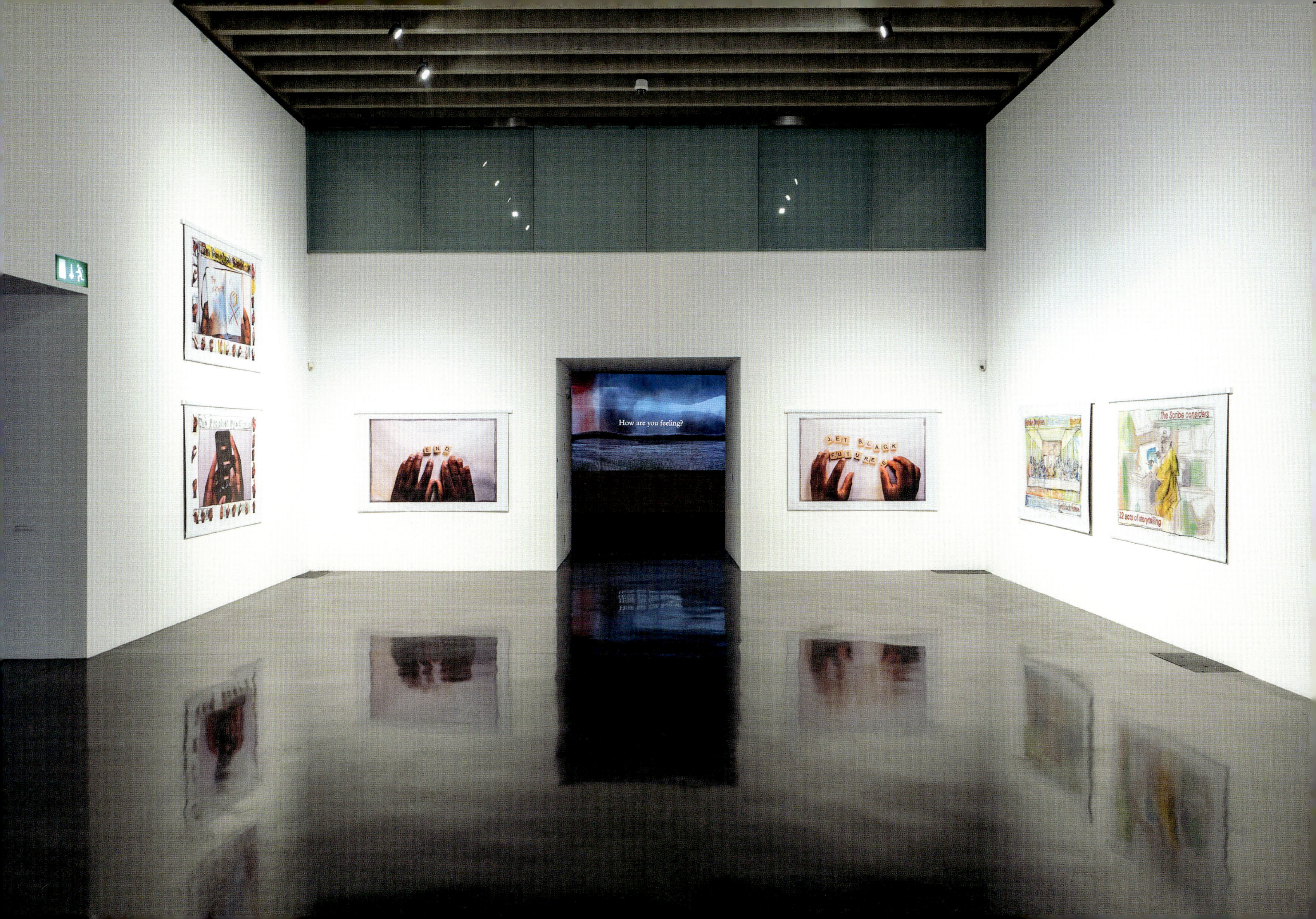
How are you feeling?
END
LET BLACK FUTURES
The Scribe considers
12 acts of storytelling

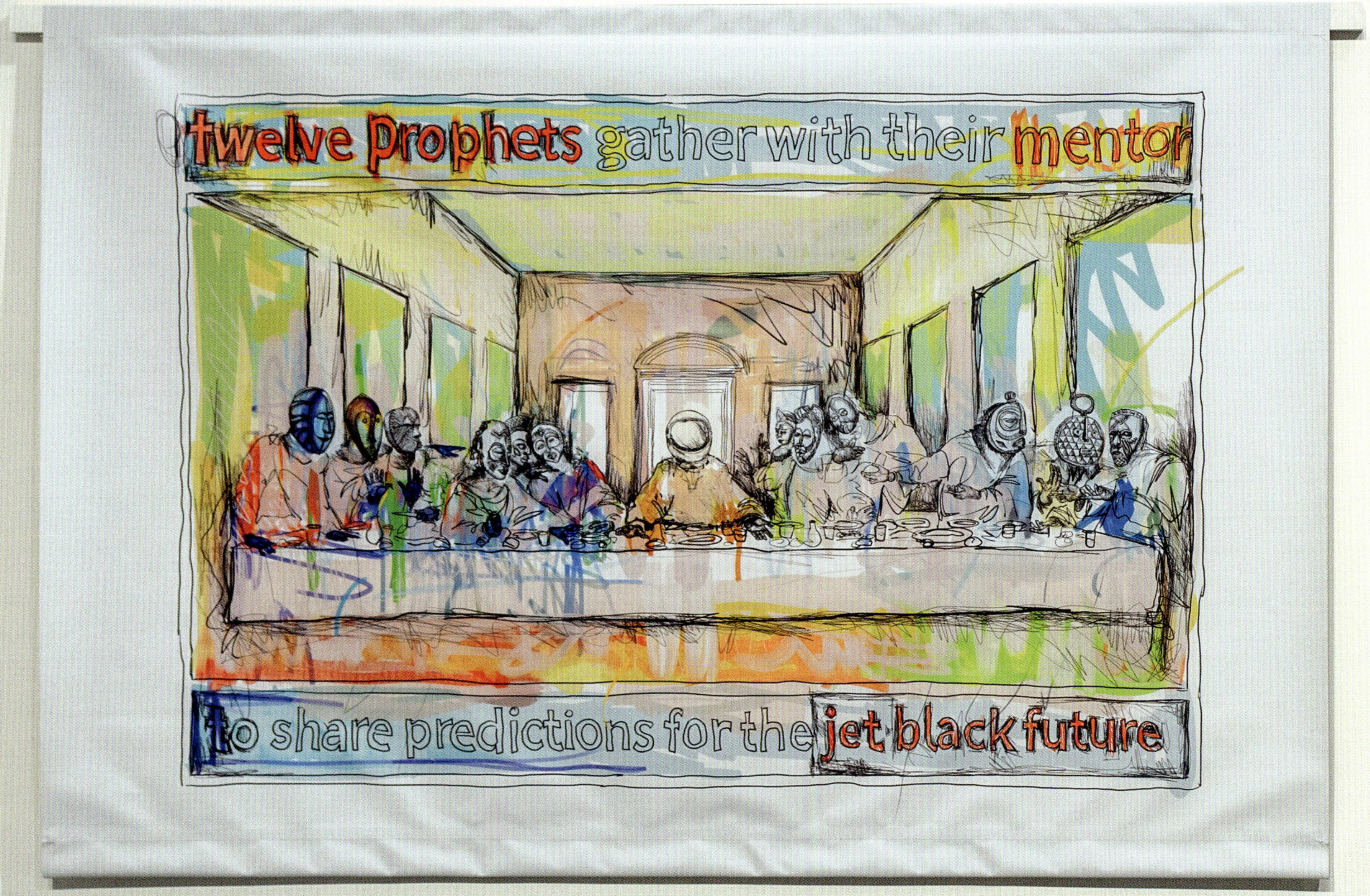
twelve prophets gather with their mentor
to share predictions for the jet black future

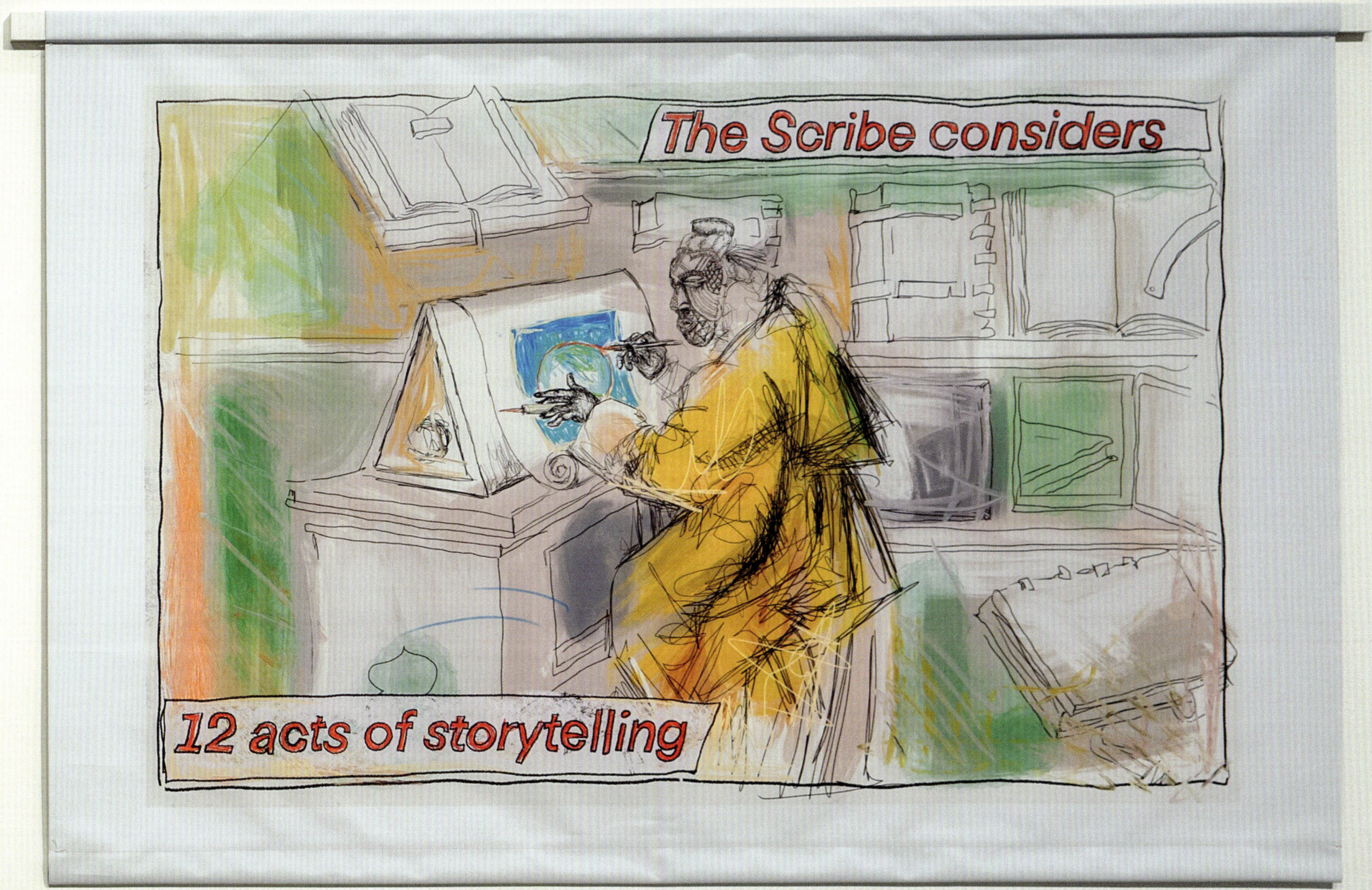
The Scribe considers
12 acts of storytelling

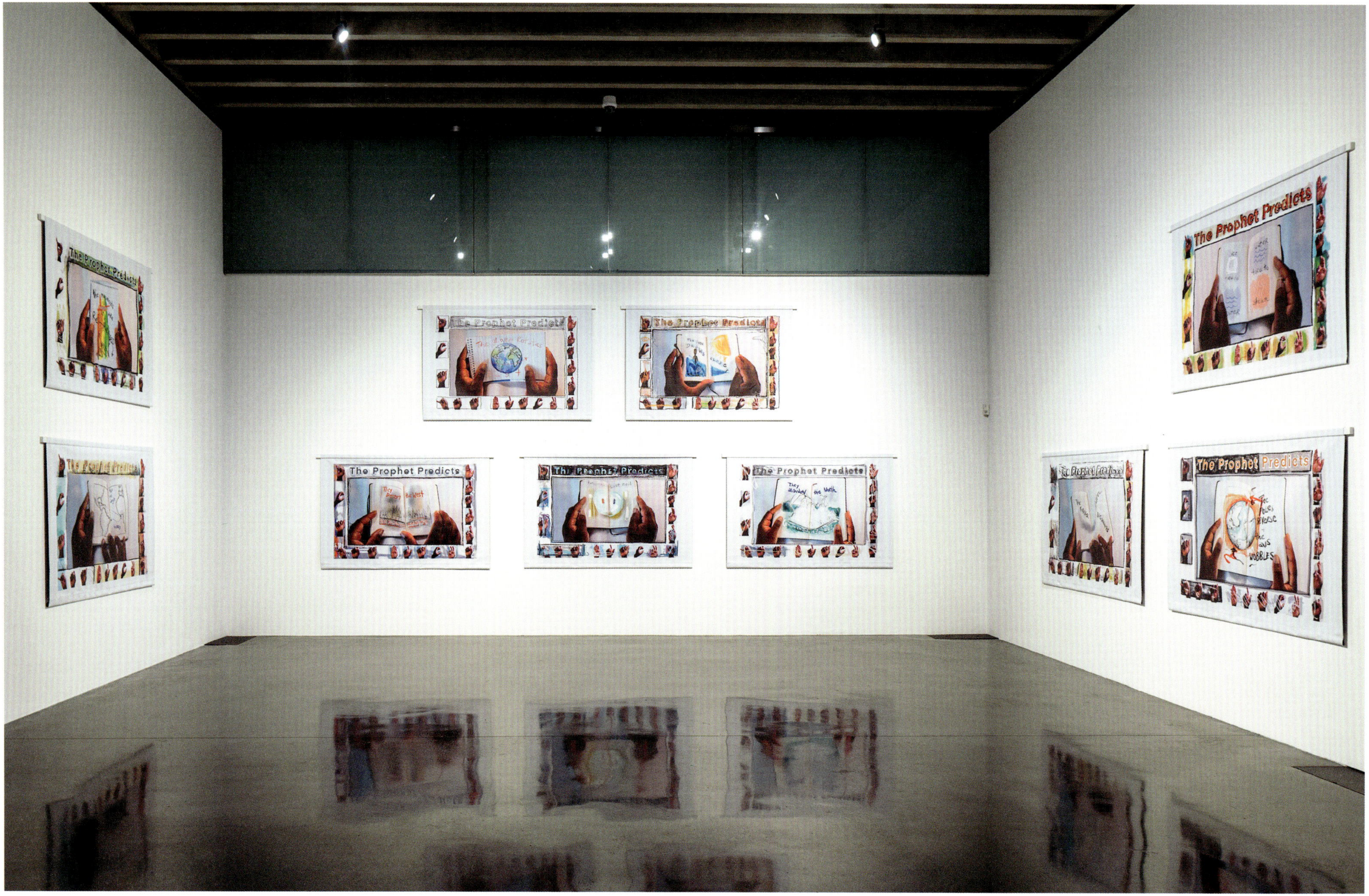
The Prophet Predicts

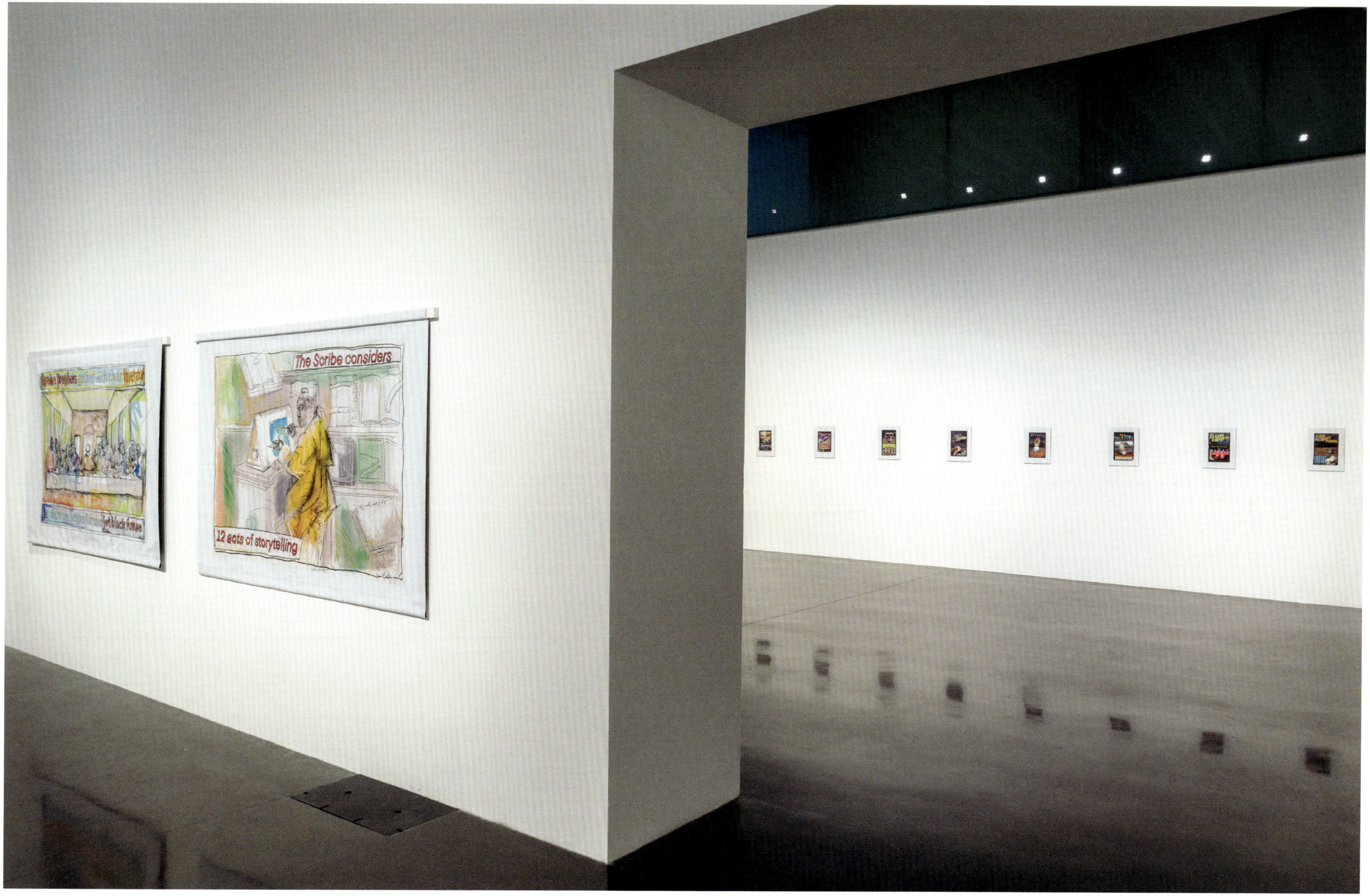
The Scribe considers
12 acts of storytelling

Pulp Fictions
2016-17

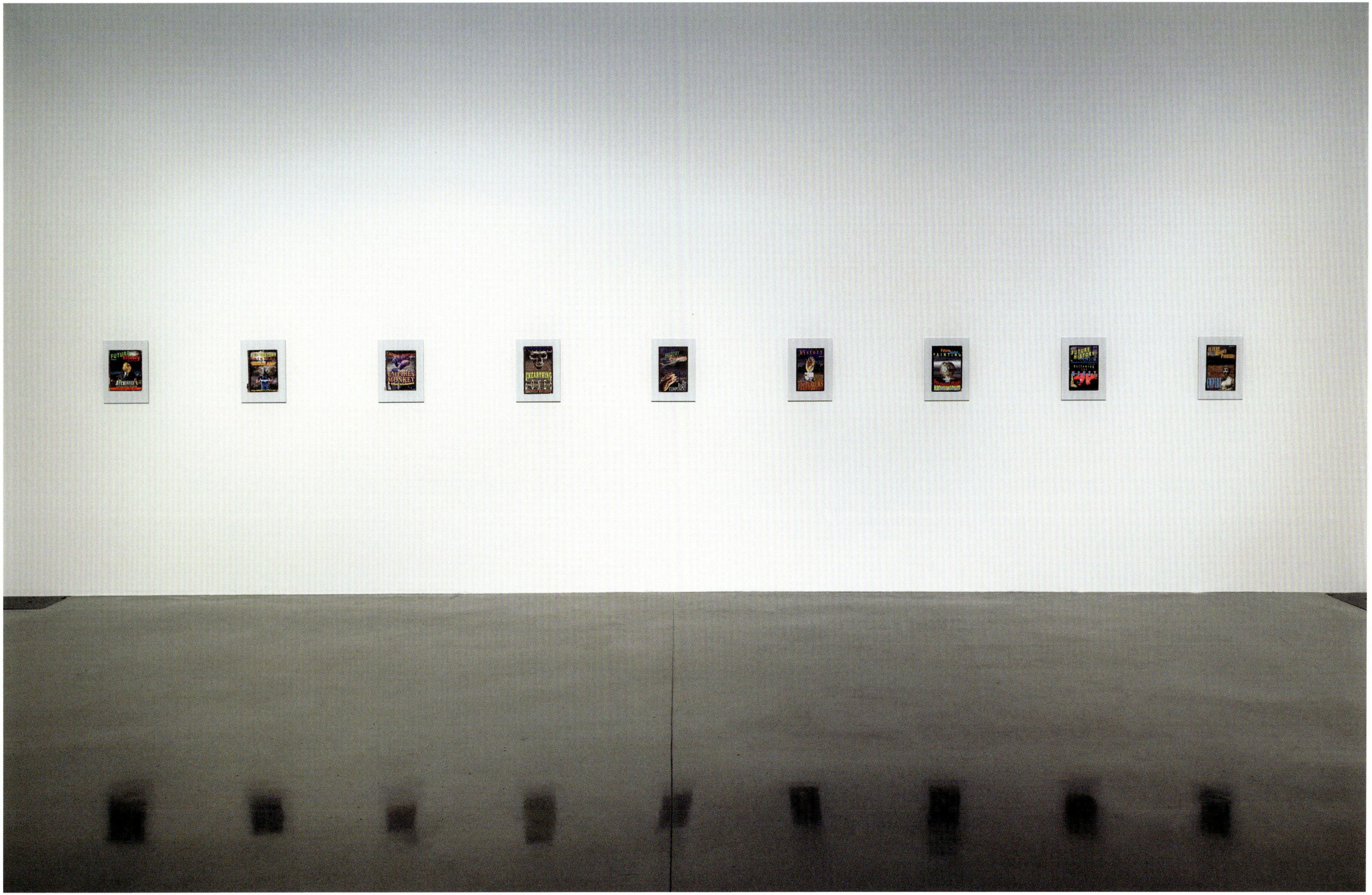

Pulp Fictions
2016-17

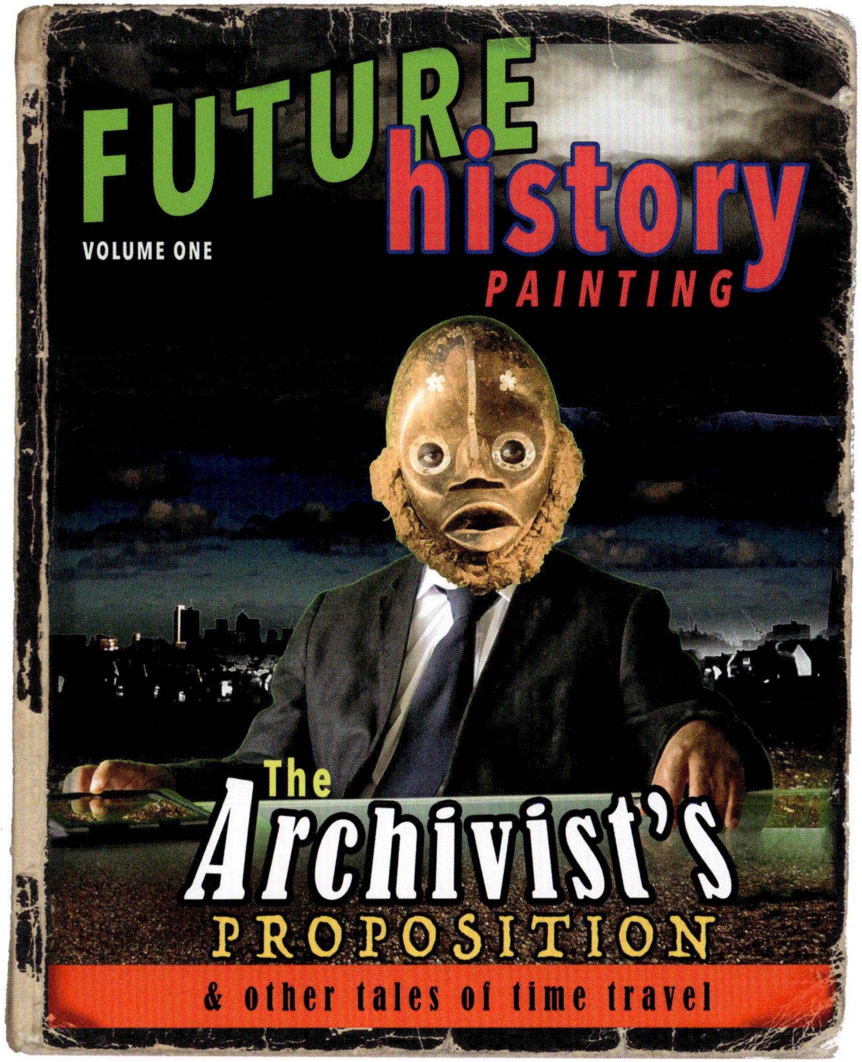
FUTURE history
VOLUME ONE
PAINTING
The
Archivist's
PROPOSITION
& other tales of time travel

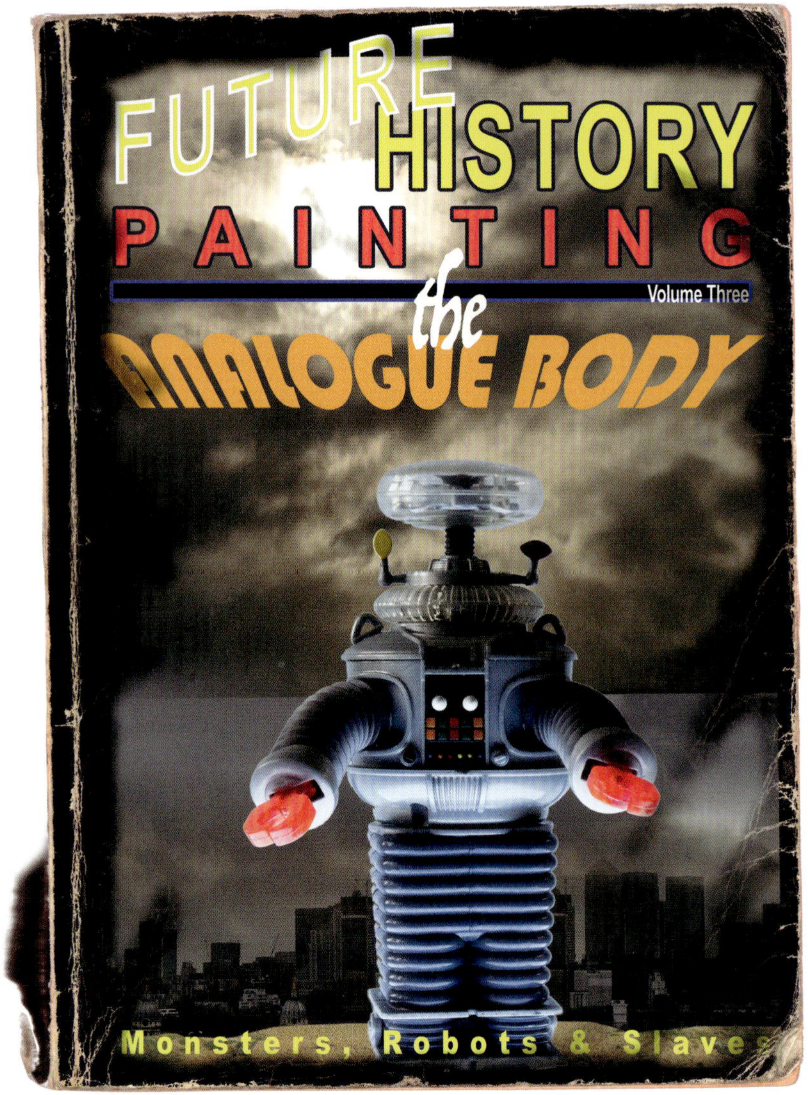
FUTURE HISTORY
PAINTING
Volume Three
the
ANALOGUE BODY
Monsters, Robots & Slaves

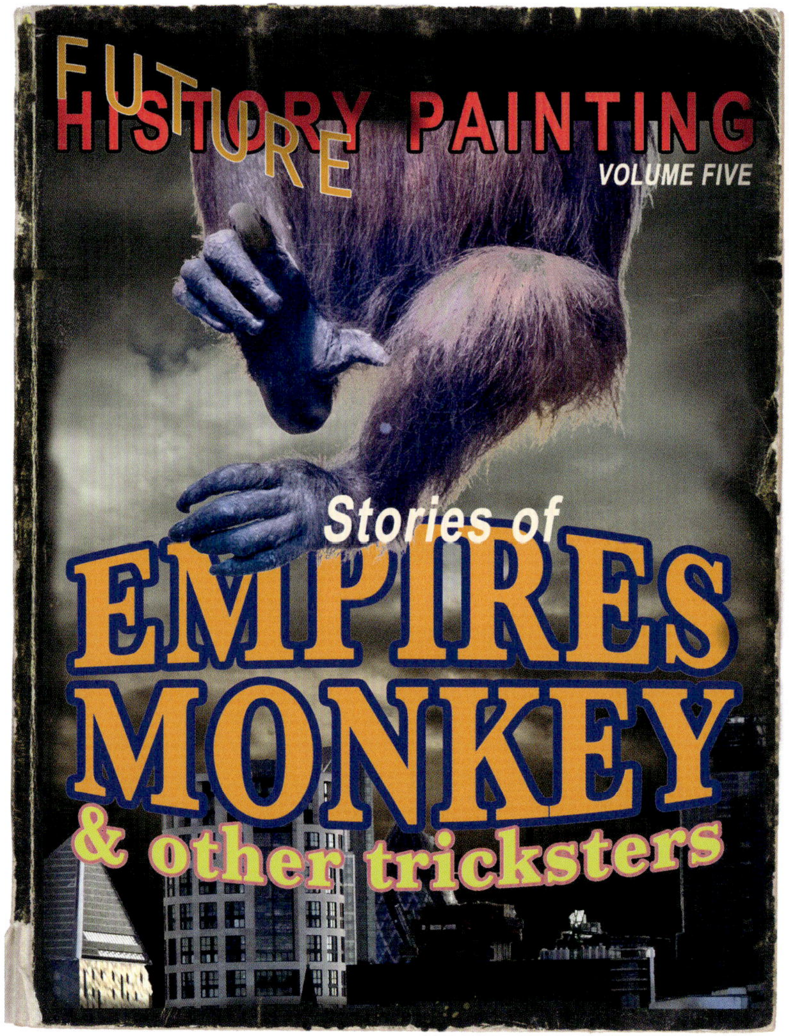
FUTURE HISTORY PAINTING
VOLUME FIVE
Stories of
EMPIRES
MONKEY
& other tricksters

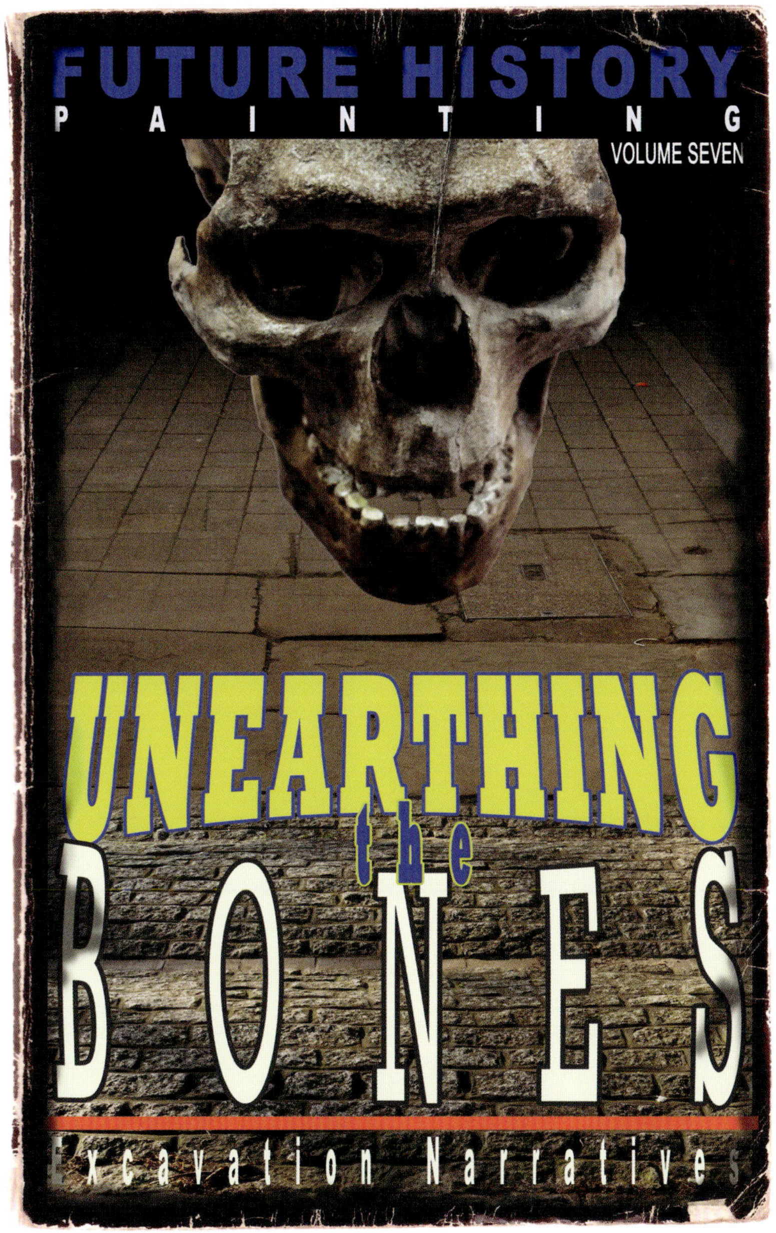
FUTURE HISTORY
PAINTING
VOLUME SEVEN
UNEARTHING
the
BONES
Excavation Narratives

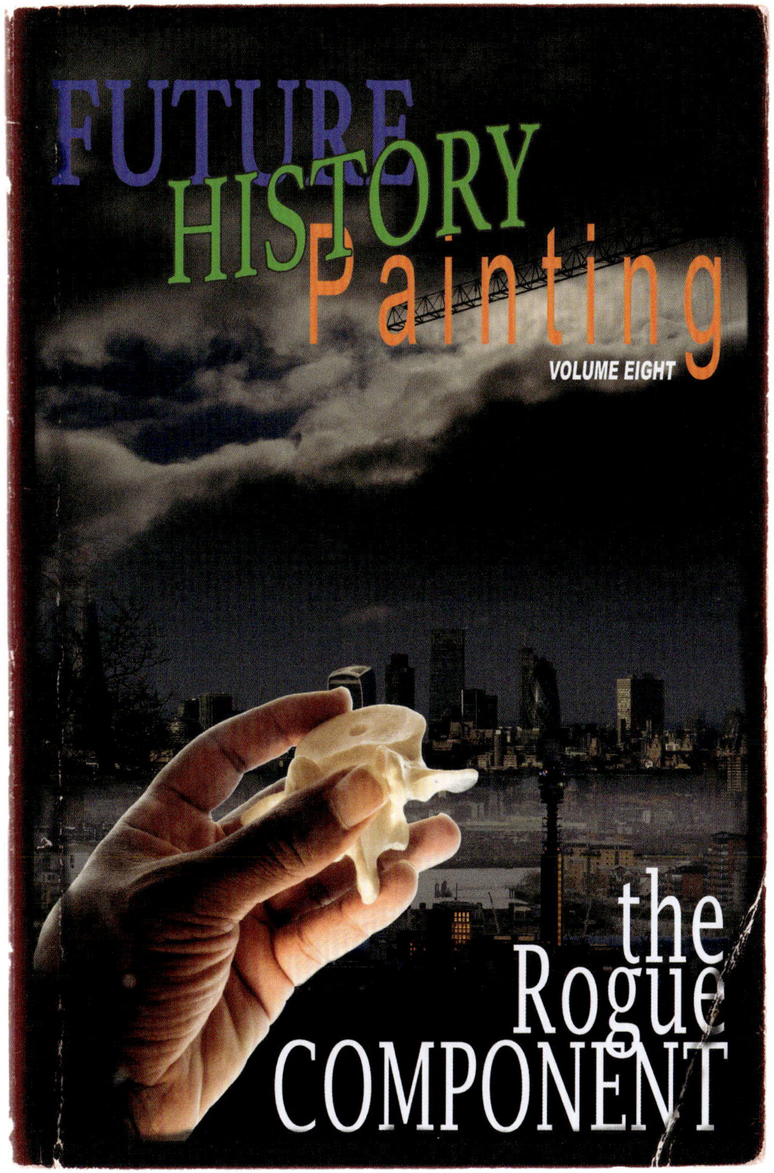
FUTURE
HISTORY
Painting
VOLUME EIGHT
the
Rogue
COMPONENT

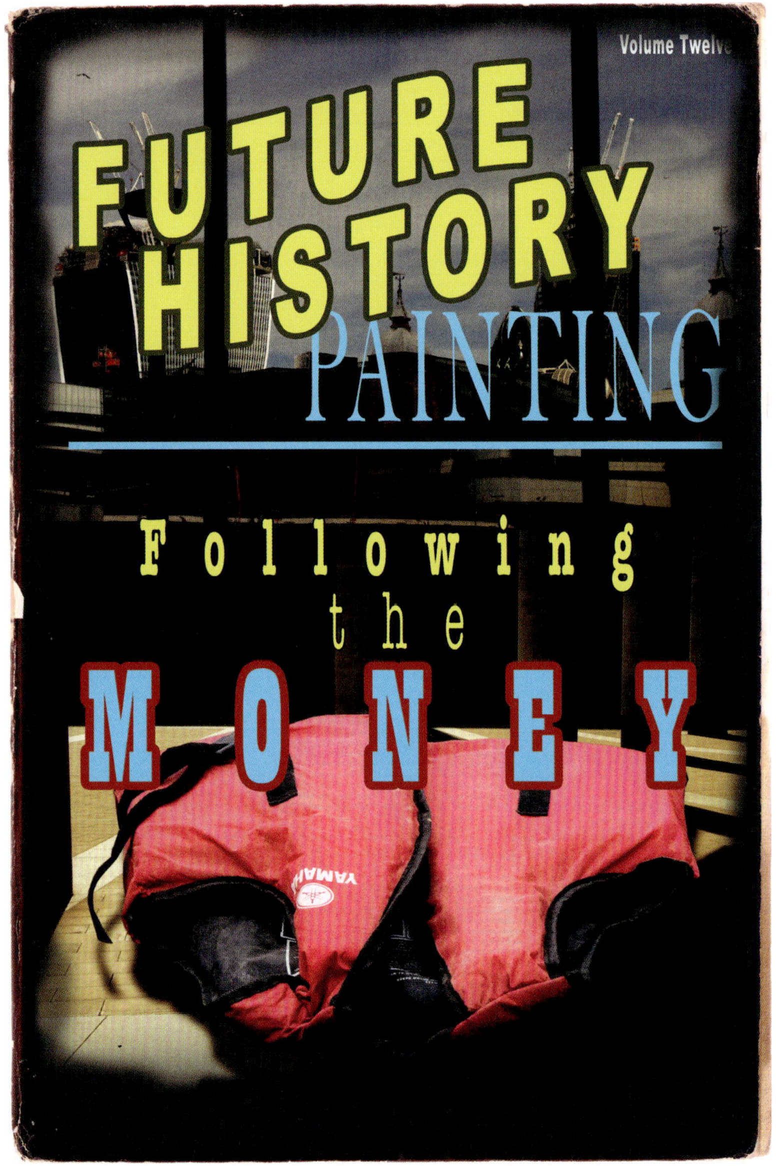
Volume Twelve
FUTURE HISTORY
PAINTING
Following the
MONEY

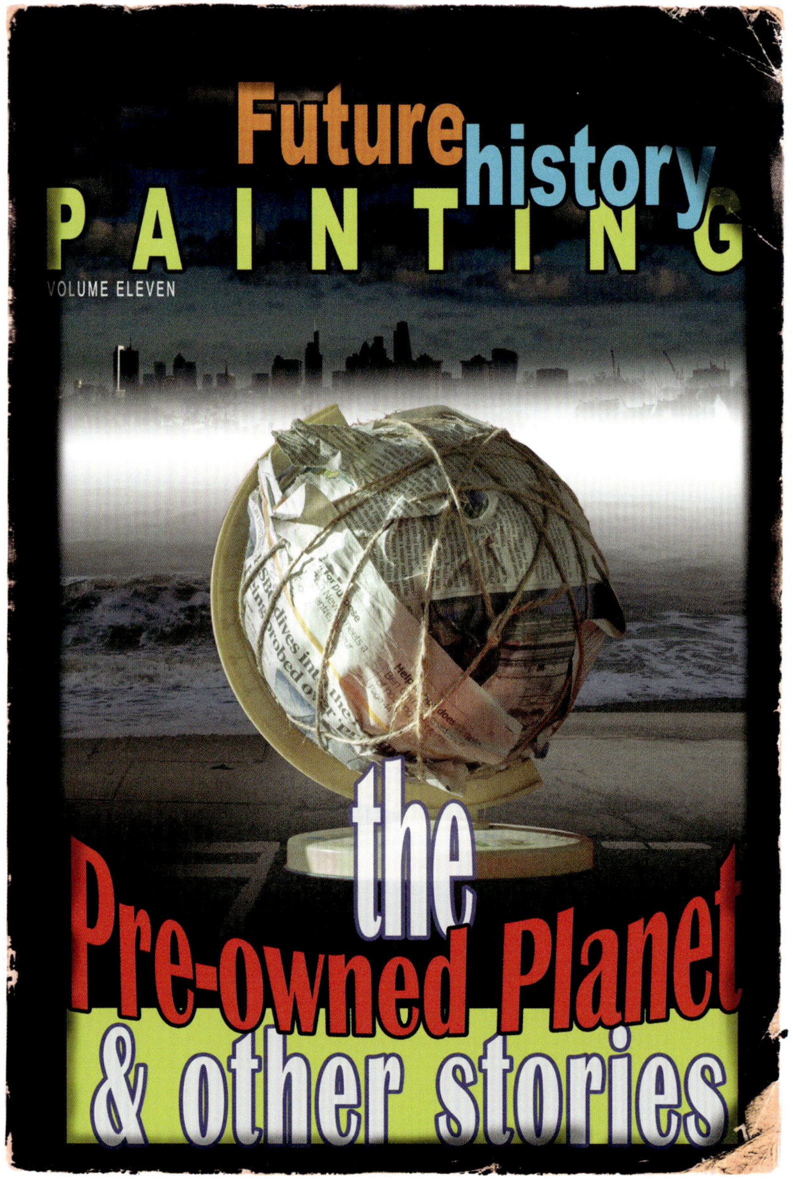
Future history
PAINTING
VOLUME ELEVEN
the
Pre-owned Planet
& other stories

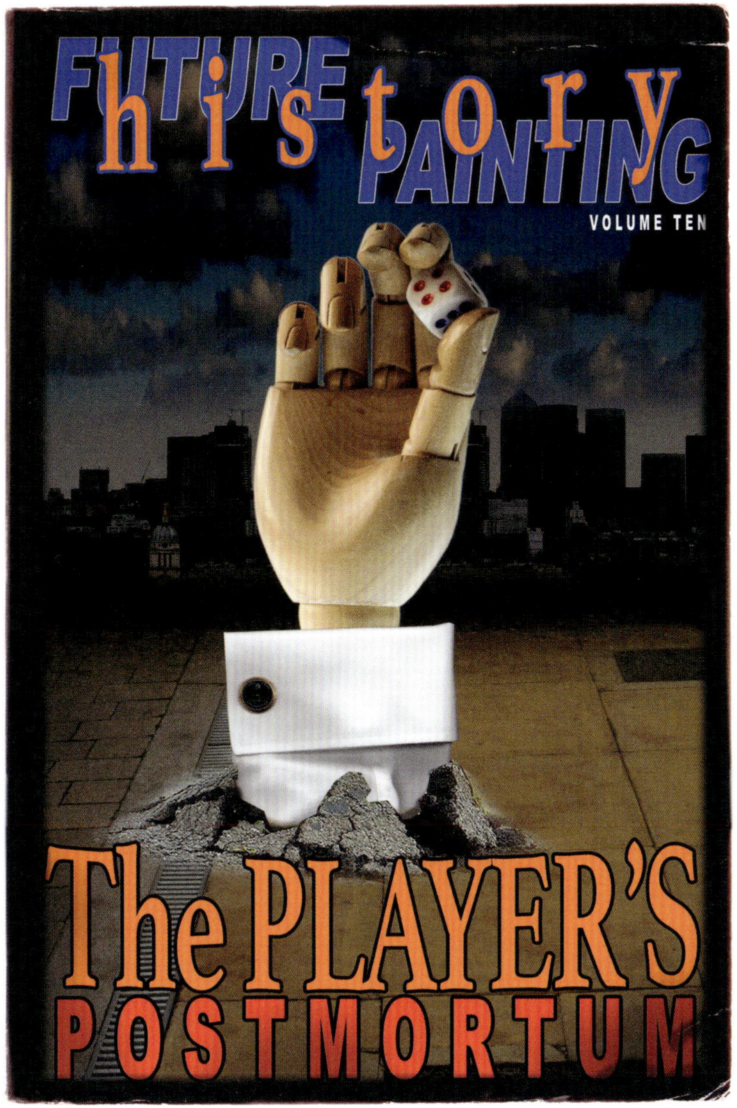
FUTURE
history
PAINTING
VOLUME TEN
The PLAYER'S
POSTMORTUM

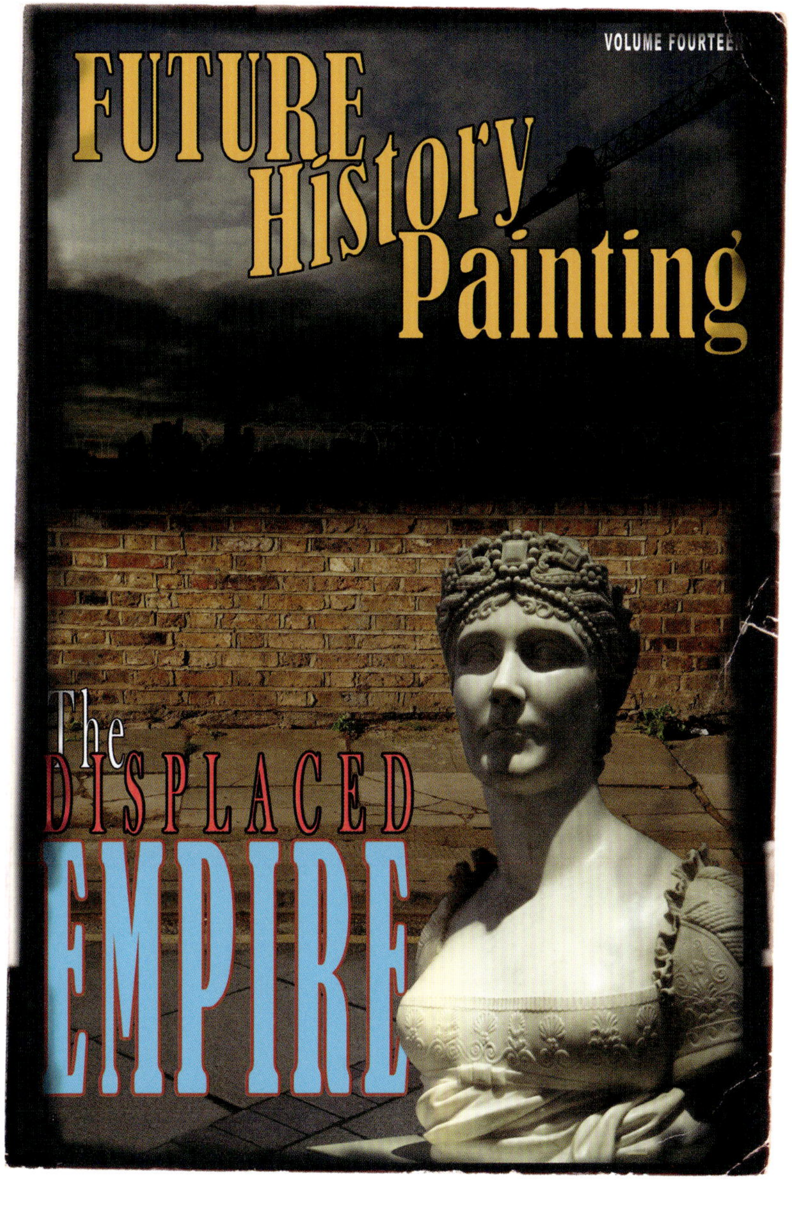
VOLUME FOURTEEN
FUTURE
History
Painting
The
DISPLACED
EMPIRE

In Search of Four Horses
2021-22

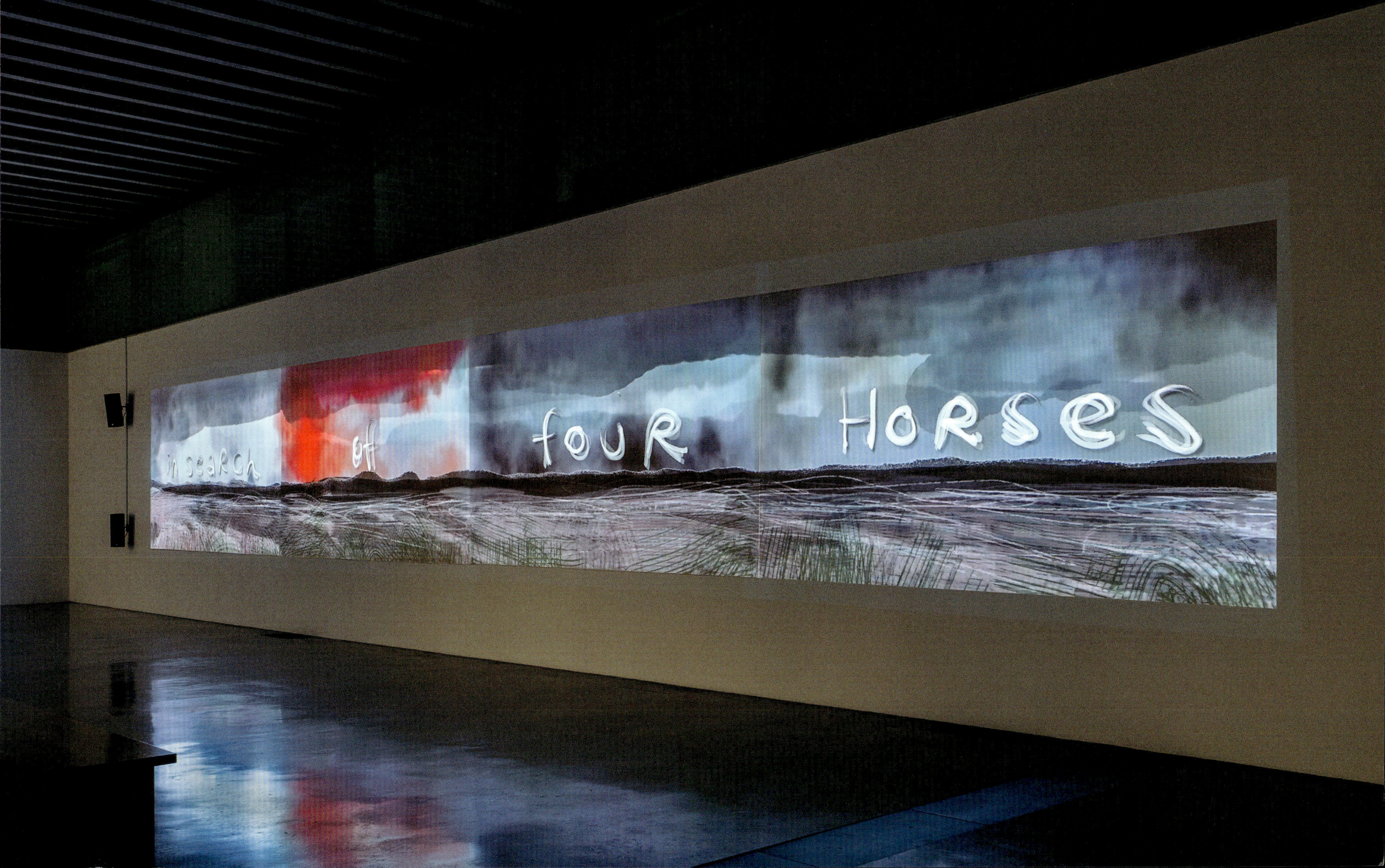
in search
of
four
Horses

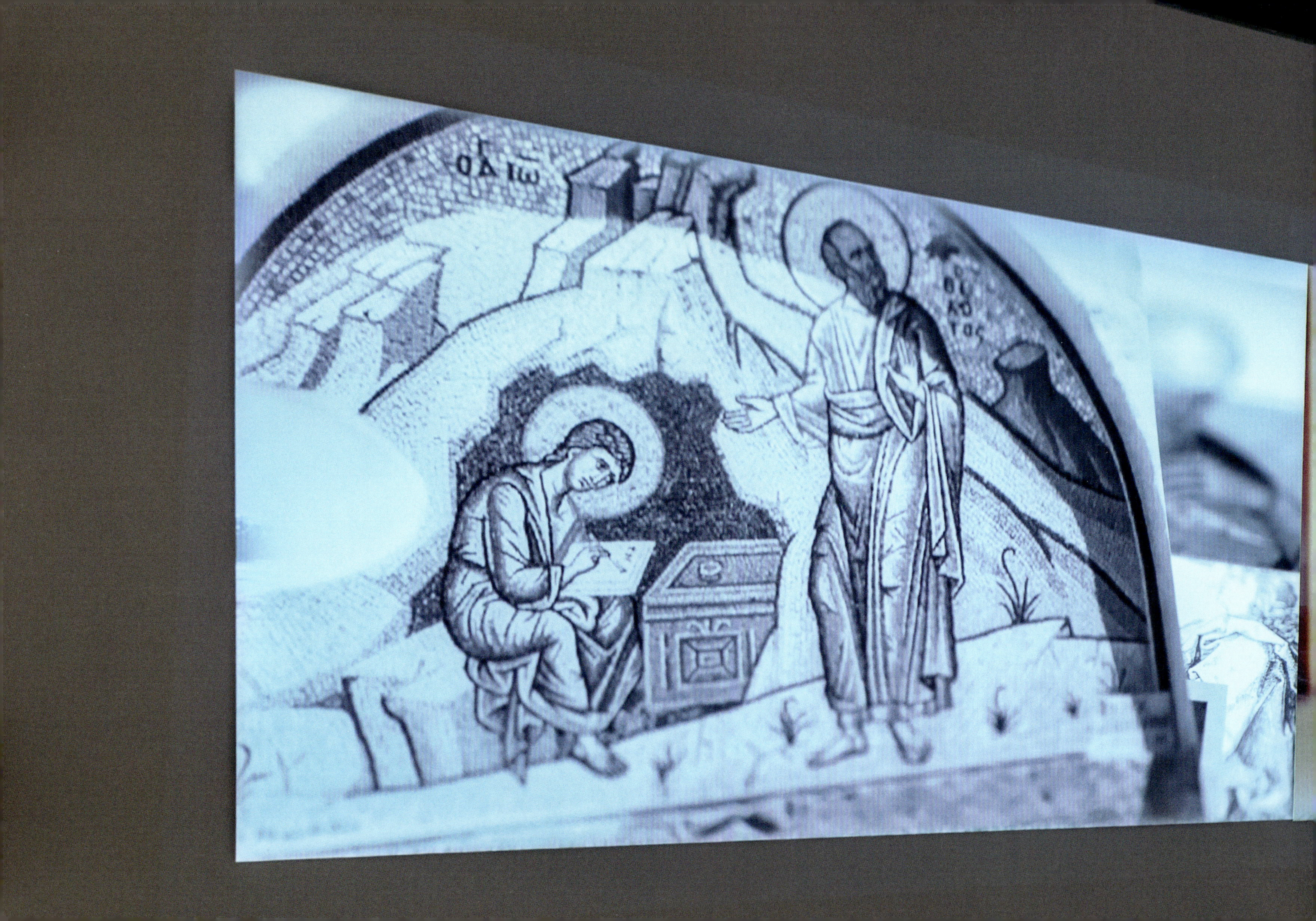

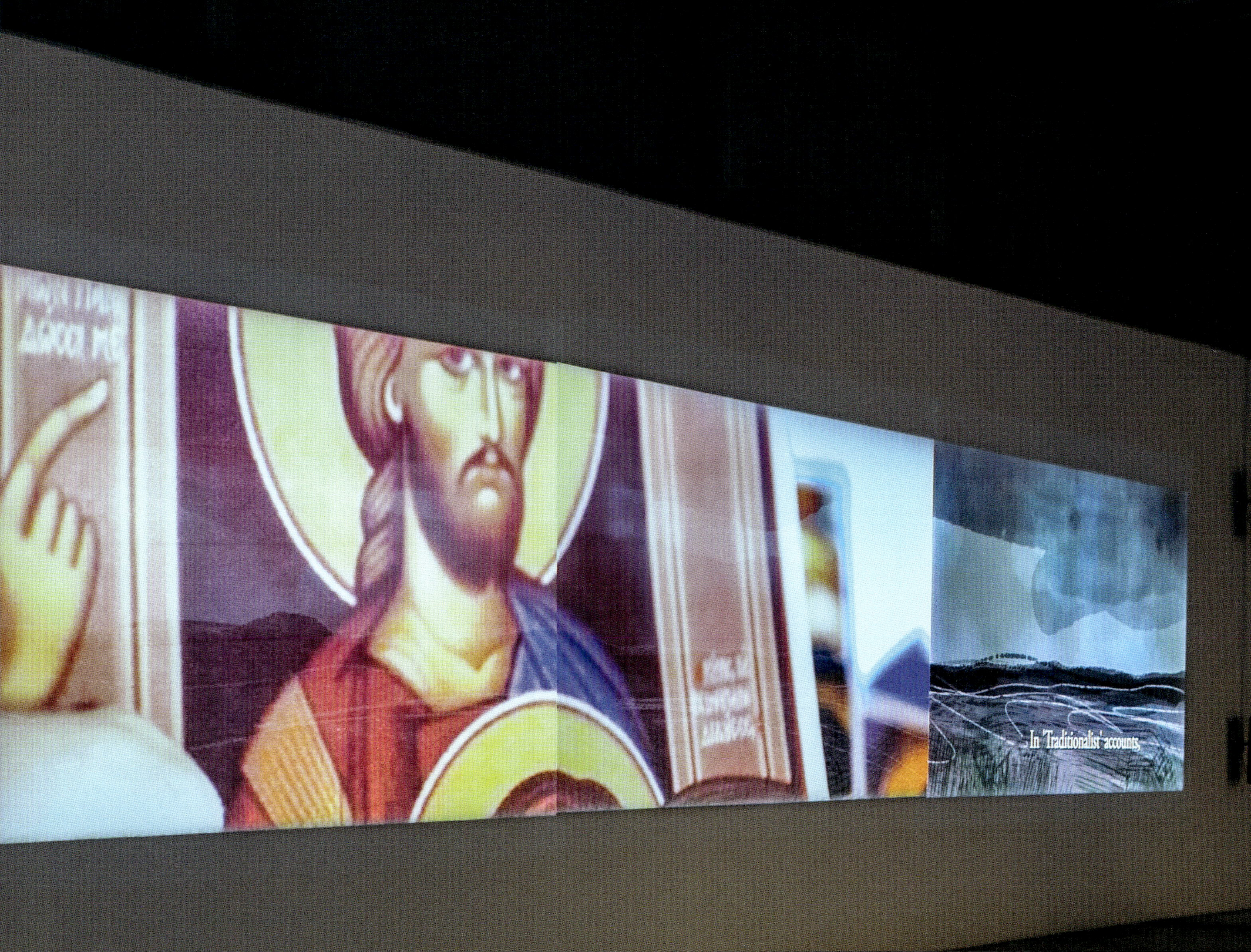
In 'Traditionalist' accounts,

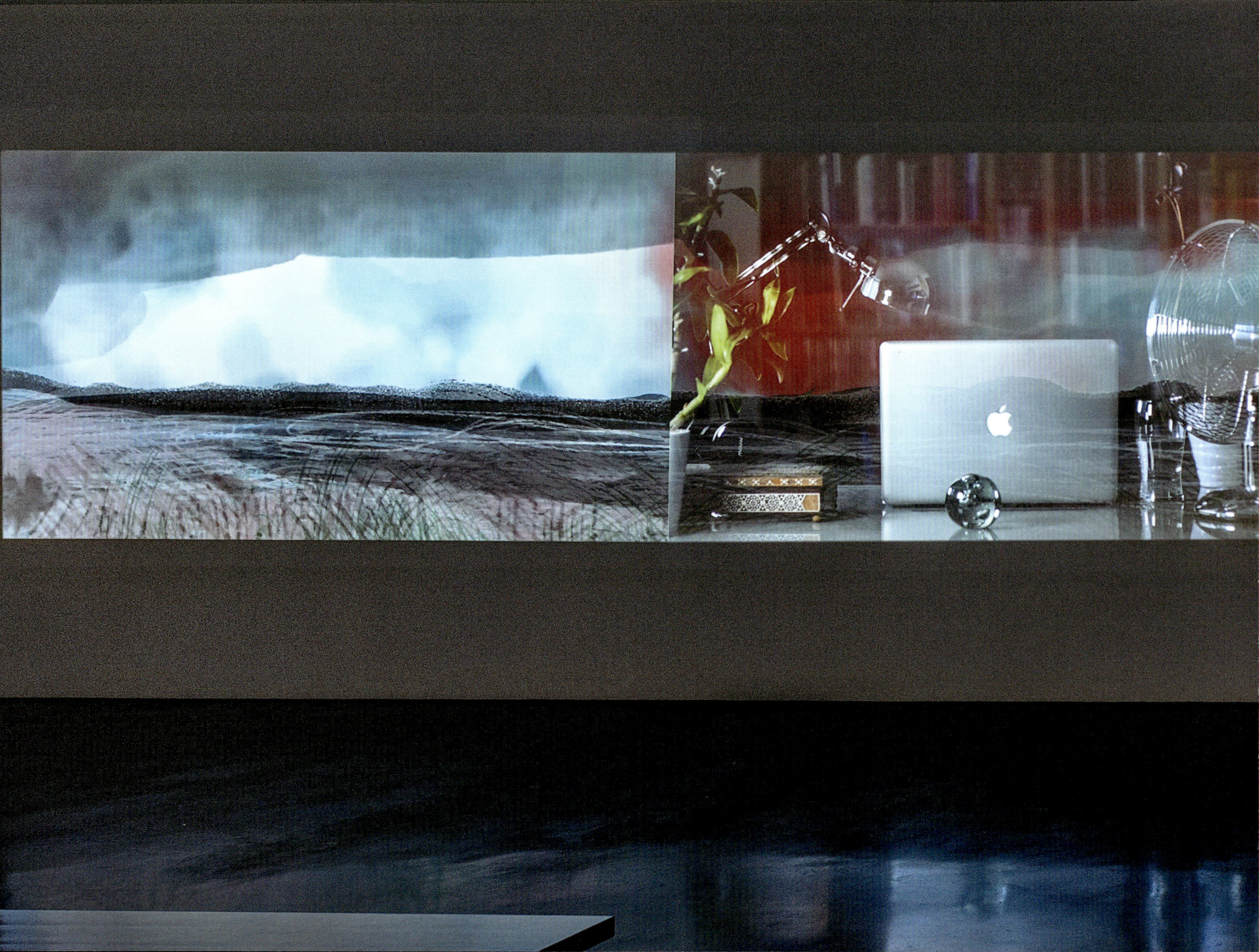

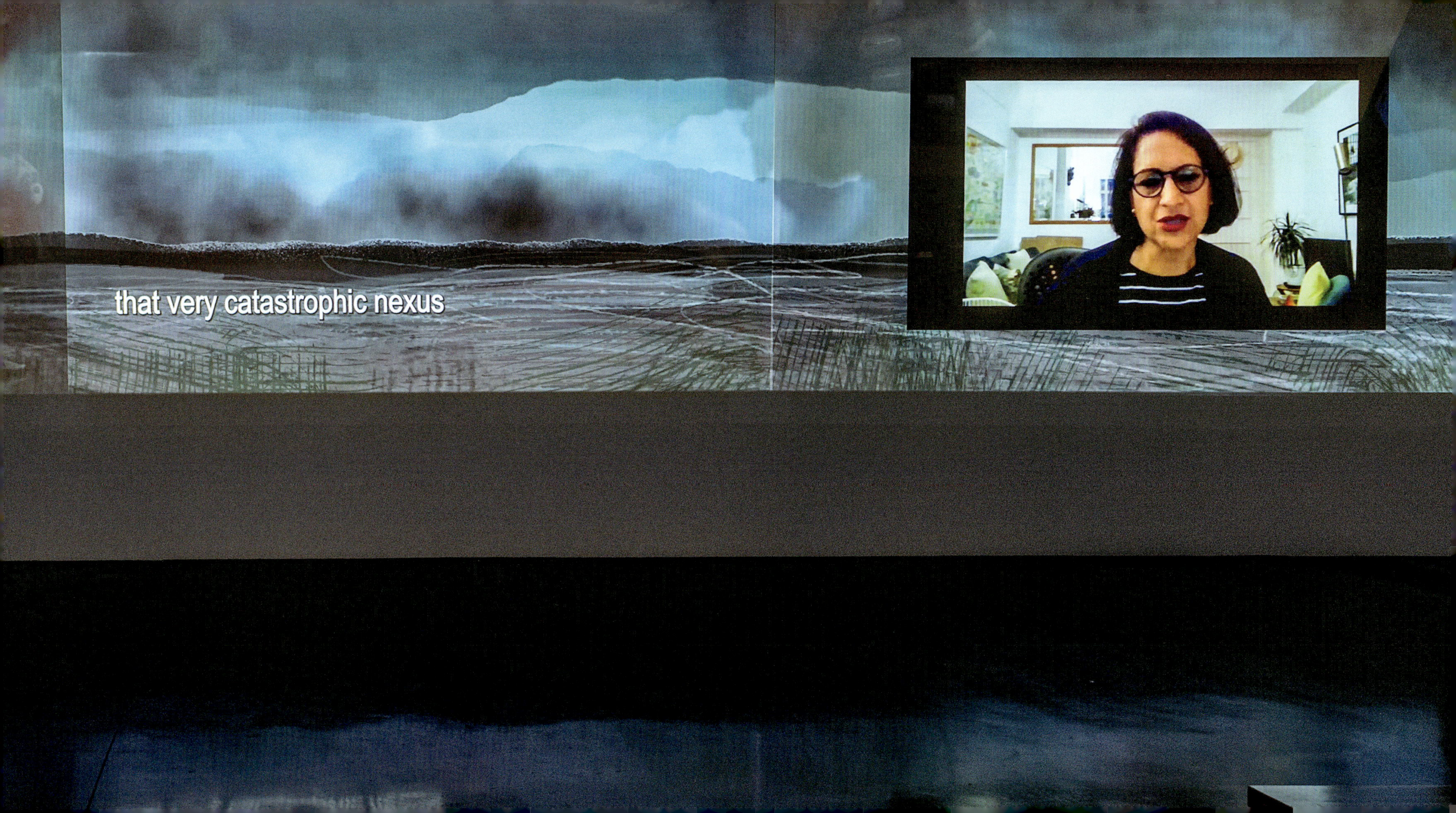
that very catastrophic nexus

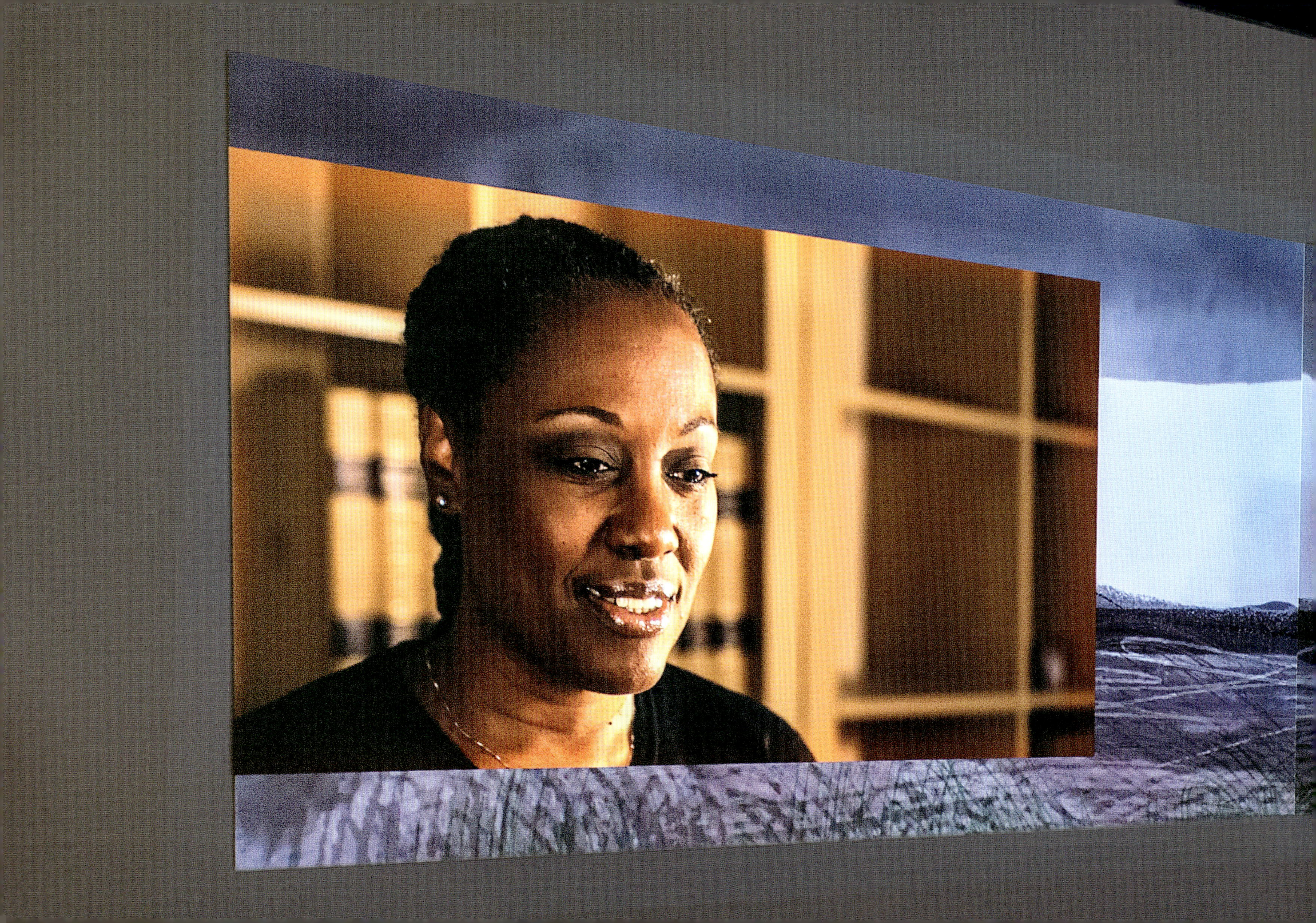

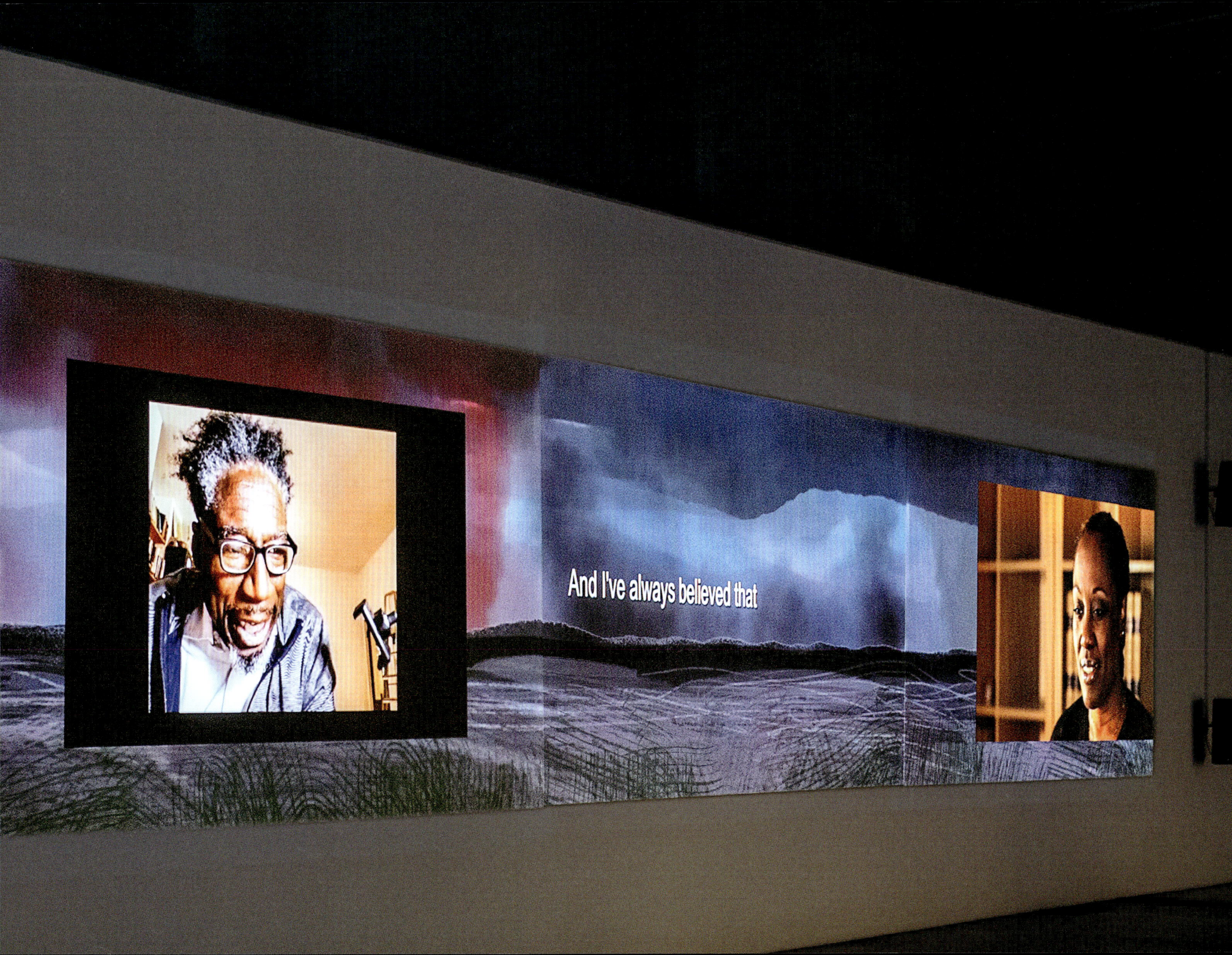
And I've always believed that

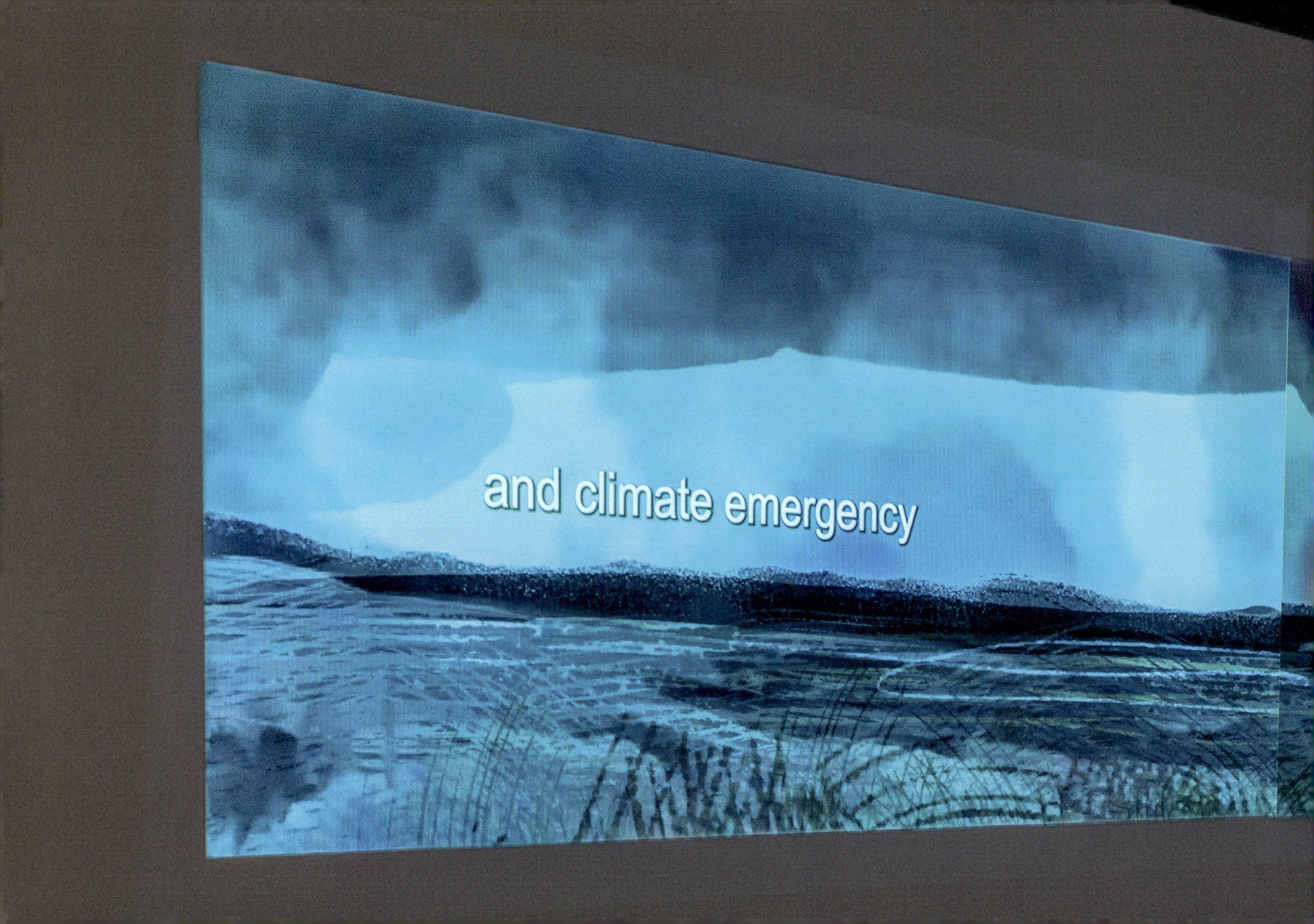
and climate emergency

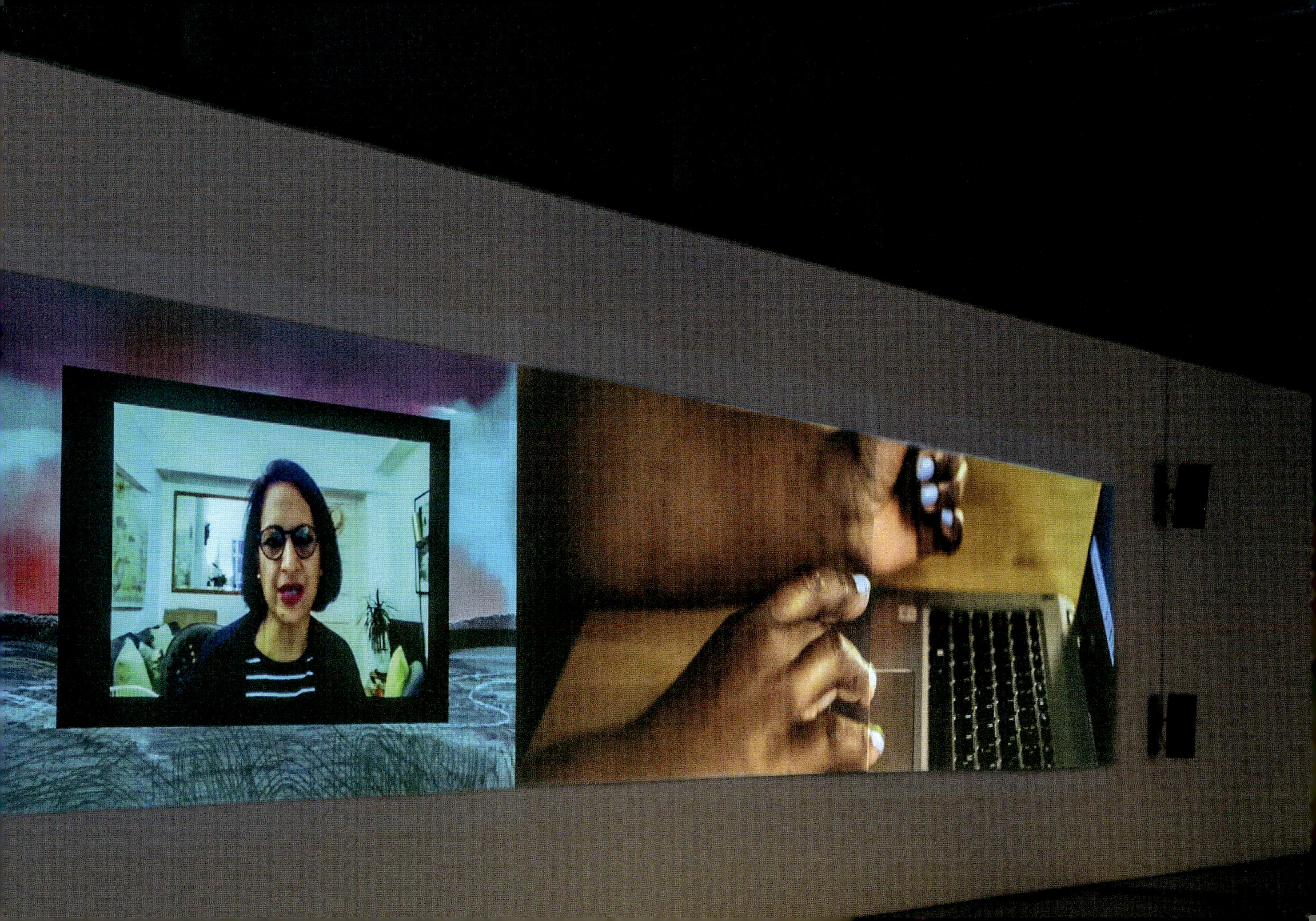

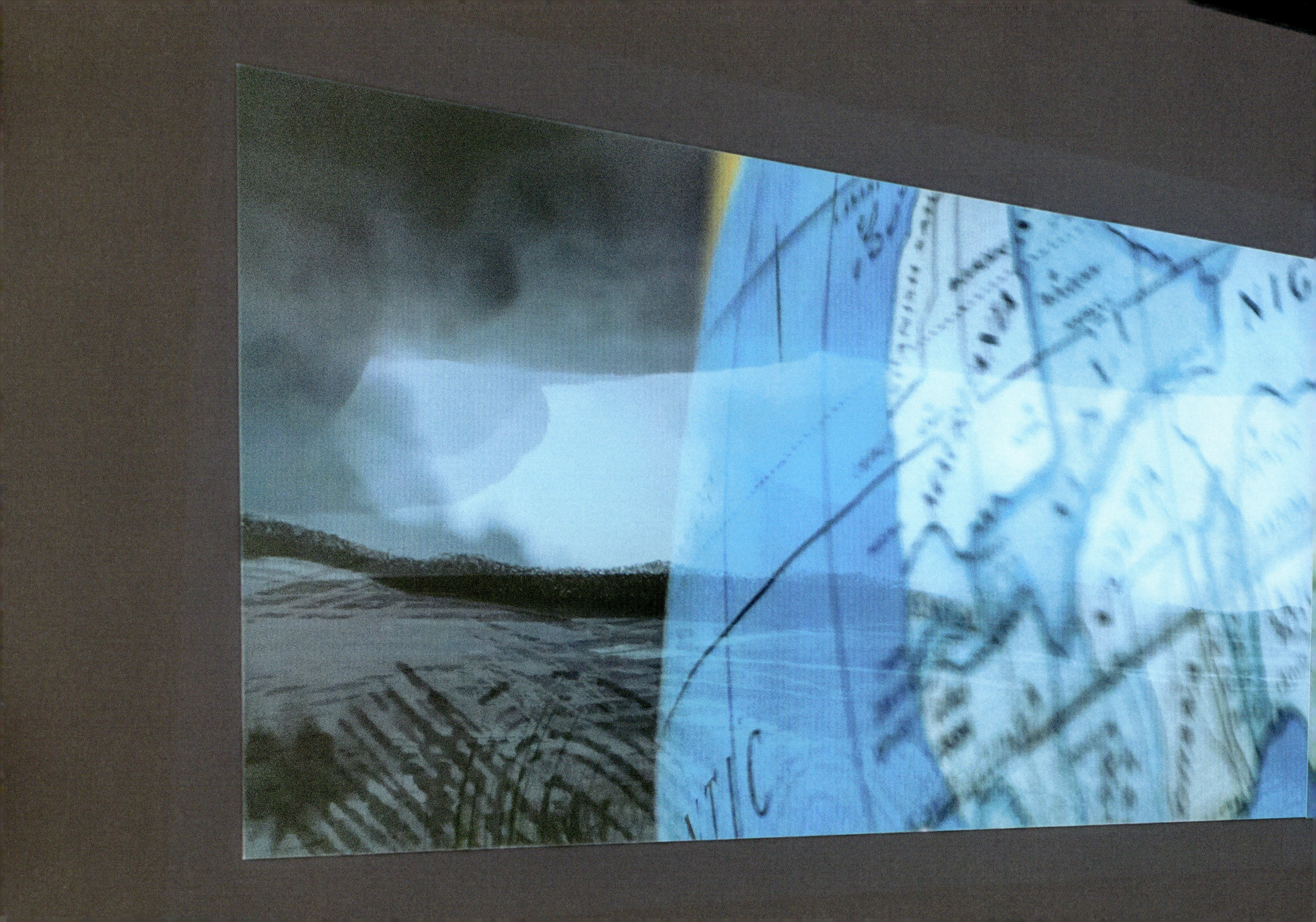

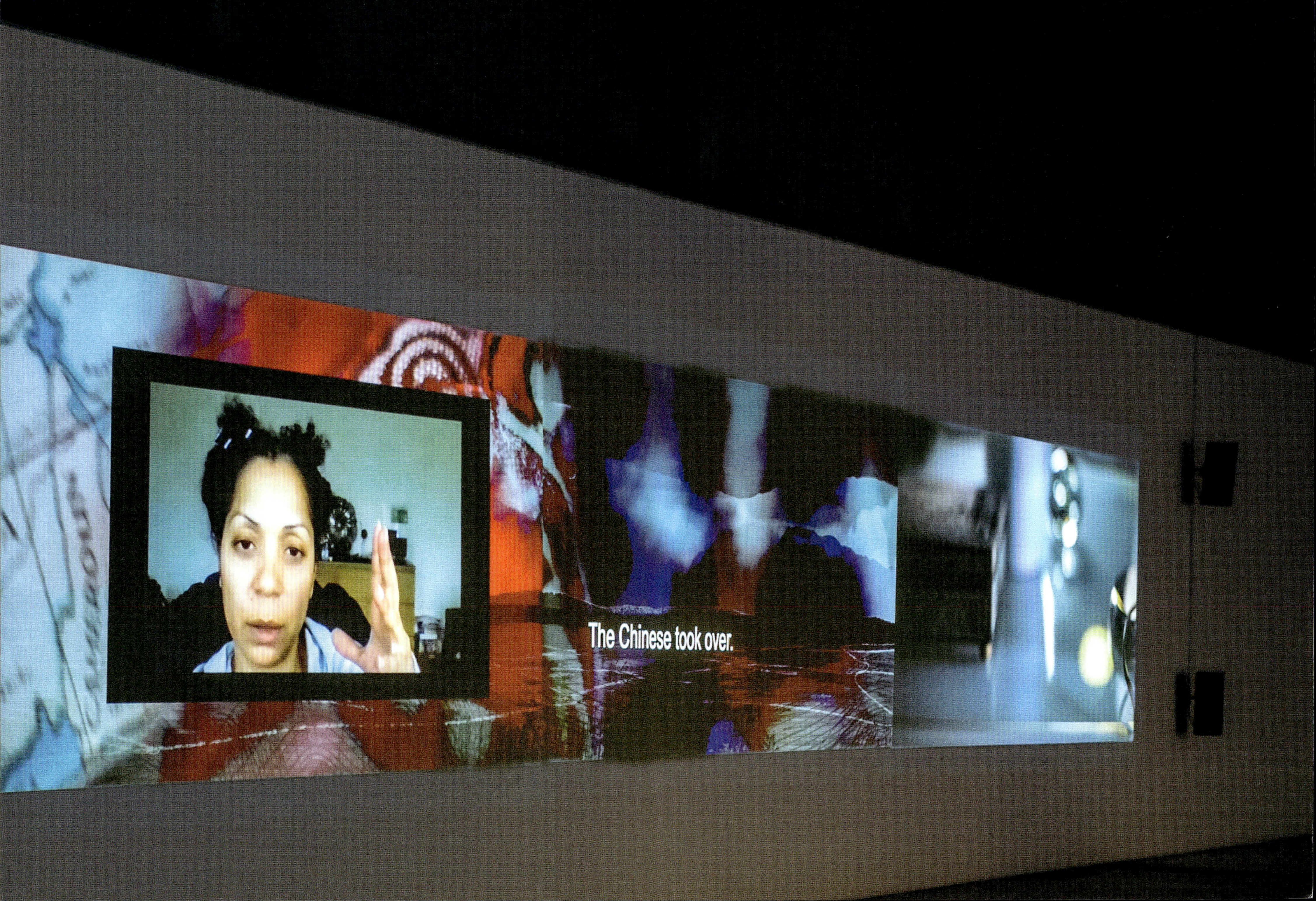
The Chinese took over.

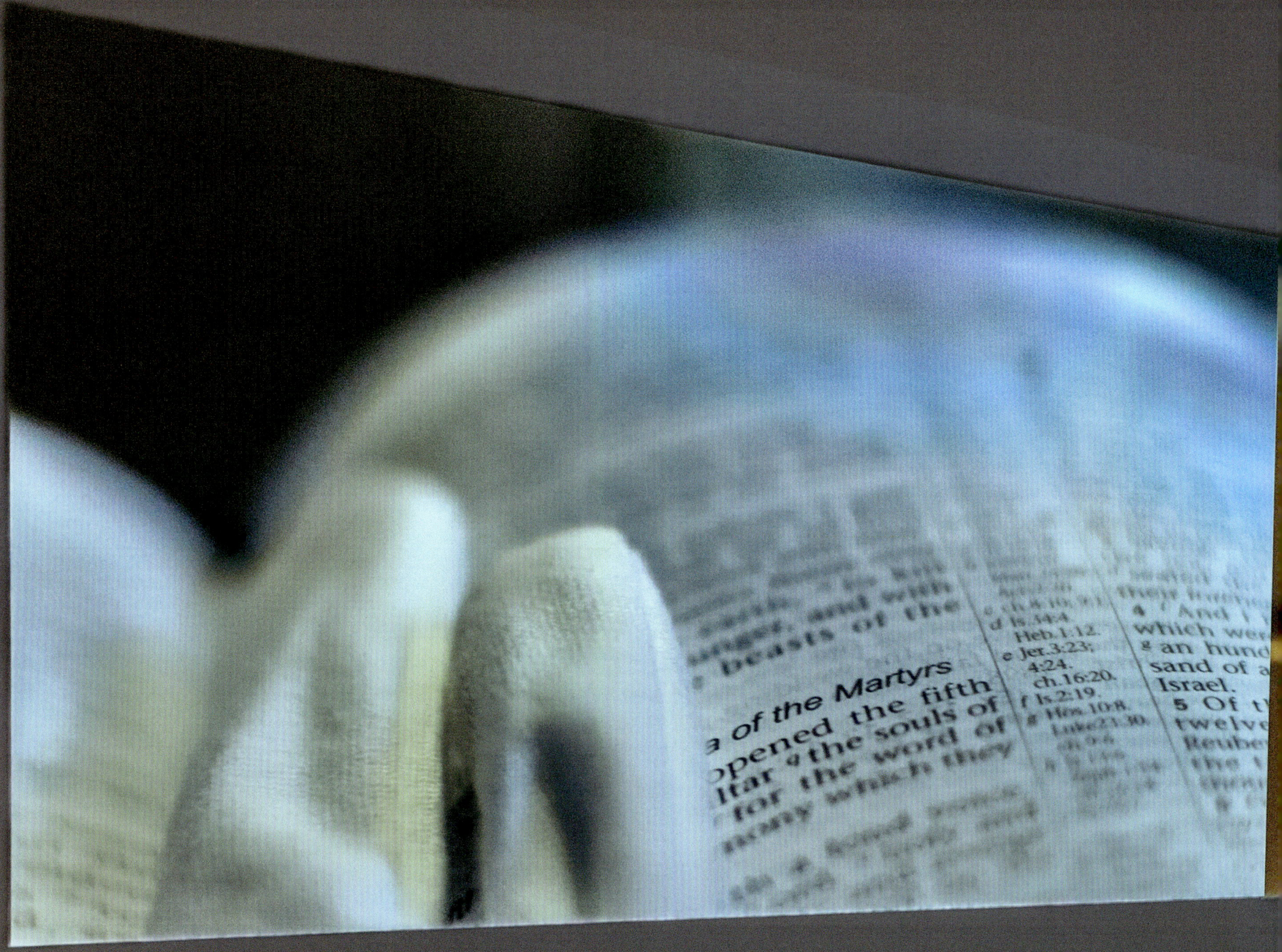
beasts of the
of the Martyrs
the souls of
for the word of
Heb.1:12.
ch.16:20.
which were
sand of a
Israel.

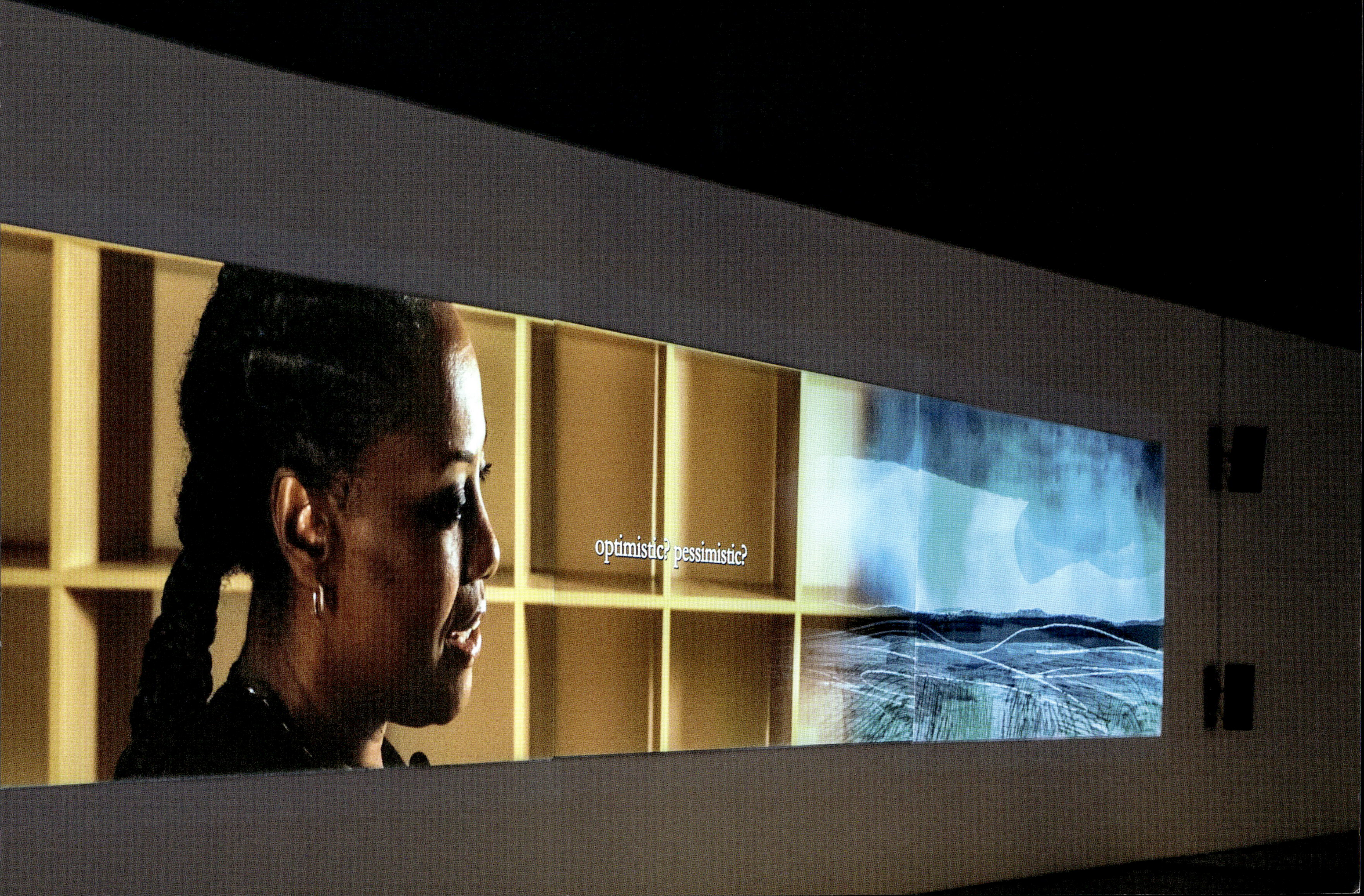
optimistic? pessimistic?

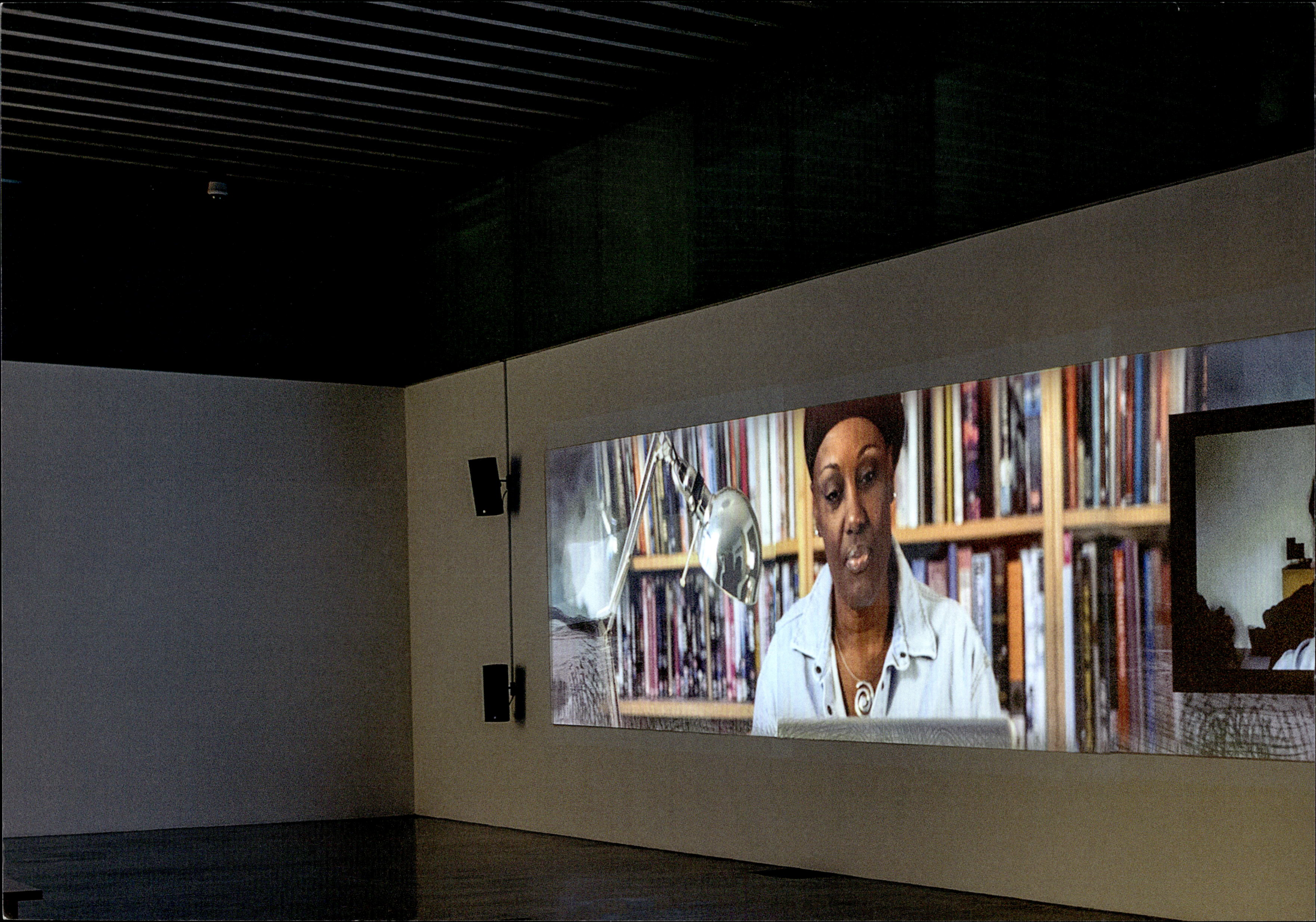

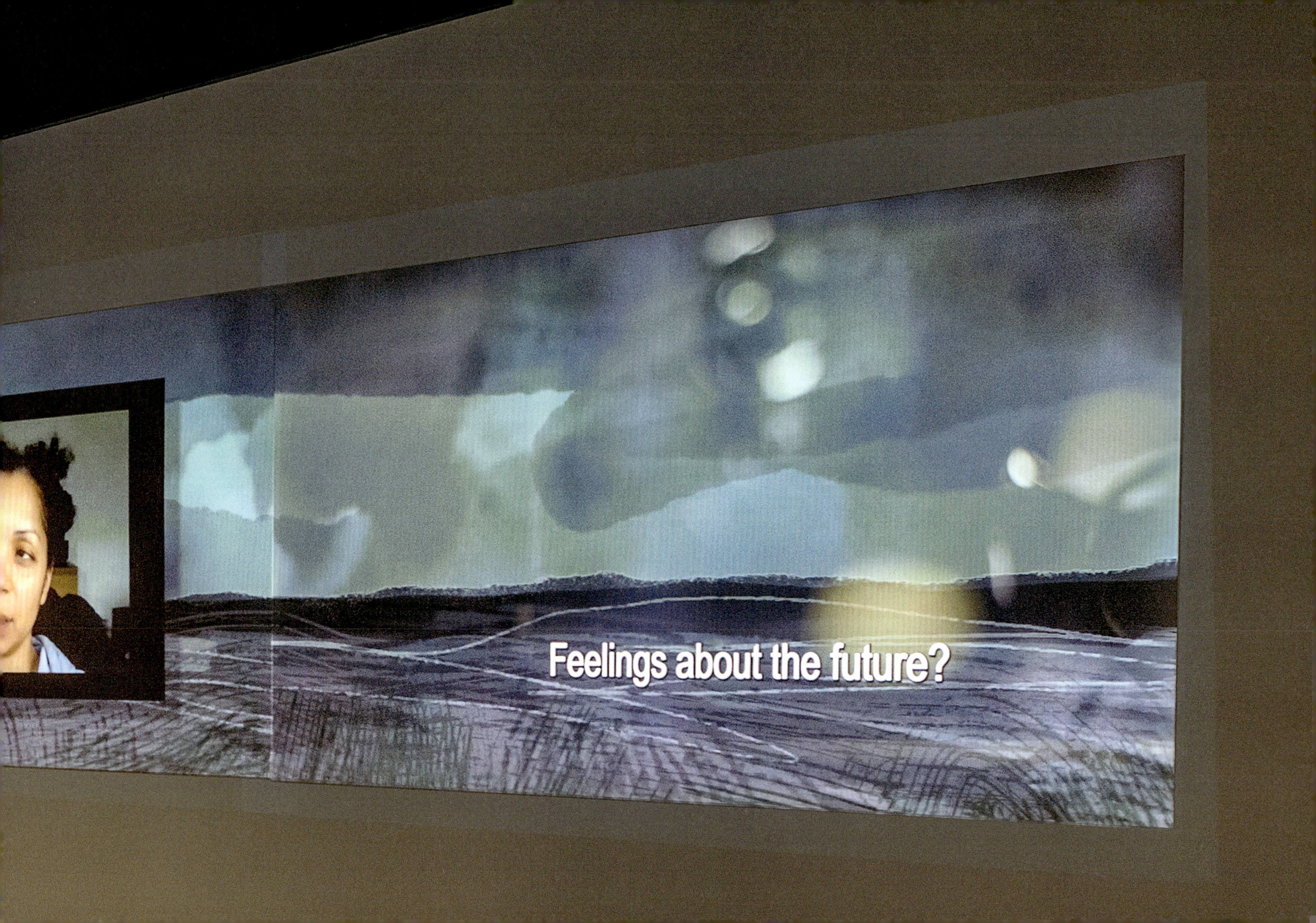
Feelings about the future?

Surveillance: Tagging the Other
1992

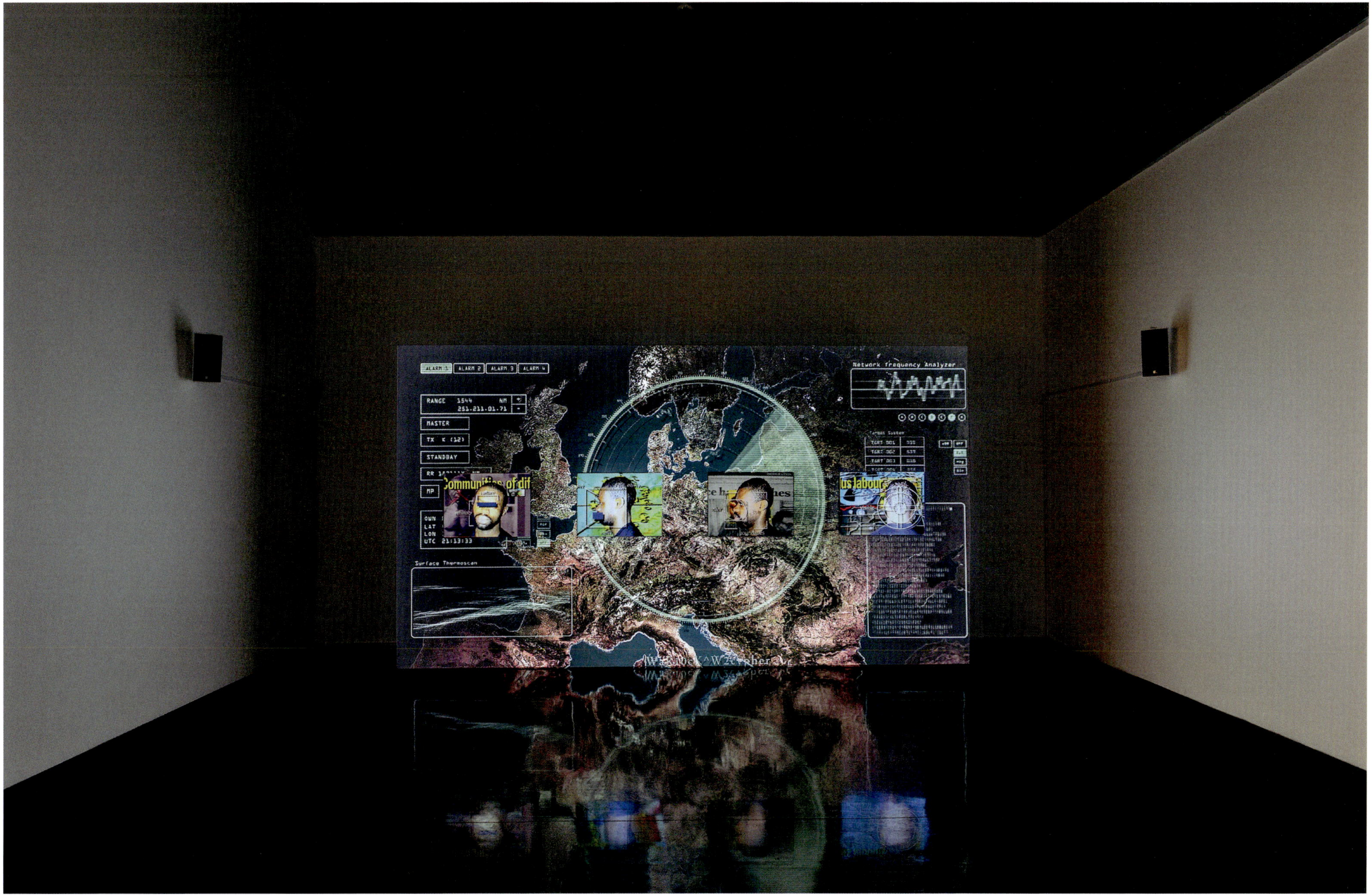
ALARM 1
ALARM 2
ALARM 3
ALARM 4
RANGE 1544 NM
251.211.01.71
MASTER
TX K (12)
STANDBAY
MP
OWN
LAT
LON
UTC 21:13:33
Surface Thermoscan
Network frequency Analyzer
Communities of dif
us labour

List of Works

p.6
Jet Black Futures
2021-22
Digital prints on banners
137 x 200 cm each
Installation at The New Art Gallery Walsall
Photo: Ilona Zielinska (Elona Photographer)

pp.12-13
The Black Assassin Saints (detail)
1982
Poster paint and screenprint on cotton duck
182.8 x 365.7 cm
Photo: Ilona Zielinska (Elona Photographer)

p.16
Poster for *Past Imperfect Future Tense*, The Black-Art Gallery
1984
Courtesy the artist

pp.21-36
Jet Black Futures
2021-22
Digital prints
Dimensions variable

p.43
The Seven Rages of Man
1984
Mixed media
Installation at The Black-Art Gallery, 1985
Courtesy the artist

p.45
***The Seven Rages of Man* (detail)**
2018
Mixed media assemblage
Dimensions variable
Installation at Graves Art Gallery, 2021
Photo: Andy Brown. Courtesy of Sheffield Museums Trust.

p.46
The Seven Rages of Man
2018
Mixed media assemblage
Dimensions variable
Installation at Wolverhampton Art Gallery, 2019
Photo: Ilona Zielinska (Elona Photographer)

p.48, p.50, p.51
***The Seven Rages of Man* (detail)**
2018
Installation at Wolverhampton Art Gallery, 2019
Photos: Ilona Zielinska (Elona Photographer)

p.54
Go West Young Man
1987
One of 14 photographs, gelatin silver print on paper mounted onto board
84 x 56 cm each
Tate
Photo: Tate

p.55
The Four Horsemen of the Apocalypse
1984 (earlier version)
Mixed media
Installation at Battersea Arts Centre
Courtesy the artist

p.57
The Black Assassin Saints
1982
Poster paint and screenprint on cotton duck
182.8 x 365.7 cm
Photo: Ilona Zielinska (Elona Photographer)

p.58
The Four Horsemen of the Apocalypse
1984
Acrylic on un-stretched canvas
275 x 152.5 cm each
Middlesbrough Collection, MIMA, Middlesbrough Institute of Modern Art.
Purchased with assistance from the Art Fund and the Arts Council England/
Victoria & Albert Museum Purchase Grant Fund
Photo: Ilona Zielinska (Elona Photographer)

p.61
***The Four Horsemen of the Apocalypse* (detail)**
1984
Acrylic on un-stretched canvas
275 x 152.5 cm each
Middlesbrough Collection, MIMA, Middlesbrough Institute of Modern Art.
Purchased with assistance from the Art Fund and the Arts Council England/
Victoria & Albert Museum Purchase Grant Fund
Photo: Ilona Zielinska (Elona Photographer)

p.64, p.65, p.67
In Search of Four Horses
2021-22
Four channel video installation with sound
Installation at The New Art Gallery Walsall, 2022
Photo: Ilona Zielinska (Elona Photographer)

pp.70-71
Body Politics: Works from 1982-2007
Installation at Wolverhampton Art Gallery, 2019
(featuring *Surveillance: Tagging the Other*, *Go West Young Man*
and *Trade Winds*)
Photo: Ilona Zielinska (Elona Photographer)

p.73
Trade Winds
1992
Video installation
Dimensions variable
Installation at Wolverhampton Art Gallery, 2019
Photo: Ilona Zielinska (Elona Photographer

pp.74-75
Surveillance: Tagging the Other
1992
Mixed media installation with four monitors, projection and sound
Dimensions variable
Installation at Wolverhampton Art Gallery, 2019
The New Art Gallery Walsall Permanent Collection. Presented by the
Contemporary Art Society through the Rapid Response Fund, 2020.
Photo: Ilona Zielinska (Elona Photographer)

p.77
The Black Assassin Saints
1982
Poster paint and screenprint on cotton duck
182.8 x 365.7 cm
Photo: Ilona Zielinska (Elona Photographer)

p.78
The Four Horsemen of the Apocalypse
1984
Acrylic on un-stretched canvas
275 x 152.5 cm each
Middlesbrough Collection, MIMA, Middlesbrough Institute of Modern Art.
Purchased with assistance from the Art Fund and the Arts Council England/
Victoria & Albert Museum Purchase Grant Fund
Photo: Ilona Zielinska (Elona Photographer)

p.79
***The Four Horsemen of the Apocalypse* (detail)**
1984
Acrylic on un-stretched canvas
275 x 152.5 cm each
Middlesbrough Collection, MIMA, Middlesbrough Institute of Modern Art.
Purchased with assistance from the Art Fund and the Arts Council England/
Victoria & Albert Museum Purchase Grant Fund
Photo: Ilona Zielinska (Elona Photographer)

p.81
Body Type 1 & 2
1982
Pencil drawings on paper
120 x 89 cm each
Wolverhampton Art Gallery
Photo: Luke Unsworth

p.83, p.84, p.85
The Seven Rages of Man
2018
Mixed media assemblage
Dimensions variable
Installation at Wolverhampton Art Gallery, 2019
Photo: Ilona Zielinska (Elona Photographer)

pp.86-87
Go West Young Man
1987
14 photographs, gelatin silver prints on paper mounted onto board
84 x 56 cm each
Tate

pp.88-89
Go West Young Man
1996
Computer animation
Courtesy the artist

p.90
The Nation's Finest
1990
Video stills
Courtesy the artist

p. 91
The Nation's Finest
1990
Video
Installation at Wolverhampton Art Gallery, 2019
Photo: Ilona Zielinska (Elona Photographer)

p.93
The Perfect City
2007
Video
Installation at Wolverhampton Art Gallery, 2019
Photo: Ilona Zielinska (Elona Photographer)

pp.94-95
The Perfect City
2007
Video stills
Courtesy the artist

pp.97-101
The Trophies of Empire
1985
Photographic slides transferred to video
Courtesy the artist

p.105
Searching for a Jet Black Future
2021-22
Digital print on banner
400 x 300 cm
Installation in the Window Box, The New Art Gallery Walsall, 2022
Photo: Ilona Zielinska (Elona Photographer)

pp.106-107, p.109, pp.110-113
Jet Black Futures
2021-22
16 digital prints on banners
137 x 200 cm each
Installation at The New Art Gallery Walsall, 2022
Photo: Ilona Zielinska (Elona Photographer)

p.115
Pulp Fictions
2016-17
Digital prints on Dibond
29.7 x 21 cm each
Installation at The New Art Gallery Walsall, 2022
Photo: Ilona Zielinska (Elona Photographer)

P117-121
Pulp Fictions
2016-17
Digital prints
Dimensions variable
Courtesy the artist

pp.123-137
In Search of Four Horses
2021-22
Four channel video installation with sound
Installation at The New Art Gallery Walsall, 2022
Photos: Ilona Zielinska (Elona Photographer)

p.139
Surveillance: Tagging the Other
1992
Mixed media installation with four monitors, projection and sound
Dimensions variable
Installation at The New Art Gallery Walsall, 2022
The New Art Gallery Walsall Permanent Collection. Presented by the Contemporary Art Society through the Rapid Response Fund, 2020.
Photo: Ilona Zielinska (Elona Photographer)

This publication accompanies the exhibitions;

Keith Piper
Jet Black Futures
14 January – 24 April 2022
The New Art Gallery Walsall

Keith Piper
Body Politics: Works from 1982-2007
10 October – 1 December 2019
Wolverhampton Art Gallery

The New Art Gallery Walsall
Gallery Square
Walsall
WS2 8LG
UK
thenewartgallerywalsall.org.uk

Wolverhampton Art Gallery
Lichfield St
Wolverhampton
WV1 1DU
UK
wolverhamptonart.org.uk

Middlesex University London
The Burroughs
London
NW4 4BT
UK
mdx.ac.uk

Texts © Anjalie Dalal-Clayton, Keith Piper, Deborah Robinson
All images © Keith Piper

ISBN: 978 1 907363 17 7

Distributed by:
Cornerhouse Publications
2 Tony Wilson Place
Manchester
M15 4FN
UK
cornerhousepublications.org

Book design by Victoria Bithell Design
Printed in the UK by Gomer Press

In Search of the Four Horses commission supported by;

Publication supported by;

Supported by a Publication Grant from the Paul Mellon Centre for Studies in British Art

ISBN 978-1-907363-17-7